Leonardo Schiocchet
Living in Refuge

Editorial

In times of increasingly impactful climate crises and ceaseless violent conflicts, new dynamics of forced migrations evolve every day. National policies are not the sole defining drivers of these dynamics, and scholars have to acknowledge international and transnational networks, relationships and sets of obligations that shape the realities independently of nation states' responses. The complexity of the matter has spread academic and public debates far and wide, ranging across issues of identity, social belonging, law, rights and duties, ethics and morality, heritage, economic and development models, religion and culture, war and peace and a myriad of other imperative topics. Few other general contemporary social processes have prompted as much debate as forced migration has today. This series aims to transit between topics, disciplines, modes of engagement with reality, theoretical proclivities, and different social scenarios and case studies pertaining to the realm of forced migration. Transcript's Forced Migration Studies Series publishes monographs and edited volumes on forced migration worldwide, engaging with theoretical-methodological developments whilst also examining concrete case studies. It is multidisciplinary and focuses hprimarily on the contemporary world.

The series is edited by Leonardo Schiocchet and Maria Six-Hohenbalken.

Leonardo Schiocchet has a PhD in anthropology (Boston University, 2011) and a Habilitation in social and cultural anthropology (University of Vienna, 2022). He is a researcher at the Institute for Social Anthropology (ISA) at the Austrian Academy of Sciences (ÖAW), a member of the Refugee Outreach & Research Network (ROR-n), and principal investigator of the FWF project The Austro-Arab Encounter. Since 2005, his work has focused on social belonging processes among Arab forced migrants.

Leonardo Schiocchet

Living in Refuge

Ritualization and Religiosity
in a Christian and a Muslim Palestinian Refugee Camp in Lebanon

[transcript]

Published with the support of Austrian Science Fund (FWF):
PUB 793-G.
Research results from: Austrian Science Fund (FWF): M 1797-
G22 and P31077-G29

FWF

Der Wissenschaftsfonds.

Bibliographic information published by the Deutsche Nationalbibliothek
The Deutsche Nationalbibliothek lists this publication in the Deutsche National-
bibliografie; detailed bibliographic data are available in the Internet at http://
dnb.d-nb.de

First published in 2022 by transcript Verlag, Bielefeld
© Leonardo Schiocchet

Cover layout: Maria Arndt, Bielefeld
Cover illustration: Leonardo Schiocchet, Nahr el-Barid refugee camp,
    Lebanon, 2007

Print-ISBN 978-3-8376-6074-6
PDF-ISBN 978-3-8394-6074-0
https://doi.org/10.14361/9783839460740

Contents

Part I – The Refuge: Nationhood & Religion

Part II – Ritual, Time and Resistance

Introduction

This book is a comparative ethnography of one Muslim Palestinian camp, Al-Jalil, and what, before 2011, was the last Christian Palestinian refugee camp in the world, Dbayeh in Lebanon. It introduces a ritualization approach for understanding two contrasting patterns of social belonging. In Al-Jalil, social life was symbolically militarized, largely revolved around Palestinian political parties and social movements, and was characterized by overt ritualization of quotidian life. Dbayeh, in contrast, was symbolically demilitarized, and ritualization was much less prevalent. Processes of belonging in Dbayeh also combined both Palestinian and Lebanese elements. Scholars often tend to attribute the differences between the two camps mostly to religion. This study instead proposes a focus on the intersectionality of religiosity, nationhood, refugeeness, and politics as framing much of the camps' daily routines.

This book tackles the intersection between the anthropology of forced migration, religion, and the Palestinian people, and contributes to each of these fields by organically merging their distinct literatures. To the anthropology of forced migration, it offers a uniquely intersectional contribution that highlights the complexity of processes of social belonging processes and avoids the reification of categories like religion and nationhood. To the literature on religion, it offers a unique synthesis of what has been widely assumed to be contradictory theoretical and methodological approaches: on the one hand, the research on piety and moral self-cultivation largely inspired by Talal Assad's approach and, on the other, the everyday life of religious communities approach presented by Samuli Schielke, among others. In addition, the book highlights the ubiquitous implications of large-scale protracted processes of displacement and the specificities of the Palestinian case. The proposed ritualization approach offers a unique contribution to the scant literature within the study of rituals, nationhood and social movements among Palestinians, epitomized by Laleh Khalili's invaluable work. Finally, the manuscript also contributes to the literature on Palestinian refugees by offering a unique and dense socio-historical portrait of two refugee camps about which there is almost no recorded literature and that have changed considerably, especially after 2011 and the ensuing influx of Syrian refugees to Lebanon.

This manuscript is primarily based on my ethnographic fieldwork in Lebanon, carried out in situ for 24 months between 2006 and 2010, and secondarily on fieldwork carried out among Palestinian refugees, some originally from Al-Jalil and Dbayeh, from 2010 to 2019 in Lebanon, Brazil, Denmark and Austria. The theoretical insights developed in this book emerge out of deeply rooted fieldwork highlighting the complexity of each actual situation and context, as the passage below demonstrates:

*

I was in the most popular coffee shop in Al-Jalil Palestinian refugee camp, smoking *argile* (hookah), drinking tea, and playing cards with the local youth, when a man appearing to be in his mid-fifties, whom I will call Abu Niẓam, entered the place. The café itself was the trendiest around because it was the only one where one could go to play cards. His presence was quite unusual, as customers were typically much younger. Everyone was slightly uneasy since they feared that the man had come to reprimand them for their improper behavior of smoking and playing cards, as many had done before him. Mine was a corner table, as far from the door as one could be in that small place. Abu Niẓam started by talking privately with one youth and then another, but in no time his thoughts were made loud and public. I was not inconspicuous, given that anyone there could spot my foreignness by my looks and because everyone in the camp knew almost everyone else. Yet, silently playing cards, I was hoping to go unnoticed. The man spoke about the importance of not discussing politics in the café, so as to maintain Palestinian unity. 'Politics', for him, meant the everlasting Fatah/Hamas divide discussed to exhaustion in the camp. It was not, for example, jumping from the table yelling, "the Palestinians have the right to return to their land," since on this everyone agreed. The problem, then, was not politics, but generating *fitna*. While this word may mean simply *strife*, its association with Islam and Arab history also evokes Devilish temptations to divide the pious. Thus, while politics was potentially the realm of *fitna*, Palestinianness was imagined as concrete, unique, and beyond politics.

With this example, I do not mean to suggest that Palestinians think of their own politics as being itself beyond politics, only that people like Abu Niẓam, and most in that café, would typically see their national belonging as a given rather than as a dynamic, negotiated construct. Even though this book emphasizes Palestinian diversity and the dynamics through which this diversity is created and transformed, it takes into consideration that most Palestinians, as most other people, do not tend to see it this way, which in turn influences contextual dynamics of social organization and belonging like the ones I analyze here. Al-Jalil's relatively small size allowed for close community ties and for the existence of a committee composed of "the most important political faction leaders" (as I was told), who generally managed to secure peace inside the camp, even if conflicts could not always be prevented.

The next time I went to the café, a hand-sketched sign hanging on the wall confounded me. It read, *mumnu'a al-din*[1] (religion is prohibited). By whichever means the sign made its way to the wall, a parallel between *politics* and *religion* had been traced. Neither was necessarily bad but bringing either to the public sphere could lead to *fitna*, and that café was not the right place for it. To people like Abu Niẓam, religion was so much out of place there that some frequently felt compelled to complain that the place might be fostering immoral behavior. It seemed that *fitna* could make its way in through politics. In the mind of the two young owners, however, religion was also a realm that could lead to *fitna*, and as such it needed to be avoided in their establishment. This relegation of religion to the private sphere is part of what is generally understood by the term *secularism*, while in Western political discourse there is no equivalent term for the relegation of politics to the private sphere. Though not openly acknowledged by the residents, politics, religion, and nationhood were very much intertwined in Al-Jalil. While one's Palestnianness and Muslimness were generally taken for granted, identity was complicated by ideas of the "good" and the "bad" Muslim or Palestinian, conceptualizations closely linked to ideals of Muslimness and Palestinianness.

On that same night in the café, possibly in deference to my obvious presence, Abu Niẓam announced that *al-Qaḍiyya al-Falastyniyya* (the Palestinian Cause) was "one and the same for Christians and Muslims alike." A young man whom I will call Hassan, the son of a local politician, burst out in a fit of rage as he contradicted Abu Niẓam's claim. In an invective filled tirade, he argued that Christian Palestinians had done nothing for Palestine. The dispute

---

[1]   ممنع الدين

took on significant proportions as the crowd took turns defending one side or the other. I avoided the discussion by playing cards and listened quietly until it seemed wise to leave. On my way out, despite having always had a friendly relationship with Hassan, my efforts to shake hands and say goodbye went ignored. Days after the incident, however, he was back at being polite, generous, and affectionate to me. What could have prompted him to behave unsociably that day? Ironically, it was Abu Nizam himself who had brought up politics, at first insisting that one should not talk about it in such a setting to avoid *fitna*, and subsequently finding himself on one side of a discussion in which his very argument about Palestinian unity was challenged. However, little did he know that I may have been the catalyst to Hassan's agitated reaction.

Less than a month after that night, I prepared to move to Dbayeh, the last remaining Christian Palestinian refugee camp not just in Lebanon, but anywhere else. A few days before the incident in the café, I had told Hassan about my impending move. As Hezbollah had just staged their short-lived invasion of Beirut, we were discussing the prospects for another Israeli invasion. Most Al-Jalil inhabitants anticipated another war in the summer. In this context, Hassan saw my departure to Dbayeh as self-serving, and accused me of running away from the war and leaving my Al-Jalil friends to their own destiny. It may be difficult for some readers to imagine Palestinians mobilizing religious difference as a main marker of ethical behavior and Palestinianness itself, since it is by no means a common position among Palestinian intellectuals. However, it was not uncommon in places like a café in a refugee camp with no Christians, located on the outskirts of Baalbek. It was generally believed in Al-Jalil that Dbayeh residents, being Christian, had all become wealthy Lebanese, living in privileged social conditions; nonetheless, Hassan's reaction to my move was by far the strongest one I had witnessed. Some had encouraged me to stay in Al-Jalil, saying I was better off there, but this was usually meant to keep me in their camp rather than to dismiss Christian Palestinians. Many also wished me good luck, and many others simply did not know of Dbayeh's existence. To me, this last reaction was the most intriguing. Were many other Palestinian refugees in Lebanon also this oblivious about Dbayeh and its residents? How did Dbayeh's refugees fit into the larger picture? How did they understand their own Palestinianness? My location in Al-Jalil afforded too narrow a perspective to be able to answer such questions.

To defend his unifying positioning in the café that night, Abu Niẓam raised an interesting point: the Christian leader of the PFLP, George Habash, had recently died, and each Palestinian refugee camp in Lebanon held commemorations in his honor. I witnessed one such event myself, enacted as a symbolic burial of Habash in Shatila, a well-known Palestinian refugee camp in Beirut. In the procession carrying a fake coffin covered with the Palestinian flag, a chorus of veiled women bearing posters of Habash sang: *la illahu illa Allah, wa Muhammad rasūl Allah* (there is no God but God, and Muhammad is God's messenger).[2] Al-Jalil itself was filled with posters honoring Habash as a martyr and it was in this context that Abu Niẓam asked whether George Habash was indeed a martyr of the Palestinian Cause, to which all present seemed to answer positively. Hassan seemed confused, though, and did not answer. I will never know whether Hassan knew then that Habash was a Christian, but the case is illustrative of how Muslim Palestinian refugees in Lebanon at times conflate Palestinianness and *the cause* with Islam.

This story illustrates how religion, national politics, and belonging can be conflated in the quotidian of Palestinian refugees in Lebanon. Though, in Al-Jalil, religion, politics, ethnicity, nationalism, and more informed social belonging in ways that allowed for differences in being Palestinian. However, the environment of the camps also generated dispositions, affects and sensibilities that, in turn, shaped identity, behavior, and action.

*

The following seven chapters deliver ethnographic accounts of social life in two Palestinian refugee camps in Lebanon. They aim to discuss Palestinianness and the relative space of religion through the subtle but pervasive ways in which notions such as *fitna* come to be part of the local vernacular politics (White 2002) repertoire embodied by most. This comparative ethnography of a Muslim refugee camp and what was then the last remaining Christian Palestinian refugee camp in Lebanon emphasizes the intersectionality of social belonging processes through a ritualization perspective. The framework of the book is rooted in a ritualization approach which seeks to understand two contrasting processes of belonging as they emerge in the two camps, encompassing differences in social organization and belonging.

In 2008, while the Lebanese population was about 4,224,000, according to UN World Population Prospects (2009), UNWRA counted about 450,000

---

2   This is the Sunni *shahāda* (literally, the witnessing), or the Islamic profession of faith that marks both conversion and subsequent reiterations of piety in Sunni Islam.

Palestinian refugees registered in the country (2013).[3] The last number is not totally inscribed into the first one because only Lebanese citizens are counted as part of the Lebanese population. Unfortunately, there is no official data on the number of Palestinian refugees registered with UNRWA who also have Lebanese citizenship, but this number is known to be very small, except when compared to the much smaller Christian Palestinian refugee population. What is also known is that about 53% of these refugees still inhabited the twelve official Palestinian refugee camps in Lebanon between 2006 and 2010. Despite their large numbers, Palestinians experienced significant hardship in Lebanon during the time of my fieldwork. Not only were their rights very few (Akram 2002), but they also faced widespread prejudice. For instance, many Lebanese still held the Palestinians responsible for the Lebanese Civil War (1975-1990), while others branded them as terrorists or simply considered them an undesirable, uncivilized horde, a hindrance to Lebanon's economic and social development. In this context, refugee camps tended to act as safe havens for Palestinians. They were symbolic centers to the lives of many Palestinian refugees, including those who, for whatever reasons, no longer lived there. This was so much the case that the camps were frequently conceptualized as Palestinian territory despite their location within Lebanese territory. This, in turn, exacerbated the tensions between the refugee population and Lebanese society at large. The camps, however, were not completely isolated from their surroundings. Palestinians and locals alike tended to conceive the refugee camps as providing some form of symbolic continuity, both with the land of Palestine and with the Lebanese lands surrounding them. Moreover, they were not homogenous entities, a common misconception. This book highlights the opposite: many were the variables contributing to diversity and even conflict within the camps themselves, which the story above hints at.

Al-Jalil is situated in Baalbek, an area dominated by the Shi'a Hezbollah, while Dbayeh, at the time the last remaining Christian Palestinian refugee camp in the world,[4] is located in Mount Lebanon, an area almost exclusively

---

3   Since most fieldwork for this research was carried out between 2006 and 2010, I chose to present numbers from 2008. In 2013 already, however, the Lebanese population had reached about 5 million inhabitants (UN World Population Prospects 2013).

4   Since the beginning of the war in Syria in 2011, Dbayeh started to absorb a number of Syrian refugees, almost all of them Muslim, and very few of Palestinian origin (The Internationalist January 2016).

Christian and dominated by Christian political parties generally opposed to Hezbollah. The United Nations Relief and Works Agency for Palestine Refugees in the Near East (UNRWA) officially managed both camps. Social life within the two camps has been portrayed by Lebanese and Palestinians alike as radically different from each other, and my fieldwork corroborates this perspective, while also pointing out important continuities between the two camps. At the time when the fieldwork was conducted, most Palestinians and Lebanese tended to attribute differences between the two patterns of social belonging mostly, or even solely, to religion, while scholars had hardly written anything about what Palestinian refugees and local Lebanese considered to be Dbayeh's exceptionality. This book discusses how religion influenced the Palestinian sense of social belonging and presents arguments that complicate direct causal explanations, thereby rendering such accounts overly simplistic. Although religion is a significant point of reference for the refugees' beliefs and behavior and while it does help delineate the camps' distinct profiles, it is only one among other important variables influencing the camps' quotidian and constructing the multi-faceted identities and alliances that characterize the lives of people in these contrasting settings.

I argue that these camps' different contexts and specific historical trajectories were very much responsible for their distinctive characters, which cannot be understood through the lenses of religion either as dogma, as many claim – including some Palestinian refugees themselves (Christian and Muslim alike) – or as theology, as scholars of religion would perhaps be inclined to suggest. However, as I will proceed to argue in the next section of this introduction, it would also not be accurate to simply leave religion out of the picture, as if it had no bearing on people's lives, following a trend in Palestine studies claiming that religion is simply not as important for Palestinians as it is for the Lebanese. This book shows that, in practice, religion interplays with a host of other variables, especially nationalism, ethnicity, and politics, thereby generating social referents, dispositions, affects, and sensibilities that account for the contrasts between the camps' social belonging dynamics. To this end, I propose analyzing each camp's social belonging processes, especially in how they relate to religiosity and nationhood through ritualization as a broad comparative frame.

Although in the commonly used sense religiosity relates to piety, following Samuli Schielke (2010) among others, I challenge the assumption that religion manifests itself in the daily lives of people solely through piety. Therefore, this book is not about Islamic or Christian theology. It is less about religious institutions per se and more about everything else religious, or what we may call *religiosity*, meaning how referents, dispositions, affects, and sensibilities at least partially rooted in theology or seen as rooted in a religious tradition (Asad 1993) make their way into social belonging processes and everyday life along with other referents less or not at all associated with religion. In this way, this book treats religion as part of more complex knowledge idioms and not as theological schemes of the world that produce unavoidably uniform patterns of social behavior. Beyond eschatology and doctrine, it tells the story of how religion and ritualization in practice tended to enthuse and inform opposite belonging processes in a Muslim and a Christian Palestinian refugee camp in Lebanon. These understandings of religion and ritualization, although my own, are largely inspired by the work of Foucault (1975) on discipline and "power as a matter of techniques and discursive practices that comprise the micropolitics of everyday life" (Bell 2009: 199), and by Talal Asad's work on disciplinary practices, the embodiment of dispositions, religion, and knowledge and tradition (1993, 2003). Furthermore, I am also partially inspired by the work of Charles Hirschkind on what he calls the *sensorium*, a concept accounting for dispositions, affects, and sensibilities (2006, 2011), and those of Stanley Tambiah (1979, 1996), Roy Rappaport (2008) and Catherine Bell (2009, 1997) on a definition of ritualization suited to understanding the fluidity of socialization and belonging processes, and the making and mobilization of disciplinary practices, embodied dispositions, knowledge and tradition.

This book is thus about how religiosity and tradition, through ritualization, evoke meaning and action beyond the orthodoxy of dogmas and theology. Yet, it is also about social belonging in what they do not relate to religion. It is about how religion is enmeshed with other variables and experienced in quotidian life by Palestinian refugees. In other words, it is about intersectionality (Crenshaw 1989). The people presented in this book may at times experience and express this religiosity only incidentally, but with effects as pervasive as when one follows religion as dogma. This book is thus about religion only insofar as it deals with the possibility (or impossibility) of defining religion as a category (Asad 1993). In accordance with my anthropological background, I will not discuss Islam or Christianity as disembodied entities, but rather as they exist and take meaning departing from subjects both bound to historical and local contexts, and as creative actors capable of dynamic subjunctive reframing of their own life conceptions and living experiences. More broadly, this book discusses the relationship between refugeeness, religiosity, and that which tends to be most imperative to the refuge: nationhood. I use the term *refuge* in two ways. While in this case it means the time and expectations of life in exile in the broad sense, at times I will also use the term in its narrower ascription, meaning the host country, which according to humanitarian principles should serve as a safe haven, a refuge.

In sum, this book aims at contributing to the study of forced migration, religion, and rituals, particularly with regard to the Palestinian case, by elucidating the often subtle ways in which religiosity and ritualization are integral to social belonging processes, especially those intimately related to the refugee condition. It contributes to the anthropological literature on forced migration and processes of social belonging and identity by offering a unique intersectional perspective that highlights the complexity of social processes, preventing the reification of categories such as religion, nationhood, or ethnicity. Yet, it also highlights ubiquitous implications of large-scale protracted processes of displacement and the specificities of the Palestinian case. Finally, it also contributes to the literature on Palestinian refugees by delivering a unique historical portrait of two refugee camps for which there is almost no recorded literature and which have since then changed considerably, especially due to the influx of Syrian refugees after 2011. Both the long-term oral histories and the 2006-2010 contrasting snapshots of social dynamics in the two small and symbolically peripheric refugee camps (Al-Jalil and Dbayeh) portrayed here have never been published before and are in themselves significant contributions to Palestine anthropology and the anthropology of forced migration.

a. Religion, Ritual, and Comparison in Palestine Anthropology[5]

Perhaps unexpectedly, given the current widespread assault on Islam and Muslims by means of their association with terrorism and backwardness, religion and ritual are two core concepts of anthropology that have been relatively absent from contemporary anthropologists' engagement with Palestine/Palestinians. As the field grew and turned towards itself (both to within the academic field and to within the Near East as a place of inquiry – and most recently especially to within Palestine), comparison too has been largely

---

5   The argument in this section is largely a summarized adaptation of (Schiocchet 2018).

avoided. To better understand just how this happened, I will briefly outline the state of affairs within the field of Palestine ethnography.

According to Lindholm, *traditional anthropology* in the Middle East – the "largest cultural area in terms of square miles in the anthropological division of the world" – was marked by the "ethos of Islam and the austerity of social life" (1995: 805). Unfavorable to elaborated symbolic systems, the flourishing of myths, and intricate ritual performances, the Middle East gave rise instead to an anthropology of public matters such as *honor, survival, political* and *marital alliances, respect* and *authority*, and *patrilineage* (Lindholm 1995: 805). Meanwhile, generations of Orientalists focused their research on Islamic history and literature, revealing a rich urban cosmopolitism (ibid.) tied to the *Golden Age* of Islam (Kassir 2006). This division into an ethnographic egalitarian, current, and peripheral Middle East, and a rivaling Orientalist textual, historical, central and status-conscious Middle East survived until the assault of Edward Said's *Orientalism* in 1979, which rendered both approaches "morally suspect." Said's main argument was that both traditions deployed representations composing imaginative geographies that served a colonial project of domination. While "Orientalism was a rationalization of the colonial rule" (Said 1979: 39), anthropology was an instrument for the reiteration of the "binomial opposition of 'ours' and 'theirs' with the former always encroaching upon the latter" (ibid: 227). What Lindholm emphasized is the fact that, to Said, both the textual and the empirical lines of study by Westerners "denied humanity to Middle Eastern people by turning them into exotic 'Others' to be gazed at and objectified" (1995: 806). It is clear that by the mid-1990s, old premises were largely abandoned, and there was space for a new theory of social life in the Middle East. Lindholm protests that Said's view of culture is merely "hegemonic and disciplinary" (Clifford 1988: 263), and that there was no outcry against this perspective in anthropology because it fit well within the "anti-comparativist and anti-essentialist" trend of anthropology at the time (Lindholm 1995: 807). While today I side with Said on his view of culture, I also agree with Lindholm that Said's *rhetoric of opposition* had little in the way of alternatives, as it was more focused on denouncing anthropology instead. However, Said's mistake was to blame on anthropology as a whole what should have been blamed on the historical engagement of anthropologists with those they studied. That is, what Said could not have anticipated was the potential inherent to anthropology to assimilate his criticism and re-fashion the discipline accordingly.

The most popular response to the crisis proclaimed by Lindholm was that of "social biography, novelistic narrative and personal accounts," which he characterized as being at the core of postmodern, or *new*, Middle Eastern anthropology. This trend, epitomized by Lila Abu-Lughod's *Writing Women's Worlds: Bedouin Stories* (1993), was to him the prototype of the "crippling" response to the crisis as he opposed her call "for the 'undoing' of old Middle Eastern anthropological categories." Lindholm acknowledges that Abu-Lughod's project is "more affirmative" than Said's, which he describes, largely using her own words, as consisting in giving "positive content to her subjects through 'a narrative ethnography' consisting of 'wonderfully complex stories' which 'challenge the capacity of anthropological generalizations to render lives, theirs or others', adequately" (Lindholm 1995: 810). Nevertheless, he denounces Abu-Lughod's stance for rejecting what I understand as being the main ingredients to comparison: *detachment, abstraction,* and *generalization,* which Abu-Lughod considered to be alienating (Lindholm 1995: 810). He explains, following Abu-Lughod and others following this trend, that to compare inescapably implies asymmetrically departing from a position of superiority, given that at the very least the anthropologist is the one who sets the rules of the game. Or, in her own words, "at the very least, the self is always the interpreter and the other the interpreted" (Abu-Lughod 2008: 13). In sum, to Lindholm the "radically particularistic [...] moral assumption" that one should not compare, when to him anthropology is intrinsically comparative, would have led today to a total absence of theorization. While this did not happen ultimately, Lindholm was right in lamenting that bolder theorization, particularly that stemming from broad geographical and thematic comparison, is relatively lacking in the field of Middle East anthropology and particularly that of Palestine anthropology today.

Another way to approach the mid-1990s anthropological context would be to construe it as a period of introspection necessary to reevaluate the practice of anthropology in a changing world. Indeed, much has changed, and while I evaluate the effects of that rebellious moment as crucially positive, and today I inscribe my own anthropology more in tune with this *New Middle Eastern Ethnography* than with that defended by Lindholm in the mid-1990s, perhaps it is time to reconsider one of Lindholm's main qualms, what he calls "radical particularism." In seeking to reinvent and rid itself of the shackles of its colonial past, did anthropology cripple its own comparative vocation? In trying to redefine humanity, was it reduced to a cultural critique of the normative?

Nowhere else does Said's critique of Orientalism (and perhaps even Asad's critique of the colonial encounter) reverberate as much as in Palestine anthropology. Thus, this is precisely where we should head to consider these questions further. One notion left out of Lindholm's 1993 considerations is that the New Middle East Anthropology has indeed become more Middle Eastern. Having largely subscribed to the postcolonial anthropology project myself, I consider this an accomplishment. Khaled Furani and Dan Rabinowitz also expressed a similar position in a piece published in 2011 in *The Annual Review of Anthropology* (2011). In an effort to trace the history of Palestine ethnography, these authors welcome the making of Palestine as a site for the production of theory, rather than just Otherness. One of their main arguments is that after the Oslo and the Madrid peace processes in the 1990s, ethnographic research on Palestinians, which today is largely associated with Palestinian activism, saw a sharp increase. One could counter that, at least until 1992, this increase in the number of studies relative to other fields and the association of such studies with activism are only partially corroborated by in-depth bibliographical studies (see, for example, Strijp 1992; 1997) and ongoing discussion within the field (Allan 2014; Schiocchet 2016). What is safe to say, however, is that Palestine anthropology is now much closer to the Palestinians' own grasp.

According to Furani & Rabinowitz, there have been four different, partially overlapping modes of approaching Palestine as a site for inquiry since the late 19th Century. The first was the *proto-anthropological* approach, and it was prevalent until the late 1940s. It was external, proto-ethnographic, and featured the bible as its legitimizing text. The second was also external, but secularized. Dominating from the early 20th Century until the late 1940s was the *Orientalist* approach, which incorporated participant observation and fieldwork, and brought about a change in nomenclature. Instead of Holy Land and Mohammedans, popular terms are Palestine, primitives, race, Muslims, Orientals, and Arabs. It was permeated by Social Evolutionary and Functionalist assumptions, and concerned with stability, rule, integration, differentiation, and evolution of social forms, alongside the documentation of disappearing cultures (what has been termed *Salvage Anthropology*). The third mode of approaching Palestine is called *absent Palestine*, and it was characterized by very little engagement with the Palestinian subject, or even its concealment. This mode was predominant between 1948 and the late 1980s, or between the foundation of Israel and the First Intifada. Two areas in particular glaringly demonstrate the absent Palestine: peasant and refugee studies were both understood as hazardous in that they would reveal Palestinian attachment to the land, and therefore absent, leaving the field open to Zionist anthropology focusing on Palestinians as "traditional" but naming them Arabs instead (Furani & Rabinowitz 2011).

Similarly to Lindholm, Furani & Rabinowitz contend that Edward Said's *Orientalism* precipitated a radical change in the field, while also adding Talal Asad's *Anthropology and the Colonial Encounter* to this genealogy.[6] Both books were published in the late 1970s and foreshadowed the fourth and most recent mode of engaging Palestine as a site in the late 1980s. This largely corresponds to what Lindholm called New Middle East Ethnography, which the latter authors prefer to call *post-structural*. Here, no longer silent and self-evident, the state becomes an object of inquiry to "a new generation of anthropologists who begin to question Israel's effort at repressing Palestinian nationalism and normalizing its racial and colonial character." Palestine and Palestinians reemerged as subjects, especially through themes such as *memory, refugees, resistance, national identity, colonial predicament*, and *gender*, but also through *law, prison, bureaucracy*, and a host of new topics (Furani & Rabinowitz 2011; Furani 2011). Meanwhile, Palestinian native ethnography finally began to flourish in the late 1970s due to a double political and epistemological shift in response to, respectively, the 1967 Arab-Israeli War and the "crisis" ushered in by Said and Asad. Alongside these two authors, Palestinian ethnography also engaged figures such as Michel Foucault (as Edward Said and Talal Asad had already done), Del Hymes, and Eric Wolf. To Furani, the entirety of postcolonial, post-structuralist, postmodern anthropology – and I would add post-Zionist studies – offers what he calls, paraphrasing Said this time, an *enabling vocabulary* to study the Palestinians, the most consequential of which is *memory* (2011).

Yet, I would like to highlight that, along with memory, *refugeeness* is also central to most ethnographies about Palestinians, especially among those working in Lebanon, as we shall see from a brief inventory. Most ethnographers of Palestinians at some point worked on memory, and some of the most relevant of these are: Sharif Kanaana (2000, 1989), Bishara Doumani (1995), Ted Swedenburg (1992, 2003), Susan Slyomovics (1998), Lena Jayyusi (2007, 2002), Lila Abu-Lughod (2007), and Rema Hammami, (2003). However, even more revealing is the number of Palestine ethnographers working on the Middle East that tended to engage with refugeeness directly, most associating it with *memory, suffering, resistance, national identity*, and/or *gender*. Some of these are: Rosemary Sayigh (1979, 1994, 2007), Julie Peteet (1987, 1994, 1996a, 1996b, 2005), Laleh Khalili (2005; 2007), Rhoda Ann Kanaaneh & Isis Nusair (2010), Rochelle Davis (2010), Lori Allen (2013), Moslih Kanaaneh (Kanaaneh, Moslih; Thorsén, Stig-Magnus; et al 2013), Randa Farah (2003,

---

6   It is important to notice that Furani was himself a student of Asad.

1998, 1997), Lotte Segal (Segal 2014a, 2014b), Ruba Salih (2013), Lori Lybarger (2007), Nell Gabiam (2006), Amanda Dias (2013), Gustavo Barbosa (2013), and myself (Schiocchet 2013, 2015). Few are those anthropologists approaching Palestine via bolder theoretical and comparative frameworks. Some of the most interesting in this sense are by Didier Fassin (2008) and Michel Agier (2008, 2011), who only wrote on Palestinians *en passant*, the latter only recently becoming interested specifically in Palestinians. Other examples are Dawn Chatty (2010), Randa Farah (2009) and Are Knudsen (2001; Knudsen & Hanafi 2011) – with Chatty coming from Middle Eastern mobility and Arab Studies toward Palestine as a site, and Knudsen being also interested in Islamism and South Asia. As final examples, Ilana Feldman's work (2008) directly engages suffering, humanitarianism and governmentality, and Diana Allan (2014) emphasizes economic survival over nationalist discourses, while also engaging refugeeness, resistance (as economic in this case), and suffering. Though it would not be accurate to claim that these studies are confined to only the aforementioned topics, they do feature prominently. The prevalence of these themes is not simply the result of European theory, self-critique, and guilt, but also emerged in praxis through the anthropological encounter that turned many anthropologists into engaged observers (Sanford & Angel-Ajani 2006), and through engaged observers who influenced an entire generation of anthropologists.

Palestine ethnography today seems to be concerned primarily with how Palestinians are confined to oscillating between repression and resistance, as epitomized by what Furani calls "narratives about the national struggle" (2011), or what I would call the Palestinian polysemic engagement to *al-Qadyia al-Falastynyia* (the Palestinian cause). To Furani and Rabinowitz, this means that attention is taken away from other topics such as environment, land alienation, employment, language, sexuality, piety, food, and health (Furani & Rabinowitz 2011; Furani 2011). While this argument does not reflect the current state of sociology, law, linguistics, human geography, and other academic disciplines, it is a relatively accurate picture of the main trends within contemporary anthropology of Palestine and/or Palestinians.

A more thorough review of the literature would reveal that these less popular topics do figure in Palestine anthropology, albeit not prominently. What matters most for our current discussion is that religion and piety are integral to the work of a few authors, such as Are Knudsen (2003a, 2003b), Nasser Abufarha (2009), Glen Bowman (2013, 2011a, 2011b), Lory Lybarger (2007), Amalia Sa'ar (1998), Bernard Rougier 2007), Christian Suhr (2013), and Anya Kublitz

(2016), but mostly not through the same lens I propose here. For instance: Lybarger, who incidentally is one of the few authors in Palestine anthropology interested in comparison, juxtaposes two refugee camps in Palestine, one of which he characterizes in terms of its attachment to religion, the other in terms of its attachment to secularism, thereby still treating religion mainly as a dogma; Sa'ar treats religion as sectarian belonging; Rougier, who is not an anthropologist per se, describes 'Ayn el-Helweh refugee camp in Lebanon as if it were completely defined by a Salafi take-over in detriment of everything else that may influence the refugees' lives; Suhr, while addressing social practices, beliefs, and piety in particular among the Muslim community (of which most is Palestinian) in Gellerupparken, Aarhus/Denmark, is engaging the anthropology of Islam, having no direct engagement with Palestine anthropology as a field; and Kublitz deals with generations of immigrants in Denmark who once identified as Palestinians and "became" Muslims, thus still emphasizing the distinction between religious and secular (national) spheres. In sum, most of those tackling religion in Palestine anthropology still to a greater or lesser extent treat it as a distinctive domain of social life. All these authors bring outstanding contributions to the field, and both in what they excel and what they lack, they reinforce the need to treat religion and ritual as embedded in the quotidian and discussed within the frame of Palestine anthropology. Thus, however plural, there are still some quite visible tendencies in contemporary anthropology of Palestine/Palestinians, and religiosity does not figure preeminently. What this book shows, however, is that religiosity and ritualization, embedded as they are in the quotidian, are pervasive in the lives of Palestinian refugees in Lebanon, and I would suggest, of Palestinians, refugees or not, elsewhere. Thus, this book can be read as a case for more serious engagement with religiosity and ritualization in Palestine anthropology.

Owing to Said, Asad, Abu-Lughod, and others, memory, dispossession, struggle, refugeeness, diaspora, citizenship, statehood, the relationship between resistance and agency, and, binding them all, suffering, are some of the main themes of current Palestine ethnography, even more so than in Middle Eastern ethnography at large. Asad and many of those influenced by him, such as Saba Mahmoud, Charles Hirschkind, Mayanthi Fernando, and other anthropologists mostly working on the Middle East or on Muslims, have been emphasizing the embodied, affective, and experiential dimensions of religion and the work of disciplinary practices and embodied dispositions, affects, and sensibilities in the quotidian, but Palestine anthropology has yet to absorb this trend more thoroughly. Among the possible reasons for this is the fact that both Palestinians themselves and scholars working on Palestine/Palestinians have historically spent considerable amounts of energy in rebuffing the critique that religion is that which defines the Palestinian question, the Palestinian cause, Palestine, and Palestinians, as Furani & Rabinowitz's scenario justifies (2011).

Similarly, talking about ritual in Palestine studies is still partially taboo. This may be so as a reaction to non-anthropologists' (and some anthropologists') perception of the term as tied to Orientalist literature and the colonial practice of anthropology of Palestine/Palestinians before Edward Said. While one could make a strong case for that, this may not be the sole or most important factor, and my suggestion remains in the realm of speculation. In one way or another, more or less emphatically and overtly, some scholars have pointed to the potential conceptual power of ritual, such as Julie Peteet (1994), Laleh Khalili (2004; 2005; 2007), and Diana Allen (2014). However, to my knowledge, I am the first proposing the usefulness of the less normative concept of *ritualization* instead (Schiocchet 2011; 2013, 2015). Ritualization encompasses much of what other authors in Palestine anthropology have been discussing under the rubric *memory*, since many of them, such as Rosemary Sayigh (2007), Lena Jayyusi (2002, 2007), and Randa Farah (1999), are interested in the dynamics of how memory is mobilized to inform social practices. The main difference, perhaps, is that ritualization is a process of redundancy creation and mobilization, and thus does not focus on normative conceptions highlighting the realm of the intellect, but rather emphasizes the inextricable connection, relative to context, between embodied affects, sensibilities, dispositions and techniques, and thinking, reflecting, and doing.

Perhaps it was fortunate that I only learned about Laleh Khalili's *Heroes and Martyrs of Palestine* (2007) after having defended my Ph.D. dissertation in 2010,[7] and thus after having already sketched out my own perspective on ritualization in the Palestinian refugee camps in Lebanon. I say fortunately because Khalili's book is extraordinarily compelling, and had I learned about it prior, I may not have developed my own theoretical framework independently from hers. Yet, as it turned out, this book's perspective was developed in parallel to Khalili's groundbreaking study.

Other works by Khalili had already influenced me while I was conducting fieldwork in Lebanon. I was struck, in particular, by her *Grassroots Commemorations: Remembering the Land in the Camps of Lebanon* (2004) and her *Places of*

---

7   Even though I was officially awarded my diploma only in 2011.

Mourning and Memory: Palestinian Commemoration in the Refugee Camps of Lebanon (2005). Having been in the Palestinian refugee camps in Lebanon and seen how pervasive such commemorations were, I wondered why only a few authors in the field discussed such events in the same way as Khalili. She was then and is today, perhaps, the foremost authority on the subject. Her work gave impetus and breadth to my own. Yet, while Khalili and I were drawn to the same subject – and she noticeably earlier than me – the theoretical perspective guiding this book is almost entirely different from hers.

In sum, this book is in close dialogue with Khalili's and corroborates her insights on just how pervasive *the performative aspect* of life in the Palestinian refugee camps is. Today, there is a tendency to move away from what are considered nationalist stories and commemorative practices, as epitomized by Diana Allen's *Refugees of the Revolution* (2014). However, I uphold that Khalili's work on ritual and nationalism remains a touchstone of Palestine studies, all the while heeding Allen's call to relativize the weight of the Palestinian nationalist discourse in the quotidian of the refugee camps. Khalili's study centers on "the struggles, failures and triumphs of a nationalist movement in imagining the nation" (2007: 214). The thread she follows throughout is the construction of memory, stories, and commemorations by Palestinian institutions. Yet, it seems Khalili frequently realizes the book is in fact about much more than what fits in neatly with her theoretical frame. For example, in the introduction, she states:

> I argue that while particular events are 'remembered' as the shared basis of peoplehood, the construction and reconstruction of these events, the shifting mood of commemorative narratives, and ruptures in commemorative practices surrounding these events all point to a far less stable notion of historical or national memory – and consequently national sentiment – than some might think. (ibid: 3)

Subjects' richly diverse lives do not neatly reproduce collective stories and memory as delivered in a top-down fashion by Palestinian political institutions. Yet, if Khalili at times acknowledges this, as the above quotation illustrates, the narrative of the book highlights nationalism and nationalist institutions to the detriment of all else. Another quotation on the same page illustrates this point: "Ultimately, this study wants to know why representations of the past are so central to nationalist movements and sentiments" (ibid: 3). Commemorations are not simply controlled by elites, though profoundly shaped by Palestinian political forces. Commemoration, like so much more in the camps, is not just about nationalism, but about nationhood. Khalili often uses nationalism and nationhood interchangeably, the first framing the later. In doing so, her narrative thread obfuscates an important part of the dynamics of national belonging in the camps. Allen also tends to subsume nationhood under nationalism, but her answer instead is to push both to the periphery of social belonging processes to the detriment of what she considers economic imperatives of survival. Thus, she disregards the extent to which nationhood (and with it, nationalism) really is pervasive, and just how much the nation in exile is embedded in Palestinian subjunctive and embodied in Palestinian subjects.

While acknowledging the excellence of Khalili's and Allan's works, this book seeks to disentangle the knot between nationalism, nationhood, and everything else not nation related, by examining the nuances in which the Palestinian nation is not only imagined, but also lived in the refugee camps in Lebanon alongside other forms of belonging and traditions informing people's lives. In doing so, I depart from Khalili's most basic insight that ritual is pervasive in the camps, and attempt to show that symbols and narratives are less substantive than Khalili's theoretical model supports, and that less normative rituals are just as pervasive as nationalist commemorative practices. Nationhood, I maintain, is subjective, produced only in practice and context, and it is profoundly shaped by sensibilities, dispositions, and affects through the ritualization of daily life, rather than by substantive symbols and discourses alone. The ritualization of daily life, thus, owes to more than just the mnemonic mobilization of stories, and narratives involving the nation are often also informed by religiosity, ethnicity, folklore and more, rather than being mainly political in character. In sum, I acknowledge that *Heroes and Martyrs...* already hints at the possibility that there is much more to performance than a normative storyboard, and so, rather than doing away with it, I intend to develop Khalili's argument further.

To conclude this brief discussion of Palestine anthropology, although I do agree with Abu-Lughod that, in the early 1990s, anthropology had yet to come to terms with the devastating critique mobilized by authors such as Said and Asad in the late 1970s, today we are in a different historical moment. The time is ripe to widen the breadth of topics discussed in the field. While richly detailed and particularistic accounts are always welcome, this is not the only project that the field can entertain. To emphasize heterogeneity and expose highly normative accounts of Palestinian refugees in Lebanon, for instance, we must compare different ethnographies, and engage in multi-sited comparative ethnography (Hannerz 2002), as this book proposes. Comparative ethnographic work should not be seen as intrinsically contrary to the particularistic approach, but complementary. While the latter has been the focus of debate for decades, the former is heavily underrepresented, largely left to geographers, sociologists, and political scientists. Current Palestine anthropology rarely acknowledges that a comparative contextual approach can act as an antidote where a more essentialist approach itself may incur overgeneralization.

Palestine anthropology, just as anthropology at large, does need contextual tools. It must recover comparison so as to remain critical, to transcend yet not expect a supposedly apolitical stance, but to gain perspective. Irrespective of which new topics we decide to explore from here on out and of which comparisons we decide to pursue, we must not forget the commitment we assumed with what Lindholm once called 'new' Middle Eastern ethnography. Maintaining the thrust of Western cultural critique is essential to the future of anthropology and giving voice to the suffering of others should be integral to the ethics of ethnography. However, as with any other anthropological project, it also has its pitfalls. Radical particularism is sometimes a form of essentialization, and the absence of comparison is often a disadvantage. If what was necessary in the 1980s was a disavowal of nationalist projects and Western imperialism, today we need further distancing from the humanitarian discourse and its injunction to abstain from portraying anything else beyond the *bare lives* of others for fear of casting a shadow over it.

Alongside the school of thought emerging from the work of Abu-Lughod, another valuable response to Lindholm's "deep crisis" was the postcolonial approach represented in the work of Talal Asad[8] and others. While Lindholm did not particularly favor Asad's model at the time, its influence in anthropology at large has been considerable. In this sense, it is also prudent to remember that many authors who in the mid-1990s were closely associated with more radical forms of particularism have been increasingly opening up to at least limited grounded comparison, when not subscribing completely to new metanarratives such as postcolonial theory. Palestine anthropology has also become more amenable to insights from postcolonial studies, even though not so much by adopting internal, regional, or global comparison, as by locating

---

8   Even though Asad would probably refute locating his contribution squarely within the realm of postcolonial anthropology, this has been one of the major trends associated with his work.

Palestine directly within the realm of postcolonial theory. Lindholm reminds us that anthropology is inherently comparative, and I suggest that it is only when context and comparison are integral to the picture that anthropologists are truly localized and engaged. Rather than being a tool of disengagement, fruitless abstraction, and ungrounded speculation, qualified comparison is not only compatible with postcolonial studies, but necessary to provincialize Europe (Chakrabarty 2007) and thus indispensable to the critique of Western reason itself.

While the scope of this book's comparative approach is admittedly narrow, I hold it to be a necessary step toward discussing the imagined Palestinian community at large. Here, I aim to not only argue that religion, nationhood, and refugeeness are often inextricably linked to the *secular* rallying for the Palestinian cause – as I have already claimed elsewhere (Schiocchet 2015, 2013, 2011) – but also to deliver an ethnographic account of how precisely this happens. Meanwhile, I have also studied groups of Palestinians in other locations besides Lebanon, mainly Brazil, Denmark, Austria, and the West Bank, and edited a collection on Palestinians in Latin America and in the Near East in comparative perspective (2015). The study presented here is therefore only one in a series, and I intend to further expand this work's comparative horizon at a later time.

b.   The Political context

It must be noted that the political situation in Lebanon was particularly tense between 2006 and 2010, even by Lebanese standards. This was reflected in the overall expression of political, ethnic, national, and sectarian alliances, and, more generally, in the way people related to each other, both inside and outside of the refugee camps. The ritualized hyper-expression of identity I describe here, and the extent to which suspicion and trust shaped social belonging processes must be understood as perhaps particularly intense due to political turmoil. However, it should be acknowledged that even this period represents merely another chapter in the violent contemporary history of Lebanon and of the Palestinians, as it has prompted embodied dispositions, sensibilities, and affects for many decades.

Animosity, tension, and actual conflict had been escalating since the start of my fieldwork, which began only months following the assassination of the Lebanese Prime Minister, Rafiq al-Hariri, and the subsequent Syrian military withdrawal in 2005, and continued until the parliamentary elections in the summer of 2009. Al-Hariri was a charismatic figure of Lebanese Sunni origin raised in Saudi Arabia. After the end of the Civil War in Lebanon, he largely financed the rebuilding of Beirut through a number of companies in civil construction, urban cleaning, and other sectors of the economy. Having become the most prominent and powerful anti-Syrian figure in the country, he was backed by most Western international leaders, and mainly by the Sunni and Druze Lebanese communities, along with large sectors of the Christian community – which then constituted the parliamentary majority of the Lebanese government despite being a minority in the Lebanese population. According to these groups, and quite likely, the Syrian government was directly involved in his killing. International pressure led to Syrian military withdrawal from Lebanon, taking with it a number of political institutions and social and military control apparatuses, including the core of the intelligence service. The parliamentary majority and their supportive communities immediately accused Hezbollah of facilitating or at least overseeing Hariri's killing. Hezbollah publicly condemned the assassination and categorically denied any involvement.

The parliamentary majority was soon after led by Saad Hariri, Rafiq al-Hariri's son, who relocated to Lebanon from Saudi Arabia after his father's death to assume the vacant leadership role in al-Hariri's political party, *Tayyār al-Mustaqbal* (Future Movement). The Druze leader Walid Jumblat, and the leaders of the Christian parties, namely the Lebanese Forces and The Phalange,[9] joined forces with Saad Hariri shortly after the assassination. On the other side, Hezbollah and the other main Shi'i political party, *Amal*, were joined by the Christian General Michel Aoun, who returned from his self-imposed exile in Paris to lead *al-Tayyār al-Waṭany al-Ḥurr* (Free Patriotic Movement), and other leftist secular parties, such as the Lebanese Communist Party and al-*Ḥizb al-Sūry al-Qawmy al-Ijtimā'ay* (The Syrian Social Nationalist Party; or simply SSNP).

The political idiom uniting each one of these groups of parties hinged upon their support for or disapproval of Syria, and their political discourse carried heavy religious, mainly Sunni and Shi'i, undertones. Smaller confessions, such as the Christians and the Druze, with their numbers and bargaining power at that time already overshadowed by those of the Sunni and the Shi'i, had to opt for political alliances with one of the more powerful groups.

---

9   The Phalange, the Maronite Christian party founded in the 1930s, was up to the beginning of the Lebanese Civil War the dominant political force in Lebanon.

The anti-Syrian alliance of Saad Hariri was also known as *March 14*, follow-ing an event in 2005, the so-called Cedar Revolution, which took place after al-Hariri's assassination, in protest of Syrian military presence in Lebanon. In contrast, the pro-Syrian alliance was called *March 8*, in reference to a po-litical demonstration on March 8, 2005, to celebrate Syria's role in stabilizing the country after the Lebanese Civil War and in strengthening Lebanese re-sistance against the Israeli occupation of Lebanon.

Although the idiom of this polarization was frequently expressed simply as "pro" and "anti" Syria parties, the goals of each faction were particular and complex. For example, the Phalange, the Lebanese Forces (L.F.), and the Fu-ture Movement supported the Syrian intervention during and right after the Civil War, whereas Hezbollah and Aoun directly met Syria with war at the time. The Free Patriotic Movement of Michel Aoun started out as part of the March 14 block, but on February 6, 2006, it signed a memorandum of under-standing with Hezbollah which put the movement in the opposite camp. As yet another of many possible examples, the Communist Party and Hezbollah were initially inimical due to conflicting ideologies, one being secular and the other religious. Finally, after the parliamentary elections in 2009, the Druze leader Walid Jumblat conveniently announced his withdrawal from the March 14 block, stating that its agenda had become too "pro-Western" and less "Arab" focused. In other words, even if the political arena appeared to have only two sides that were expressed according to the "Syrian formula," in reality there was no permanent direct ideological resemblance among the parties grouped on each side, and nobody could predict with certainty how political alliances would unfold even in the near future. These alliances were primarily strategic and political in character, while social belonging was still very much defined by the ethnicized religious tones of the confessions. While the pro-Syria group was mainly associated with the Shi'a, the anti-Syrian coalition was largely as-sociated with Sunni Islam. At the time, the Christians were politically frac-tured, with the Aoun group primarily highlighting the Arab anti-Imperialist nature of its Lebanese identity, as Christian groups on the other side tended to express their Lebanese identity by aligning it with Western and Christian values.

Such was the political climate when I arrived in Lebanon at the end of May 2006 to begin my field research. What I did not expect, though, was that the political situation would soon even further deteriorate. On June 25, 2006, Hamas kidnapped Gilad Shalit, an Israeli soldier, killing two more soldiers and wounding four others. Israel responded with its largest offensive in Gaza since the Second Intifada (al-Aqsa). Soon thereafter, Hezbollah kidnaped two more Israeli soldiers on a cross-border raid. The Israeli answer was a full-scale war against Lebanon.

In a genuine, if momentary, bridging of sectarian and political divides, all sectors of the government and the majority of the Lebanese population condemned the Israeli attack and proceeded to help its direct victims. Nonetheless, some factions, both within government and in society at large, saw in the war an opportunity to weaken Hezbollah and strengthen their own grip on the country. The war pitted the Israeli IDF against Hezbollah, as the Lebanese army did not enter the war due partly to a lack of equipment, and even more so out of fear of splitting into confessions, thereby scaling up the conflict and plunging the country into civil war once again.

This war was commonly seen in the West as a war of Israel against Hezbollah. In practice, Amal and other small leftist political groups not well known in the West also joined the war on Hezbollah's side, while the only Palestinian group to directly join the conflict was the Marxist Popular Front for the Liberation of Palestine *(al-Jabha Sha'abiyya li-Taḥrīr Filastyn*, or PFLP), which had only a symbolic role and lost only two militiamen. The Israeli government stated that it was helping to liberate Lebanon and the Lebanese from Hezbollah,[10] and the Israeli Prime Minister Ehud Olmert never officially declared war against the state of Lebanon. However, the Israeli army violently attacked Lebanese civilian infrastructure, destroying the Rafiq al-Hariri international airport, all bridges and major roads in Lebanon, many silos containing fuel or food, and entire Shi'a majority villages and cities, such as Tyre, Bint Jbeil, and Qana[11] (Hovsepian 2007).

This war was locally known as *Ḥarb Tammūz* (July War; or simply the 2006 War) and lasted for thirty-four days. Its consequences were tremendous in Lebanon. In addition to the large number of causalities, the war destroyed a considerable part of the country's infrastructure and deeply undermined the Lebanese economy. Until the end of my formal fieldwork in the summer of 2009, the government was still rebuilding that infrastructure. For example, daily electricity restrictions continued, rationing four hours of electricity alternated with four hours without in most cities except the Beirut area, where rationing did not take such extreme proportions. Politically, the war

---

10   I read this in Arabic on a flyer dropped by an Israeli plane onto the streets of a mixed
      neighborhood in Beirut.

11   All of which also had a significant number of Christians.

in effect strengthened Hezbollah's grip on the country after what was locally considered to be its military success. Although many Lebanese held Hezbollah responsible for provoking the war, in the opinion of the great majority of Lebanese, the Israeli response was disproportionate, especially since it was by no means limited to the destruction of Hezbollah's infrastructure and elimination of its personnel.

Upon returning to the USA, another consequential event took place in Lebanon, this time involving the Palestinians more directly. On May 20, 2007, the Lebanese police raided a house in Tripoli which was ostensibly used by militants of an Islamic neo-fundamentalist group called Fatah al-Islam[12] with headquarters inside the Nahr al-Bared Palestinian refugee camp. According to UN data from 2003, Nahr al-Bared was home to 31,023 Palestinian refugees. Fatah al-Islam members were fewer than 300 in total. Nevertheless, when members of Fatah al-Islam opened fire against the Lebanese police, they triggered a major armed confrontation in the area surrounding the refugee camp. Fatah al-Islam members stormed a Lebanese checkpoint at the entrance of the camp, killing 27 Lebanese soldiers plus a number of civilians. The faction was already unpopular even in Nahr al-Bared. As I heard from camp residents, it had been trying to impose its version of Islam upon residents, and it treated Palestine as just one more front for jihad. After the conflict started, both Fatah and Hamas offered to enter the camp and dismantle the group for the government. Lebanese authorities, however, rejected this offer, as they saw official Lebanese intervention as being of utmost necessity. Hezbollah vehemently condemned the neo-fundamentalist Salafi group, which began to be seen as an implant in Lebanon to counter Hezbollah influence. This time, Hezbollah did not take matters into its own hands, but expressed support for the Lebanese army, calling its fallen fighters "martyrs of the national cause."

The Lebanese government chose to address the problem by deploying the army and began a siege of the camp that lasted about four months. According to the Lebanese army, Fatah al-Islam leaders were mainly Iraqi, Algerian, and even Lebanese. They sought to establish themselves in the Palestinian camps due to the sites' strategic value both as hideouts and as fertile ground for recruitment to Islamism and Islamic neo-fundamentalism. Many Palestinian refugees were considered to have lost their direction in life, to have no

---

12   A split from Fatah al-Intifada – which is already a split from Fatah – that, unlike its predecessor, did not have many Palestinians in its leadership and was not secular and/or socialist.

expectations or hope for the future, and to be living in abject poverty. However, there is little evidence that their efforts at recruitment were successful. Nonetheless, the camp was completely leveled to the ground during the four months of siege, which lasted until September 2. Most of the displaced people went to live with friends and family in other Palestinian refugee camps across Lebanon.

I returned to Lebanon a couple of months after the end of the conflict in Nahr al-Bared. This time, when I left the airport, I went straight to al-Jalil refugee camp where, among others, I met some of the Nahr al-Bared refugees now living there and a Palestinian man with whom I had spent much time during the war in 2006. In my absence, another political development had occurred: the Lebanese could not agree on elections following the end of President Emile Lahoud's term. Both the March 14 and March 8 factions were suspicious of one another and would only accept a new election under their own conditions. As a consequence, for the whole second period of my stay in Lebanon, which lasted a bit more than 10 months, the state had no president, and this issue greatly heated up the political arena and helped to shape the processes described in this book.

c.   The Structure of the Book

Bearing the "religion as the cause" thesis in mind and the overall ritualization perspective, this book is divided into two parts, each one contributing key elements to the main discussion. *Part I* presents the broad ritualization approach. As one of the main differences between the camps, social life in the Muslim camp, al-Jalil, was profoundly ritualized, while social life in the Christian camp, Dbayeh, was hardly so, or at least not collectively so. In this way, ritualization emerges as a central topic to the discussion on the camps' distinct characters and the influence of religiosity.

Chapter 1 contextualizes my own long and ongoing process of negotiating suspicion and trust among my fieldwork interlocutors. It is self-reflective, problematizes my position, and introduces relevant general methodological specifics about the historical and local contexts. This chapter opens the discussion on suspicion and trust that is an intrinsic part of social dynamics in the contexts I present throughout the book, and which will be resumed in the final chapter prior to the conclusion.

Chapter 2 briefly discusses how Palestinian referents, dispositions, affects, and sensibilities affect the framing of time, before presenting succinct oral historical accounts of each camp. The historical trajectories thus delineated help identify the main elements that led to social differentiation between the two camps, and events that shaped the way refugees from each camp appropriated and re-appropriated religious and non-religious referents, affects, dispositions and sensibilities and how that came to affect their sociality. Subsequently, I discuss social belonging in each camp through a ritualization perspective by focusing on Palestinianness and on how religiosity influenced each camp's contexts.

Chapter 3 describes social dynamics in the Muslim camp. Al-Jalil's social dynamics had strong centripetal attributes that tended to connect most camp residents. The camp was militarized, and social dynamics revolved around Palestinian political parties and social movements. This environment accounted for a strong sense of collectivity; it fueled collective expression, restricting individual expression and imposing a certain social pace and format to quotidian life that stimulated ritualization. Nonetheless, this did not always entail social cohesion. The ritualized pace, or rhythm of daily life evident in this camp, is what I call a *ritual tempo*, which can be understood also as a social forum shaping, maintaining, and transforming sociality. Ritual tempi relate to sets of public ritualized practices and discourses ranging from simple day-to-day social interaction to specific calendars of events. A given ritual tempo socializes members of the community around a set of values, practices, and behaviors, helping demarcate the boundaries of the community vis-à-vis others, and organize community history, thereby providing frameworks for understanding the world. These tempi inscribe religion as much as religion itself inscribes ritual, further strengthening social bonds and helping to shape common socio-political goals, moral values, national imagination, and even common conceptions of time and space.

By contrast, *Chapter 4* delineates the social dynamics present in the Christian camp. Dbayeh was marked by centrifugal social tendencies. This camp was completely demilitarized, and the local tempo of daily life combined both Palestinian and Lebanese elements. Social life was much more dispersed, and the collective configuration of discourses and practices tended to be much weaker. Concomitantly, common socio-political goals, moral values, national imagination, and common conceptions of time and space were not as strongly expressed. The *tempo of daily life* – as defined by Rosemary Sayigh (1994) – was much less ritualized. Even though religion did provide a common frame alongside nationhood, it was not coupled with an element singularizing the group *vis-à-vis* its Lebanese surroundings, as was the case of nationhood in al-

Jalil. In fact, in Dbayeh, religion tended to provide a common denominator with the Lebanese surroundings, enabling the Palestinian refugees to carry on with their lives despite the historically hostile environment.

Quotidian social interaction in Dbayeh did not revolve around a public articulation and assertion of Palestinianness, but precisely the opposite; Palestinianness was expressed privately, thus ensuring that it did not manifest itself in the public sphere, thereby creating new conflict or opening old wounds between the Lebanese Christian surroundings and the Palestinian (Christian) camp. Between 2006 and 2010, Dbayeh community social life was much more dispersed because of different categories of belonging (non-*muwāṭan* Palestinian, *muwāṭan*, and non-*Aṣl Falastyny* Lebanese - respectively: Palestinians who do not hold Lebanese citizenship, Palestinians who do hold Lebanese citizenship, and Lebanese with no Palestinian origins). Such categories designated the level of incorporation of individuals on a *continuum* from Palestinianness to Lebaneseness. Dispersal was increased by the diffuse physical environment of the camp, an absence of the Palestinian institutions brought by the PLO, Dbayeh inhabitants' attachment to Christian values, and their own perceptions of themselves. All these forces pulled the camp's social dynamics away from formalized and shared forms of ritualization, as the book demonstrates.

Part II discusses the making and maintaining of general referents, dispositions, affects, and sensibilities affecting the framing of time underlying social dynamics in both camps, and of a Palestinian conception of resistance with religious undertones, whereby existence is equated to resistance. *Chapter 5* presents Palestinian general referents, affects, dispositions, and sensibilities affecting the framing of time. While the general notion is tributary to the same historical events and conditions – especially in *al-Nakba*, "The Right of Return," and present refugeeness – each camp developed different tendencies based on desirable outcomes to its present undesirable condition. *Al-Nakba*, or "The Catastrophe" in Arabic, is what Palestinians called Israel's independence and their subsequent existence as refugees. The Right of Return refers to a United Nations resolution calling for "the return" of Palestine refugees. Although such a resolution was not binding – like all United Nations resolutions – and ultimately rather vague, it was appropriated by many Palestinians as a utopian event, tending to influence the framing of time especially among those groups and individuals who prescribe or wish for a return.

Chapter 6 introduces the concept of *al-ṣumūd*. The term can be translated in English as "steadfastness"; it means "resistance" in Arabic, but it is distinguished from other forms of resistance, such as *muqāwama*. While *muqāwama* refers to a more "active" resistance, as in, for example, defending a homeland with weapons, *ṣumūd* denotes a more "passive" kind of resistance, such as to continue to uphold national or religious traditions despite unfavorable conditions. In Islam, *ṣumūd* is associated with several divine attributes, and in spite of having been secularized by the PLO especially during the times of the Lebanese Civil War, *al-ṣumūd* continues to carry religious undertones for the Palestinian refugees among whom I researched. The Palestinian general referents, affects, dispositions, and sensibilities affecting the framing of time described above and *al-ṣumūd* were tightly interwoven, thereby reinforcing each other. Both of these concepts underpinned feelings and actions, profoundly impacting social belonging processes and thus representing important ways in which religion was experienced in daily life.

Chapter 7 connects the discussion on a disposition toward suspicion presented in *Chapter 1*, to one on ritualized politico-moral economies of trust embedded in most interpersonal interactions. Religiosity here is more or less important for entrustment, depending on subject and context. In most cases, politics and family ties are just as relevant, and often even more so than religiosity. While all societies may develop their own economies of trust, cultural and situational elements define every particular local case. Both camp environments presented in this book show an inclination towards suspicion associated with the refugee condition, similar to what the authors of *Mistrusting Refugees* (Daniel & Knudsen 1996) first noticed among Palestinians, but also elsewhere in the world. Such a disposition reinforced the intensity of economies of trust in refugee camp social life, constituting a strong force shaping its dynamics. In other words, the condition of refugeeness heavily influenced such economies of trust, which thus worked as a boundary maintenance mechanism influencing the making, maintenance, and transformation of groups' constituencies and alliances. While generalized suspicion is the theme of *Chapter 1, Chapter 7* focuses on local entrustment systems.

Thus, if religiosity tended to galvanize different social belonging processes in the two camps, a disposition towards suspicion associated with the refugee condition was susceptible to be equally central to both and actively shaped each of the camps' economies of trust. Nonetheless, ritualized local economies of trust in each camp were impacted by religiosity to varying degrees depending on context and regardless of the camp or religion, while still expressing broader socio/cultural/historical contexts, and thus emphasizing the uniqueness of each social arrangement.

Finally, the *conclusion* brings together the ritualization and religiosity discussion, now better informed by ethnographic data. It seeks to explain how these concepts help advance the anthropological understanding of social phenomena such as those described throughout the book and makes a case for further developing these concepts via subsequent comparative work.

Chapter 1: A Disposition toward Suspicion

Between 2006 and 2010, most of my fieldwork in Lebanon was spent inside Palestinian refugee camps. I spent my days in the camps, slept in the camps, ate in the camps, and socialized in or outside the camps, usually with the Palestinian community. Given the animosity that prevails between almost all sectors of Lebanese society and the Palestinian refugees, this was a source of suspicion for many Lebanese people around me, from state officials to civilian actors of all confessions and political ideals. At the same time and for similar reasons, I also became a source of suspicion for the very Palestinians among whom I was spending my time.

The fact that the Palestinians were refugees had important consequences for their sense of belonging and for the making of social relations, both at intra-group and extra-group levels. Among the most important implications of refugeeness was an almost ever-present sense of suspicion that I will call a *disposition toward suspicion*. This disposition can be characterized as a generalized mistrust that must be overcome in order for social bonding to occur. Therefore, the experience of suspicion was of great importance in matters of social organization and identity.

In what follows, I analyze the sources and modes of suspicion and trust among Palestinian refugees in Dbayeh and Al-Jalil, ranging from a broader social conceptualization of trust to more situational and culturally specific aspects; hence, this chapter also dwells in some detail on the Lebanese political situation at the time of my field research. This serves multiple purposes: first, it helps the reader to gain a general understanding of the breadth of Lebanese political allegiances, which are major sources of both suspicion and trust for Palestinians in Lebanon. Second, it allows me to dive deeper to the level of interpersonal relations, providing a perspective from below that is complementary to my focus upon the broad social context of the camps. This, in turn, also provides a background to my field research experience and its limitations. Third, it allows me to investigate in greater depth the ways in which the politics of nationhood were entangled with religion in Lebanon, how the Palestinians were uniquely situated in this context, and how the process of entrustment was also part of the ritual tempo of both Al-Jalil and Dbayeh.

In the Palestinian case, the characteristic inwardness of the refugee experience was first imposed by the events leading to fleeing and the flight itself, and then reinforced by the Lebanese social and political exclusion of Palestinian refugees. This, in turn, led to a suspicion towards outsiders as a way to protect members of the refugee communities from the largely hostile environment surrounding them, while also reinforcing a sense of collectivity among the groups thus formed. Suspicion toward outsiders was not only a Palestinian cultural element. Some would say it is universal. However, in this case suspicion was closely related to these groups' specific condition as refugees. This chapter presents generalized suspicion as one of the stronger forces heightening the importance of trust and forming the shape of entrustment in both refugee camps compared in this book. Towards the end of this book, *Chapter 7* defines what I call politico-moral economies of trust and, in the process, articulates the relevance of suspicion, among other contributing elements, to what I will suggest is a largely ritualized economy.

a.   The Politics of Religion

Political alliances in Lebanon change at a frantic pace. As a result, it becomes difficult to distinguish political allies from opponents. Nevertheless, political belonging in Lebanon is very much constitutive of identity for both groups and individuals. In order to mitigate the unpredictability of the political sphere, individuals and groups tend to withdraw to the comfort zone of their own families, villages, and religious sects.

"Confessions" (singular *ṭā'ifa*; plural, *ṭawā'if*) is the English term, derived from the French *confessions*, designating the socio-political organizations based on religious affiliation upon which the Lebanese state system is based. It is a synonym for "sect," if sect is also understood as a socio-political institution rather than just a secretive religious group. Because of this political system, religion inevitably permeates the political sphere in the Lebanese context, even if it does not fully determine it. Such a system also accentuates the social aspects of religion, which in turn become increasingly associated with categories such as ethnicity and nationhood. In practice, politics in Lebanon is greatly shaped by confessional interests, which in turn tend to be expressed partially in religious idiom. This not only further strengthens internal confessional relations, but also ethnicizes religion.

For instance, civil marriage is still prohibited in Lebanon, and confessional authorities officially handle family law. This arrangement makes inter-confessional marriage difficult, and, in turn, the confessions are often thought of and felt as not only different religious groups, but also different ethnicities. Intra-sectarian strife, such as between Amal and Hezbollah in the 1980s or between the Jumblat and the Arslan Druze alliances, is still possible, as are political alliances such as those between the Shi'i Hezbollah and supporters of the secular Christian leader Michel Aoun, or between the Christian Phalangists and Sunni-led Future Movement. However, while alliances might appear strong at a given point in time, they shift constantly, while confessions themselves remain stable political groups. Notwithstanding a general propensity for strife, the political system encourages different political allegiances to collaborate toward similar goals, as these are largely defined in sectarian terms.

As mentioned in the introduction, the political situation in Lebanon was particularly tense during my fieldwork, even by Lebanese standards. Animosity, tension, and actual conflict had been escalating, starting with the assassination of the Prime Minister Rafiq al-Hariri and the ensuing Syrian military withdrawal in 2005. The situation was further exacerbated by the 2006 war, the destruction of Nahr al-Bared refugee camp in 2007, the long period in which Lebanon remained without a president, and the Lebanese parliamentary elections in the summer of 2009.

National and territorial boundaries of what constituted Palestine and Lebanon, Palestinians and Lebanese, were largely shaped in contrast to each other, in line with Frederik Barth's discussion of the role that boundaries and contrasts play in constituting identity (1967; 2002). Thus, in Lebanon, the Palestinians, much like the Syrians, were sometimes defined/self-defined as the primary *others* within Lebanese society, more so than other migrant communities such as the Filipinos, Sudanese, or Iraqis. Given that they constituted an important element for the definition of Lebanese identity itself, a look at the boundaries of the Lebanese nation-state helps to better understand how they were constantly being shaped, reshaped, manipulated, maintained, and transformed.

While I was living in Dbayeh, the political situation in Lebanon reached a boiling point (once more). The Lebanese parliamentary majority threatened to close Hezbollah's TV station, Al-Manar, prompting the Shi'i group to take to the streets of Beirut with its fighters and heavy weapons, clashing with Future Movement supporters and militiamen. The situation soon worsened in Tripoli, where Alawite militiamen fought in support of Hezbollah, and Sunni militiamen (including radical Salafi militias), loyal to the Future Movement, fought in the name of the government. Once more, the army played no role except for being deployed to conflict areas, typically after the clashes had already ended. In fact, whenever new clashes erupted, the army would evacuate the area so as not to be involved in the conflict, again, out of fear of splitting the military into factions and starting a new civil war. As a result of the hostilities, the army was compelled to withdraw from Beirut's most important high-end commercial center in Hamra, Walid Jumblat had to leave his home in *Verdun* due to Hezbollah's dominance in the region, Saad Hariri also ran away from his residency in Hamra, and so on. Because of fears that civil war might be imminent, no Christian militia was involved in the conflicts, as they were seen as a struggle between Sunni and Shi'i groups only.

In fact, at times I thought we were already in the midst of a civil war, but I soon learned from personal experience that what would be considered civil war in Europe or the USA was very different from what would be considered civil war in Lebanon, where the recent history of internal violence was much more extreme. While in Beirut during part of this conflict-ridden period, I heard the sounds of machine guns rehearsing their theme day after day. I avoided going to certain neighborhoods where the conflict was more intense. Like many Lebanese and Palestinians, I was used to hearing the sound of machine guns every day even before this conflict. From Dbayeh, for instance, you could often hear the Phalange training with machine guns somewhere around the neighborhood, or at least the Phalange was the conductor of that dreaded symphony in many Dbayeh inhabitants' minds.

Hezbollah eventually completed its takeover of the most important Sunni neighborhoods of Beirut after only a few deaths, broken windows, new bullet holes joining old ones in the edifices' facades, and the revenge burning of the Future Movement TV station's main building. After holding these areas for a period of time, Hezbollah proceeded to inform the public that the operation was complete, and it withdrew its forces, giving space once more to civilians and the Lebanese Army. The goal seemed clear: to prove that the March 14 claims that Hezbollah was planning a *coup d'état* were wrong. That is, by first staging it and then withdrawing, Hezbollah hoped to prove that a *coup* had not been its main political goal, and at the same time display its military might. It sought to sway Lebanese public opinion to their favor and frighten opponents into dropping their demands on the Shi'i group.

Before completing the 2006-2010 phase of my fieldwork, the Lebanese finally agreed on General Michel Suleiman as "the candidate" for presidency, indicating that the army was the only non-sectarian Lebanese institution capable of representing the interests of the nation in general. The army's neutral position vis-à-vis Hezbollah's actions against Israel in the 2006 War and during the conflicts between the two main Lebanese warring factions, and its renewed morale after its victory in Nahr al-Bared at the expense of the camp's Palestinian refugees, guaranteed the preservation of public order after Suleiman's election to office.[1] The army remained the only political reason for Lebanese people from different groups to still refer to themselves equally as Lebanese.

Palestinians themselves were very much divided in their alliances with Lebanese political factions. The general official position was to avoid direct involvement in internal affairs, so that they could maintain their political autonomy by way of an informal compromise. In practice, Hamas, Islamic Jihad, PFLP, and all the other components of the "rejectionist front" supported March 8 (the so-called pro-Syria group), while Fatah (minus its splinter groups formed after the failed Oslo Peace Process) and the rest of the Palestinian Authority supported March 14 (the so-called anti-Syria group). It is known that such Lebanese groups collaborated with other political offices in the refugee camps.[2] For the Palestinian camp residents who supported one or another of these Palestinian political blocks, the tendency was to go along with the parties' allegiances and support their respective Lebanese allies. This, however, often generated friction, as the following story illustrates.

As with all my fieldwork visits, the summer of 2009 did not pass by without surprises. It was the time of the much-awaited Parliamentary elections that would finally tip the balance of power toward one side or the other. For one month during this time, I lived in an apartment that functioned as a haven for Palestinian refugee camp youth studying in Beirut.[3] The apartment

---

1   On April 14, I went once more to Lebanon for three months to complete my fieldwork. This time, parliamentary and local elections were at stake in June 2009.

2   As shown by the demonstration I present in Chapter 3.

3   While Palestinians were prohibited from holding most jobs in Lebanon, they were still free to study, and some students were funded by endowments from donors in Arab countries (including some Lebanese sources). However, most chose not to study since by Lebanese law they were not allowed to exercise their professions in Lebanon. During

was located amidst old bombed buildings still used for habitation in a lower class area of Tariq Al-Jadideh, two blocks away from the *Jām'a 'Arabiyya* (Arab University), the richest area of the neighborhood. This neighborhood was almost exclusively Sunni, and it was almost impossible to find anyone in it who did not support Hariri, since anyone with other loyalties would most certainly hide their convictions for fear of reprisals. It was there that I heard the result of the electoral result favorable for the March 14 movement. However, not everybody was happy in the neighborhood, and my Palestinian refugee roommates kept their political convictions largely hidden.

The apartment itself was humble – there was little furniture, and the space itself, especially the kitchen, was not very clean, like most male students' apartments. It had two rooms, a kitchen used almost exclusively for tea and *argile* smoking, one bathroom, one living room, and a veranda. Four people permanently lived in the apartment during the week, although usually all of them would return to their respective refugee camps on weekends. In addition, almost every night guests would usually sleep there as well. Each room had a couple of beds, but more space was made by simply placing thin mattresses on the floor of the bedrooms and living room.

Quranic verses or Islamic expressions were written in ink on the walls and doors of the apartment, along with Hamas' flags, stickers, and posters. The person in charge of this space was Tawfiq, a young man from Al-Jalil. The son of one of the most reputable figures among the sheikhs in Al-Jalil, it was Tawfiq who invited me to live with them. He enjoyed good relations with the local Sunni community because of his father and also because of his own job at *Dār al-Fatwa*, where he was studying to become a sheikh. *Dār al-Fatwa* literarily means "home of the religious edict" and was created in 1922 to preside over confessional matters pertaining to the Sunni community in Lebanon. The mufti of the republic heads the institution, which administers mosques and religious schools throughout the country. To work at *Dār al-Fatwa* was highly respected in Lebanon, an honor not awarded to many Palestinians in the country, even though many Palestinian refugees studied there (Rougier 2007). However, Tawfiq supported Hamas and the Lebanese opposition led by Hezbollah, like most who set foot in his apartment.

---

my stay in the camps, I met, for instance, a sociologist who made a living running a backyard pastry shop, a philosopher who was on his way to becoming a sheikh, and a psychologist who ran a Palestinian cultural association.

The political situation in Lebanon – together with memories of the Lebanese Civil War and the ways in which Palestinian social, political and religious leaders positioned themselves in relation to the Lebanese parties – generated a conceptual space from which Lebanese discourses about Palestinians arose.[4] Due to the power imbalance between them, the ways in which the Lebanese conceptualized Palestinians were integral to the ways in which the latter viewed themselves in the country. As Palestinians, Sunni, and also pro Hamas, those young men in Tariq Jadideh had to make sense of their identities according to many elements in a complex process of articulation that often did not coincide with Lebanese expectations.

b. Negotiating Anthropology

For a few months at the beginning of my fieldwork, I had to go back and forth to the Lebanese General Security office to gain research permission. The officer in charge of my papers was suspicious of me from the outset, given that I was researching Palestinian refugees and that I was living in the camps. To make matters worse, I had managed to enter Nahr al-Bared – which was then off-limits to almost everyone – with an acquaintance from the camp itself who was working there as a nurse. He told the Lebanese soldiers at the checkpoint that I was working with him, and I would soon discover that the Lebanese intelligence did not approve of it. The officer in charge of my case at the General Security had short hair, military uniform, and a grim face. I could not read her. Was she Muslim or Christian? Was she Pro-Syria or not? What seemed clear, though, is that she viewed Palestinians with great suspicion. The first words she uttered to me as I stepped into her office for the first time were: "You have been talking to people you shouldn't; you have been taking photos of things you shouldn't; you have been living where you shouldn't. Who are you and what do you want in my country?" My letter from Boston University stating that I was a PhD candidate there and that I would be conducting fieldwork in Palestinian refugee camps was not sufficient to gain her trust. Neither were the hours of interrogation and reasoning. The Syrian occupation had just ceased and the Hariri assassination had plunged the country into turmoil. The Lebanese intelligence apparatus was therefore trying to regain

---

4   In a parallel example, Nasser Abufarha shows that the manner in which Israelis conceptualize and act towards Palestinians in the Occupied Territories partly constitutes the way Palestinians conceptualize themselves, even if in opposition (2009).

control over the country. I had to negotiate with her and her office for many months before receiving authorization for my research, a process involving weekly interrogations and demands. I was already living in Al-Jalil and once a week I had to travel to Beirut, where the headquarters of the General Security was located. The trip itself sometimes lasted two hours each way, and occasionally I had to stay overnight in a cheap dormitory in Beirut, proceed to General Security in the morning and only then return to Al-Jalil. Both for ethical and security concerns, I did not hide the reason for my trips from people in Al-Jalil. As a result, these trips also led to some suspicion: what was I really doing at the General Security offices practically every week?

My stay in the camps had been negotiated from the outset among local groups. During the 2006 War – and because of it – I met a Palestinian refugee from Shatila who lived with two acquaintances of mine (one American and the other French), in the same building as myself. His name was Marwan. We spent almost all of our time together during the war. Both of us volunteered in a local school that was receiving new Lebanese refugees, mostly from the South, and Palestinian refugees who had evacuated the camps. He and I also spent time in the streets on the lookout for news. From hilltops, beaches, or rooftops, we sadly and helplessly watched buildings being bombed. We ate communal meals back at the apartment building, and sometimes went to Shatila to check on his family and see if they needed anything, as they had chosen to stay in the camp stating that "they did not want to live as refugees anymore." This experience was my first contact with the refugee camps. Approximately one week before the end of the war, due to my academic commitments, I was required to leave Lebanon in the last wave of repatriations offered by the Italian government. When I came back and went straight to Al-Jalil, it was Marwan who waited for me, as he was then working in the camp. Experiencing the war together had forged a strong bond of friendship between us, which in turn made my fieldwork possible.

In Al-Jalil, I initially lived with Marwan in his one room apartment while I taught English as a volunteer for *Markaz li-Ḥuqūq al-Insān* (Center for Human Rights), where he also worked. I later decided that it would be better to rent my own place in the camp, so I could have more privacy and would not bother my friend too much, especially since in the beginning his mother liked to visit him from Shatila for two or three days at a time. After the first month, I moved to an apartment right outside the entrance of the camp, which allowed me to spend full days and nights socializing with people in Al-Jalil. I remained there for just over five months. For the last three months I lived in yet another apartment, this time inside the camp, where I paid US$100.00 in rent per month to an elderly woman whose entire family had either died or moved abroad, leaving her with extra space to rent out. I was told that, prior to my moving in, the place had been a cultural center, and once there, I noticed that a big yellow flag featuring Yaser Arafat's face served as curtains. When I left the camp to live in Dbayeh for five more months, the woman offered me the flag as a present.

Friends in Al-Jalil urged me not to talk openly about the reason behind my trips to the General Security offices in Beirut and not to even mention that I had visited Nahr al-Bared. In their view, it could compromise my research and make my life in the camp difficult. Besides, they told me there were spies for the Lebanese army, for Israel, and for many other groups, Lebanese or otherwise, within the camp population. They claimed that one of the reasons they could trust me (although they did not mention the reasons why they would not trust me), was that the spies tended to be Palestinian. In the idiom of Lebanese or Palestinian politics, their concerns were multiple: they worried about what local Palestinian non-Lebanese government supporters would think; about what Lebanese government supporters would think; and what supporters of the Palestinian authority or those supporting the rejectionist front led by Hamas would think.

According to a number of camp residents, I was the first non-Palestinian to live in Al-Jalil, as opposed to camps such as Shatila or Beddawi, both of which had community centers that at times offered accommodation for journalists and researchers. Locals informed me that for my stay in Al-Jalil to materialize, considerable negotiation had to transpire beforehand, and weekly visits to the Lebanese General Security offices would certainly not expedite matters. The only reason I could go straight from the airport to live in the camps was due to the trust developed between Marwan and I during the war of 2006. This trust was sufficient for Marwan to risk his own reputation by making the case in Al-Jalil for me to live there. Shared experiences of hardship during the 2006 war allowed for an exceptional bonding experience, which was somewhat similar in character, although different in scale, to that of those who became refugees from the same country and shared the same roof. Nevertheless, these negotiations about my status in Al-Jalil did not cease upon my arrival, nor were they limited to my relationship with Marwan.

For instance, after already having stayed in the camp for a period of time, I was approached by a local Palestinian who shouted at me that I should not be living there. He seemed unaware that it had already been decided that I could do so, or so I thought. Moreover, he was especially angry that someone would have rented an apartment to me within the boundaries of the camp. Where was I living? Who rented the apartment to me? Why was I there? I told him my story - the same story I told at the General Security offices – although I did not mention that I was going almost every week to the Lebanese intelligence headquarters. He walked alongside me inside the border of the camp as we passed the Fatah checkpoint, where armed men dressed in military uniform were talking with other Palestinians in civilian clothes. He demanded to know how I was able to find housing and walk around the camp freely. I mentioned that I was working for the *Markaz*, where I taught English, and helped them on general issues such as translating documents into English. He insisted I should leave the camp, and that no one should have allowed me there without his approval. It turned out that he was the local responsible for the UNRWA office in the camp. The reason for his disapproval, although he claimed it to be solely a matter of internal security for camp refugees, had less to do with security and more to do with his belief that I, and whoever vouched for my stay in Al-Jalil, had disrespected his authority. As such, it was a moral issue, or a matter of honor. Such questions of respect and deference were not uncommon as many local groups constantly disputed authority in the camp.

Puzzled and very worried, I mentioned the matter to the general manager of the *Markaz*. His demands were met with laughter and a certain lack of consideration from my Palestinian sponsors. The manager of the *Markaz* told me to "forget about it" since "everything that should have been taken care of was already taken care of." He also proudly told me that he would talk to the UNRWA representative personally. However, when I returned home that night, I found that contrary to the *Markaz* manager's position, Ḥājja[5] Amina, the elderly woman who had rented the apartment to me, was very worried about possible repercussions. The UNRWA representative had visited her stating his authority in the same way he had done with me. After about a week, however, Ḥājja Amina was back to smiling at me, proving to me that she was once again comfortable with my presence there. I realized that the manager of the *Markaz* had taken care of the situation – however it happened – since the UNRWA representative never bothered me again.

---

5   This is an Arabic feminine term referring to those who had taken part on the pilgrimage to Mecca (the Hajj), or as a sign of respect to the elderly.

My move to Dbayeh was even more difficult than my move to Al-Jalil, as not only did I have no contacts there, but more to the point, the Palestinians I knew from the Muslim majority camps did not know anyone in Dbayeh, save for the two Al-Jalil brothers who helped me. I first tried to enter the camp using the official route, by talking to UNRWA and then Caritas about the possibility of living in Dbayeh and doing voluntary work in exchange.[6] The rest of that story should help highlight the pervasiveness of suspicion in Dbayeh and introduce the reader to the ways in which trust was locally managed.

Although I tried to convince Caritas that I could be an asset in the camp, no one from the office seemed interested in my proposal. Virtually all of our communication had been by email, and every time I suggested I could visit their Dbayeh office, they postponed the meeting. I was repeatedly asked what I would do in Dbayeh, and my PhD project and emails simplifying the argument and offering to work as a volunteer did not suffice. After a while, I decided to explore the camp on my own. At first, the locals were puzzled about me: I looked Western and I spoke broken colloquial Palestinian/Lebanese Arabic with a strange accent. I told them that I wanted to do research about their lives and, if possible, live among them so that I could understand the nature of their community more profoundly.

For a few weeks, I took several trips like that first one, spent hours trying to meet people and prove that my intentions were noble, and that my stay in Dbayeh could be helpful in some way to the community. Then, one man's fascination with what I presented as the practice of anthropology became stronger than his suspicion, so much so that he rented out to me an apartment used by his family for business storage. That man was Charbel, and he did it just so he could sit with me and philosophize about the nature of mankind, the nature of God, and our favorite topic, the nature of his community. He often asked me about his primary interest, namely, how to make his community better, a topic I insisted was difficult for me to discuss, as I was not a social engineer. Despite moving to Dbayeh, I still visited Al-Jalil regularly which made some in Dbayeh uncomfortable. A few young men were brave enough to inquire, supposedly inconspicuously, what were my thoughts about Dbayeh, the other camps, the Palestinians, the Lebanese, the Muslims, and even the Jews. After months of fieldwork, Charbel and I had already established a close friendship. Yet, he and his associates in the camp would often, until the day I left, ask me

---

6   As I introduce in Chapter 4.

the same questions they asked me when I first set foot in the camp. They were not so much worried that I was a spy for Israel or the Americans, but about what I may be telling the Lebanese and the Palestinians in other camps about them.

These negotiations illustrate three important matters. The first has to do with how authority and social belonging were understood, distributed, and negotiated in Al-Jalil and Dbayeh. The second has to do with how authority was directly linked to one's honor, and challenges to authority were commonly perceived as direct attacks to one's honor – a topic I will develop in the next chapter. Finally, the third of these matters relates to my own presence in both camps, which had to be constantly negotiated in a way that was representative of modes of social bonding in the camps in general. As a principle, if my residence had become a problem for the community, then anyone who defended me would be perceived as guilty by association. Thus, my interlocutors in Al-Jalil, for example, showed genuine concern for my security and local public opinion in asking me to conceal the reason for my constant trips to Beirut. If I became suspicious, then at some level so would they. Any flag I raised in the camps would be understood as one raised in connection with the people with whom I surrounded myself, or better yet, who surrounded me, and any flag they raised would also become associated with me. This kind of association was mainly what allowed me to stay in the camps, since in spite of constant negotiation and suspicion, I was seen as part of my local network of friends who had their own political, ideological, and religious convictions. The Dbayeh story, in turn, illustrates how suspicion could be persistent and its direction indefinite.

Yet, it was not just the anthropologist or the outsider who gave cause for suspicion. In both camps, social cleavages and the fragility of people's lives made them wary of others. "The spies are Palestinian," I was told. Given this conceptual framework, almost no one was totally above suspicion, and trust was not absolute but contextually directed at the same subject or institution concomitantly, in a tug of war dynamics. Thus, trust became an element of strategic choice and investment, at the same time as it was expressed through the idiom of sensitivities, feelings, and morality. To trust someone or something was also to believe (yṣadeq) them. Trust was then given or withdrawn, in the same way that my Arabic would be contextually criticized or praised for being Lebanese or Palestinian as acknowledgement of distance or proximity. All camp inhabitants were constantly located and relocated on a continuum of trust, depending on their convictions, social networks, and actions. Therefore, every social relationship, even if not primarily concerned with the issue of trust and social bonding, carried along with it an element of trust surreptitiously negotiated. For instance, even being seen in the company of someone was as much a statement about one's standing in the community as it was an investment in that person. Thus, one of the most important social elements of this investment was precisely the act of vouching for someone or something, as different groups of people both in Al-Jalil and Dbayeh did for me at various moments during my stays in the camps, as the above examples illustrate.

The differing socio-historical contexts of the two camps shaped the ways in which suspicion and trust were publicly performed. In Al-Jalil, there was a tendency to deal with such investments in the form of public displays that served as clear statements of one's own position in the community, performed as both ritualized rehearsal and public expression of one's identity. In Dbayeh, by contrast, such investments tended to be less public and more situational, although also weakly ritualized.

c.   Suspicion as Disposition

Since I too was caught up in the camp's social dynamics, suspicion surrounded me and consumed much of my own energy. I started to suspect everyone: that some were monitoring me for this or that Palestinian or Lebanese political party or even for the Lebanese government; that the Lebanese government tapped my mobile phone hoping to obtain information on the Palestinians; that the Palestinians had monitored and recorded the international phone calls I made to my family in Brazil and the USA from Al-Jalil's phone center; that much of the ritualized celebrations in Al-Jalil were geared towards putting up a show for my sake; that Dbayeh inhabitants were ignoring or misleading me on purpose to jeopardize my fieldwork because they wanted to be left alone; and so on and so forth. In fact, even when American and European journalists, scholars, and tourists occasionally tried to bond with me, I would be suspicious of them.

No matter how much I tried to maintain self-control, I could not dismiss those thoughts completely. After all, I had indeed gone through heavy screening by the Lebanese government, which at one point retained my passport for about four months and made me go to the General Security offices almost every week to get it back, while interrogating me at every turn. The Lebanese also did not allow me to leave the country in 2009, stating that I had overstayed my visa. Instead of making me pay a fine, however, they ordered me back and forth to talk to army and General Security authorities all over again until, through the intervention of a friend of a friend, they allowed me to leave as long as I boarded the first flight, at that very moment, out of the country. In Baalbek, Hezbollah stopped me twice, and also detained me and confiscated my passport for a short while for a background check. However, I understood the necessity for both Hezbollah and the Lebanese government to check my background and keep an eye on me, since to them I was meddling in Lebanese affairs at a dire time. Syria had just withdrawn its occupation of Lebanon and had allegedly taken with it, as I was constantly told, the Lebanese intelligence files. Maybe this was just another urban myth, but it did reflect the general mood in the country. Therefore, while Lebanon was involved in many local, regional, and global conflicts, it did not seem to have much of a hold on what was actually happening in the country itself. This made sense to me, as I understood their efforts as an attempt to regain badly needed control of their internal affairs. The government was severely weakened by paramilitary control, and Hezbollah had its own independent intelligence and security apparatus, which it needed especially around the southern border with Israel, given the Lebanese army's weakness in the area.

Naturally, it also made sense for the Palestinians in Lebanon to keep track of affairs within their own territory, especially given their tacit agreement with the Lebanese government in which the Lebanese authorities would refrain from entering the refugee camps on condition that the Palestinians assume responsibility for solving their own matters and maintain security inside the camps. Internal conflict between Fatah and Hamas, and the eruption of fighting between Salafi neo-fundamentalist organizations and the PLO in some camps only made this necessity clearer.

In short, while I understood these dynamics, I continued to be suspicious of everything and everyone because everyone was also suspicious of me and almost everyone else. In Lebanon, fear of "allies" changing sides was constant, and thus trust was bestowed upon whoever was perceived as "closer," especially those from the same family (or clan), village, and confession. By the same logic, whatever was conceived as "betrayal" was among the most severe of offences. Thus, avoidance of betrayal in itself was a powerful force both consolidating as much as polarizing groups. I felt suspicious firstly because the general social climate in the camps was one of suspicion and mistrust. Second, since in my mind suspicion seemed justified and logical, I found little reason to dismiss it. Third, I felt that I could not possibly know who might be monitoring my actions or for what reasons, and this made me even more suspicious, as suspicion thrives on a sense of a lack of control.

This fieldwork experience was difficult and challenging for me, to the point that it left me somewhat disoriented for a while upon my return. In retrospect, I am still not completely sure of what was "real" and what was "imagined." Either way, what matters most is that I learned firsthand what it is to feel observed, persecuted, and victimized, and how the local communities I studied dealt with observation, persecution, and victimization – both real and perceived. Although my experience was much less severe than that of the Palestinian refugees, my humble experience allowed me to make sense of the Palestinian refugee experiences in Lebanon through one of its most important components: the weight of suspicion and trust in the community, and its modes of expression.

My own experience of being a cause for suspicion among the Lebanese and the Palestinians in Lebanon serves to illustrate its pervasiveness in the refugee camps. However, the political situation in Lebanon, in which the refugee condition was a nodal point, had a great impact on each of the camp's social belonging processes, and suspicion was in fact generalized. This context created imperatives that the refugees inescapably had to address, not just by reflecting upon them, but also by routinely dealing with them. Continuously dealing with suspicion then generated an embodied disposition, a certain technique, learned at least as much through the body as through the mind. Through imitation and repetition, camp residents learned scripts contained in daily routines since childhood. That is, they learned proper behavior, values, and vernacular expressions to deal with the quotidian and the unexpected through ritualization at least as much as by conscious reflection. A structural disposition toward suspicion and embodied scripts to negotiate trust were thus vital components embedded in both Al-Jalil and Dbayeh's ritual tempo.

d.   Suspicion & Refugees

Lebanon is but one example of how suspicion tends to be rampant in countries torn by civil war. In Lebanon, the matter was further exacerbated by entrenched sectarianism. As we have seen, war and sectarianism through Lebanese confessionalism reinforced each other, and both were responsible for the emergence of a disposition toward suspicion. However, the refugee condition also tended to intensify suspicion.

The refugee's identity stigmatization is a paradox according to which the refugee is precisely that which he cannot be. The stigma, being the cause of the refuge itself, overwhelms the refugee and becomes an imperative to be dealt with, one that informs much of the refugees' thoughts, reflections, and actions in the world. According to my own experience among Palestinian refugees in the Middle East, Latin America, and Europe, this overwhelming imperative can be dealt with in practice through two ideal typical tendencies. The stigmatized identity can be taken to heart and rendered positive, a process that often causes a hyper-expression of the stigmatized identity trait, as I witnessed mostly in Al-Jalil. Alternatively, it is put aside and largely effaced, often causing a hypo-expression of the stigmatized identity trait, as I witnessed mostly in Dbayeh. It is not always a question of choice between hyper- or hypo-expressions of Palestinianness.

In Al-Jalil, resettlement was not an option, and given the limited practical alternatives, resisting as a refugee through ṣumūd, and reinforcing the claim to return to the homeland constituted an almost necessary posture. In Dbayeh, by contrast, maintaining a ṣāmid posture and expressing Palestinianness was life threatening and thus virtually impossible as a public practice, even if enduring hardship was often understood and even sometimes expressed in more private settings in this way. Another strategy tended to be easier, namely, putting stock in a common religious (Christian) belonging to the detriment of a national identity, which was often seen locally as ethnic (Palestinian), in an effort to blend in or even become Lebanese. Likewise, there were also those in Al-Jalil who chose - and managed - to blend in with the local Lebanese population. Some even converted to Shi'i Islam and took up residency and a life outside the camp, and others were just socialized in Baalbek to the extent that Hezbollah's ideology and the institution itself became partially or totally their own. Yet, there were those in Dbayeh who found it hard to blend in and efface their Palestinianness, even when they expressed themselves otherwise so as to be able to live, just like it was the case in Al-Jalil. Moreover, given the Lebanese patrilineal citizenship principle, it was far easier for a woman to acquire Lebanese citizenship, as they could do so through marriage, whereas men did not have this option. Due to the local context, in both camps, whenever desired, the only possible way to do away with a Palestinianness to men was concealing it or leaving it aside, while women married to Lebanese citizens could "choose" to officially become Lebanese whenever individual circumstances allowed for it.

As I argue throughout this book, social context more than religious theology is what accounts for the difference in social belonging processes and identity expression in the Muslim and the Christian Palestinian refugee camps in Lebanon. However, I also point out that Palestinian refugees manage the contents and outlook of their religious belonging, as much as their ethnic, political, and economic belonging, thereby reconfiguring identity contextually in quotidian life. While this process is partially strategic, it is also partially embodied, resulting from feelings, fears, expectations, affects, sensitivities, dispositions and moral imperatives not always clearly defined or even articulated.

Furthermore, in the Palestinian case, nationhood is deeply infused with religious and ethnic elements. Being stateless also reinforces the national component of Palestinian refugee claims, and frequently even acts as a deterrent for Islamic neo-fundamentalist religious recruiting. Nationalism generally postulates a homogenous national culture, frequently equating that with religion and ethnicity. Israeli politics have largely associated Israel with the world's Jewry, instead of acknowledging its large non-Jewish, mostly Palestinian Arab component. Moreover, Jewish identity is at once ethnic and religious, which by a contrast imposed by the refuge, also highlights Palestinian religious and ethnic belonging.

Therefore, the Palestinian refugees' generalized suspicion was mainly geared towards:

a) Anyone who could be seen as responsible or even complacent with the creation of Israel and thus their own refugee condition. Muslims often also blamed "the Christians" for their misfortune, while Christian Palestinians often also blamed Palestinian Muslims for Islamizing their national cause.

b) The Lebanese and other Middle Eastern people in general, given the heavily disputed and highly fragmented political situation, plus the widespread local and regional practice of trying to control intelligence in the country.

c) Humanitarian organizations, since they were often perceived as an important part of an international consensus on maintaining their refugeeness. Palestinian refugees often reminded me that, after all, "the UN had created Israel" and that "the international community" had given it legality and legitimacy.

d) Scholars and journalists, given that while they might even show sympathy for the refugees, they do not always portray the situation as they should, and cases in which spies claimed to be scholars or journalists were not that uncommon. In a recent case around the time of my fieldwork, a "Brazilian" journalist filmed and obtained information in Shatila that was later broadcast in Israel. As it turned out, she was Jewish and a double citizen of both Brazil and Israel.

e) Palestinians themselves who might not only be members of rival political groups, but more importantly could be spies, as one refugee once told me, "The spies are Palestinians themselves."

To conclude, I define a disposition toward suspicion as collective, generalized suspicion, a condition that must be surpassed or put on hold in order for social bonding to occur. Therefore, the collective and individual experience of suspicion is of great importance to social organization and identity. That is, due principally to the refugee condition, generalized suspicion made subjects turn toward their own inner groups. Furthermore, the refugee condition coupled with the Lebanese socio-political context made Palestinian refugee camps in Lebanon extremely conducive settings for a disposition toward suspicion. The historical context of the Palestinian refuge, once more greatly reinforced by the Lebanese socio-political context, made religion, entangled with nationhood, an important source of identification and social organization among Palestinian refugees in Lebanon. Finally, the refugees' inwardness, as an entailment to suspicion toward outsiders, tended to lead to political polarization in Al-Jalil and social fragmentation in Dbayeh. The importance of trust, the emphasis on dealing with trust as a matter of honor, and the pervasiveness of customs emphasizing bonds of honor, such as extreme hospitality, are at least partially, or take the role of, efforts to manage the fears and concerns of war and oppression. As such, a structural condition of suspicion in both camps was pivotal for ritualized disciplinary practices allowing local economies of trust to develop, as I will demonstrate in the final chapter, towards the conclusion of this book.

Part I – The Refuge: Nationhood & Religion

Ritualization, as the interaction of the social body with a structured and structuring environment, specifically affords the opportunity for consent and resistance and negotiated appropriation on a variety of levels. (Bell 1992: 209)

The Marxist thesis is that the activities of the secular market – where all values are supposed to be measured by the strictest cannon of rationality – judgments are in fact influenced by mystical non-rational criteria. A full generation latter, Mauss (in The Gift), developing his theory of gift exchange form an entirely differently viewpoint, reached an identical conclusion. Exchanges that appear to be grounded in secular, rational, utilitarian needs, turn out to be compulsory acts of a ritual kind in which the objects exchanged are vehicles of mystical power. (Leach in Hugh-Jones & Laidlaw 2000: 167-68)

Chapter 2: Settling in Lebanon:
An Oral Historical Account

a. Palestinian Time Framing

To Lena Jayyusi, contemporary memory articulates a "past condition," "a bibliographical event," and a "historical facticity," but always from the point of view of "present interests," "viewpoints," and "subjective (even also subjunctive) modalities." She also suggests that the same can be said about history (Jayyusi 2007: 107) – a point similar to that made by George Stocking in *Race, Culture, and Evolution: Essays in the History of Anthropology* (1982), and one that resonates with Hans-Georg Gadamer's *fusion of horizons* (2005).

According to this perspective, iteration of the similar yet different – in a metonymical relation where the difference is located within the similarity – is a feature of all collective identity, "constituting, shaping, and apprehending collective fate and experience." In other words, the (re)-iterability of personal experiences makes possible the constitution of collective experiences. However, for collective memory to exist, iterability must be accompanied by "the simultaneity of the iterable narrativized event, present *within* the narrative itself, and iterated endlessly in one narrative after another" (Jayyusi 2007: 111).

The collective experience thus formed adds a layer to an individual experience "which can enhance its sharpness, its associated sense of the tragic, and the potentiality for continued remembrance through its entry into a public register." Thus, collective experience frames personal experience. The simultaneity of the experience, its iterability, and its concurrent onset implicates thus "the very identity of the bereaved," and for Jayyusi, such general features are also found in Palestinian narratives about the Nakba (Jayyusi 2007: 111). For her, these collective memories create a "subjunctive mood" that "encompasses both past and present" (ibid: 119). Memory is then often recast into this subjunctive mood, which is in turn interwoven with relationships between "past to present," "memory to the contemporary," and "both to the future," resulting in "different inflections of the relationship of the past to the present and the future, and distinct inflections of the subjunctive mood itself within memory" (ibid: 107).

Thus, Palestinian memory does not create a fixed past or "timeless symbols attesting history," which Jayyusi calls "time out of time," as much as it indexes "the vicissitudes of time," "the works of others," and "the presence and agency of the historical subject," which she calls "time within time," defined as "the pocket or fold of time unfolded, opened up," that "provides the dynamic and power of that agency. It offers not merely a vision of, but a project for, the future" (Jayyusi 2007: 130). In this way, Jayyusi emphasizes the intellectual process of conceptualizing memory through the iteration of narratives. What follows is influenced by Jayyusi's argument, but I prefer to highlight the performative quality of iteration rather than the intellectual work she ascribes to memory. I suggest that the mechanism of ritualization I described in the introduction is similar to the process of cumulative iteration Jayyusi describes through her notion of *time-within-time*; however, alongside narratives, I bring into consideration practices and techniques that discipline not only the mind, but also the body, generating dispositions, sensibilities, and affects which in turn directly frame behaviors, expectations, desires, moral imperatives, and practices, in addition to people's engagement with space and time.

Al-Nakba means "the Catastrophe" in Arabic. Palestinians employ the term to refer to the establishment of the state of Israel in 1948. The term's valences, however, extend beyond the historical event itself and may include the historical processes leading up to it and the ongoing Palestinian dispossession, which is seen as a consequence of the loss of their country. Especially for Palestinian refugees, the Nakba evokes the origin and reason for their refugeeness. Today, it is widely recognized that *al-Nakba* has become, at the individual, community. and national level, "both in Palestinian memory and history, the demarcation line between two qualitatively opposed periods" (Sa'di & Abu-Lughod 2007: 3). But to Ahmad Sa'di and Lila Abu-Lughod, strikingly little has been written about the period of Palestinian history (and memory) known as the Nakba. Editors and contributors to the pivotal edited collection *Nakba* all seem to acknowledge *al-Nakba* as a turning point in Palestinian memory, and thus in Palestinian discourses about history and identity. As the editors point out, "Although Palestinians had various forms of identity before 1948," it generally included "a sense of themselves as Palestinians" (Sa'di & Abu-Lughd 2007: 4; see also Beshara Doumani 1992 and Rashid Khalidi 1998).

However, the Nakba represents both in academic Palestinian history and popular Palestinian memory the "beginning of contemporary Palestinian history (...) the focal point for what might be called Palestinian time. The Nakba is the point of reference for other events, past and future. (...) The Nakba has become a key event in the Palestinian calendar – the baseline for personal histories and the sorting of generations" (Sa'di & Abu-Lughod 2007: 5).

Due to the disciplinary practices (narrative and otherwise) involved in shaping memory, and the protraction of general Palestinian material and symbolic dispossession, the Nakba cannot be relegated to a remote past. Recounting Nakba memories is pivotal for Palestinianness in that collective life "adjusted these memories to each other," producing a "canonization" of "some stories and symbols" (Sa'di & Abu-Lughod 2007: 7), and – I will add – individual and social practices. For Sa'di and Abu-Lughod, there are three aspects of the relationship between Palestinian memory and time that make it singular: a) There is practical urgency in remembering and chronicling the *Nakba* (among other events and periods), because Palestinian memories of 1948 serve as a basis for political claims; b) there is a sense of an ongoing Nakba, since most Palestinians still experience its effects and that of similar processes; c) the *Nakba* is seen as a marker of a generational time frame that upholds social processes of transfer (of "stories," "memories," "foods," "anger," "burden," "the great significance of the past," and "the inheritance of the identity") from one generation to another (ibid: 19).

Similarly, Rosemary Sayigh views *al-Nakba* as a constitutive element of Palestinianness, a site in memory that, citing Sa'di, she calls an *eternal present* (Sayigh 2007: 135). While history is epistemic and is concerned with a way of knowing the world, heritage is ontic, deals with a way of being in the world, and usually takes the form of ritual or myth. Heritage has no beginning or end, and it is open toward the future (Sayigh 2007: 137). Along with the more generalized approach to Palestinianness in her classic ethnographies on Palestinian refugee camps in Lebanon, Sayigh's seminal work examines gendered differences in the ways Palestinians relate to themselves and their collective past. Adopting Valentine Daniel's concept of heritage instead of history, she describes two different varieties of Palestinian narratives, one traditionally associated with men, and the other with women. She associates the Palestinian fable, or folk tale mode of narrative, *hikaya*, to the way women narrated events before the Nakba, and accounts of actual happenings, *qissa*, with men's narratives. In the Palestinian refugee camp Shatila, most women, whose oral histories of the Nakba she collected, did not recount the Nakba as a "fact in history, or as an internal conspiracy," but rather as "experience crafted into the form of *ḥikaya*." Nonetheless, the Nakba – she says – bridged much of the gap, as women also often engaged in *qissa* while describing events associated with it (Sayigh 2007: 153), especially after 1968 and the Six Days War. Moreover, she points to a generational difference in understanding and dealing with Palestinianness very much intensified by the Six Days War, which recast much of the feeling of dispossession into a need to maintain steadfastness (*ṣumud*) in the "revolution" (*thawra*). The different generations I could distinguish as a result of my own fieldwork were the *Jīl al-Filasṭyn* (the Generation of Palestine), *Jīl al-Nakba* (Generation of the Disaster), *Jīl al-Thawra* (Generation of the Revolution, highlighted in Lebanon), and the *Jīl al-Intifada* (Generation of the Intifada, which stands out in the Occupied Territories and spans the current generation). The main generations Sayigh points to when discerning modes of narrative are the *Jīl al-Nakba* and the *Jīl al-Thawra*. For her, it was only with the Generation of the Revolution that narratives of the Nakba took other forms "in recollections of camp conditions as experienced by a child, or of national commemoration days in school, or in declarations of Palestinian identity" (Sayigh 2007: 140). Furthermore, given that the generation of the revolution – very much inspired by Occidental leftist secular thought – was responsible for popularizing much of this frame, religion is only one more component embedded as much as others in such a temporal frame. Its importance is relative to every particular group and individual iteration.

Along with *al-Nakba*, Lila Abu-Lughod also recognizes that *al-ʿAwda*, meaning "the Return" in Arabic, especially for Palestinian refugees living outside the Occupied Territories,

> ...evokes nostalgia for the homeland they were forced to flee in 1948 and a reversal of the traumatic dispersion that sundered families, ruined livelihoods, and thrust Palestinians into humiliating refugee camps or individual adventures to rebuild lives armed with little more than birth certificates, keys to the homes they left behind, and the stigma of having somehow lost their country to the alien people. (Abu-Lughod 2007: 77)

Beyond collective utopia, Abu-Lughod recognizes through her own memories a personal experiential dimension to *al-ʿAwda*. Her father, Ibrahim Abu-Lughod – a well-known Palestinian political scientist, Middle East expert, and political activist – lived in the USA for many years following the events of 1948. Before leaving Palestine he even "skirmished with the Zionists," but despite having an American passport, he refused to go back to Palestine for many years fearing what he would see. At some point in his life, however, after having raised Lila Abu-Lughod in the USA, he made the decision to return to Jaffa, where he was born and raised. As she recollects, he faced his return as his personal 'Awda, which was publicly recognized and celebrated at his funeral by Palestinian personalities such as Mahmoud Darwish and Edward Said (Abu-Lughod 2007). As this personal experience of 'Awda suggests, I hold that, for Palestinian refugees, beyond nostalgia, al-'Awda is as much a marker of popular and historical time frames as is al-Nakba. Unlike al-Nakba, it is not a marker of memory, but a utopia which projects the romanticized and venerated past into the future and locates the present in-between such idealized times.

Although Sayigh does not discuss narratives about al-'Awda in particular, she assumes that a cyclical concept of history is fundamental to expressions such as "Only God moves history, not men; it is He who will eventually restore the Palestinians to Palestine" (Sayigh 2007: 143). In other words, she seems to acknowledge that al-'Awda entails the return to that which was lost in the past. Alongside gender (her focus) and the generational gap (which is not as much developed in her work), Sayigh emphasizes the necessity to identify diversity within the Palestinian experience and identity. As she states, "internal differences need to be written into the unwritten collective story" (Sayigh 2007: 136), and:

> Disparities of power or status between classes, sects and ethnicities, city and rural residents, the educated and the uneducated, men and woman: all are glossed over in nationalisms that lead to, and follow, the establishment of a state. Historians of the Palestinian people need to reflect on whether the predominant model of 'history' – with its focus on 'facts' and the 'public domain' – is inclusive enough to match the full reality of a unique difficult struggle. (Sayigh 2007: 136)

In the following pages, I will attempt just such a recognition of differences.

b.   Settling in Al-Jalil

I had already been living there for several months when I first interviewed Abu ʿAbbas,[1] a first generation (*Jīl al-Nakba*) resident of Al-Jalil refugee camp, or *Wavel*, according to UNRWA's official naming. The story I heard from him reflected the nuances of his personal trajectory, while also being strikingly similar in many respects to the stories of other first-generation refugees in Al-Jalil. I will recount Abu ʿAbbas's narrative in considerable detail to give the reader a sense of one personal story. Furthermore, I will juxtapose this account with notes from interviews with other first-generation Al-Jalil occupants to illustrate how ʿAbbas's biography reflects a broader collective narrative of displacement and resettlement in Lebanon, as recounted by numerous others in the camp.

At times, Abu-ʿAbbas would trace his origins back to the main port city of Haifa in what he still called Palestine. Whenever he wanted to be more precise, though, he would mention that he came from *Shifa ʿAmar*, a village located just some 20 miles away from today's Israeli port city. Most Al-Jalil inhabitants originated from the village of *Lubia* in the Galilee, north of Palestine. Galilee in Arabic is Al-Jalil, hence the popular name of the camp among the local residents, despite UNRWA's official naming. As Abu ʿAbbas recalled, during the Nakba, Palestinians fled to different places. In general, those from the South tended to flee to the Gaza Strip or Egypt, those from the East tended to flee to the West Bank of Jordan, and those from the center regions tended to go to Jordan and Syria, along with some others fleeing from the North. Their trajectories were not always as straightforward as that. According to ʿAbbas, in Shifa ʿAmmar different people were pushed to different places. The village was inhabited by Christians, Druze, and Sunni Muslims. He was a Sunni Muslim, as were at least by denomination all the other refugees in Al-Jalil. Almost all the Christians and Muslims from Shifa ʿAmmar were displaced from Palestine. Most of them fled to the West Bank or to Lebanon and became refugees. Christians and Muslims from Shifa ʿAmar who settled in Lebanon tended to join neighbors or kin in one of the sites where the refugees were gathering. But this general trend was by no means without exception. Groups of Shifa

---

1   To protect the people whose lives I discuss in this book, all names are fictitious, unless explicitly stated otherwise.

'Amar residents also fled to different places in Lebanon.[2] Some of his former village neighbors took alternative routes and wound up in other places in the Middle East. Moreover, a few in his village "made agreements with the Zionists," and remained in place or went elsewhere (especially Haifa) in what became Israel. Local Druze often chose this path, as they tended to follow their political leaders who struck deals with the newly established Israeli government and armed forces. As a result, today the Druze community of Israel enjoys many privileges, such as, for example, what Abu 'Abbas and others saw as the (financial) "opportunity" to serve in the Israeli army.

From Shifa 'Amar, Abu 'Abbas fled to *Bint Jbail* in South Lebanon, along with relatives and neighbors. He recalled that "there was nothing; no hospital, nothing." He suffered from the cold, as they had no clothes or blankets to protect them from the hardships of winter. He remained there for two months, deciding to move with a group of Palestinian refugees stationed in Bint Jbail to *'Anjar* in the Beq'a Valley, some fifty kilometers away from Beirut on the Beirut-Damascus road and close to the *Masn'a* crossing. 'Abbas then moved to *'Anjar* because of a rumor touting vacant houses in the area. Once there, he indeed discovered a few empty houses, but also that the village harbored a large group of Armenian refugees. During our conversation, he did not remember if the Armenians were there by chance or if they had been settled there by Lebanese authorities. However, his narrative matched the known fact that thousands of Armenians coming from Turkey had been resettled to *'Anjar* between the 1920s and 1930s (Sfeir 2008; Verdeil et al. 2007).

Around September of 1948, clashes erupted in *'Anjar* between the Armenian and the Palestinian refugee groups. Abu 'Abbas could not remember the reasons precisely, but they were related to the occupation of the empty houses. The clashes took significant proportions. As a result, the roads around *'Anjar* were closed and the Lebanese authorities drove the Palestinian refugees away from the Armenian settlement. The Palestinian refugees then went to where they thought would be best. Once more, neighbors and kin tended to stay together. He and his group decided to go to another Palestinian settlement in the Beq'a valley, known by the name of *Ghoro*. UNRWA did not exist at

---

2   Abu 'Abbas remembered that although Palestinian exiles were frequent even before the post-Nakba international recognition of the Israeli state, the only organized resistance to Israeli occupation was mounted by the *Jeysh al-Inqath* (Salvation Army) – an "army" of Arabs from Palestine, Lebanon, Syria, Jordan and Iraq that started its operations in the *"el-Filastyn el-musta'amarat"* (Occupied Palestine).

that time, and the only existent *marākaz al-khudma al-ijtimā'iyya* (social work centers) or *jam'ayāt* (associations, such as the Red Cross) during the first year after the Nakba was the one headed by the Grand-Mufti of Jerusalem, Hajj Muhammad Amin Al-Husseini.[3]

Abu 'Abbas only gradually remembered the presence of the International Red Cross in the area. This lapse perhaps was due both to the fact that the Red Cross did not work with all the refugee groups coming into Lebanon, and that Hajj Amin's charisma (despite his polemic character) occupied a central position in Abu 'Abbas's memory. However, from 1948 to 1950 the International Red Cross was in fact the main organization that assisted Palestinian refugees, providing them with tents, clothes, water containers, and food (as detailed in AJIAL 2001).

Meanwhile, Palestinian refugees who had also been in *'Anjar* prior to the group's expulsion joined other refugees in a similar situation and settled in a French barracks close to the main entrance of Baalbek. The barracks was named after a general who once commanded the battalion stationed in the Beq'a Valley, General *Wavel*. In 1948, these barracks remained in French hands and officially "unused" by the Lebanese government (in Abu-'Abbas' words, "the soldiers were using the barracks just to relax"), and neither Abu 'Abbas nor others I spoke with remembered the arrangement through which French authorities first took in a few Palestinian refugees.

Many of those who left *'Anjar* with Abu 'Abbas went on to join other Palestinian refugees in the Wavel barracks, and in 1952 UNRWA transformed the site into a Palestinian refugee camp. At the time of our interview, Abu 'Abbas did not mention any other reasons for the transformation of the French barracks into a refugee camp for Palestinians, but the deal was struck as part of the armistice negotiated in 1949 between Lebanon and Israel, in which Lebanon agreed to refrain from settling Palestinians close to the Israeli border (Sfeir 2008). Although Wavel is still the official name of the camp for both UNRWA and Lebanese authorities, its dwellers, most of them from Galilee, named the camp Al-Jalil. As I found out from Abu-'Abbas, unlike most other Palestinian refugee camps set up in Lebanon, Al-Jalil was not a "rich man's land" donated or sold to UNWRA. Prior to the establishment of the camp, the land had been government property. According to him, UNRWA was able to

---

3   Al-Husseini was then also the leader of the Palestinian resistance, known at the time as the "National Movement."

buy such land from "these rich people" or to rent it from the Lebanese government due to "money coming from all over the world" to support the UN
General Assembly Resolution 194 from 1948. The resolution called for a "right
of return" for Palestine refugees (al-Ḥaqq al-'Awda, in Arabic) and it was the
document that gave rise to the symbolic notion of Al-'Awda, as previously discussed in relation to the Palestinian framing of time.

Since Ghoro had no schools and was close to Al-Jalil refugee camp, its
young refugees attended the newly built UNRWA school in Al-Jalil. The physical proximity of the camps and the shared experience of nationhood, dispossession, and displacement brought a number of Ghoro refugees closer to
the community from Al-Jalil. Abu 'Abbas's stay in Ghoro only lasted for a brief
period. The site was soon reclaimed by the Lebanese army, in part due to
pressures from the Christian right-wing party Katā'eb al-Lubnāniyya.[4] He left
Ghoro and resettled in Rashidieh, another site originally created by the French
authorities to receive Armenian refugees.

Rashidieh today is the southernmost Palestinian refugee camp in
Lebanon. It is located five kilometers south of the Lebanese city of Tyre
and only some fifteen kilometers away from the Israeli border. According to
what I learned from other Palestinian refugees, the "new camp" was added
to the original Rashidieh site in 1963. It had been established explicitly to
receive families arriving from Ghoro and from El-Buss Palestinian refugee
camps. Abu 'Abbas did not remain in Rashidieh for too long either. After a few
months, the Red Cross transferred him to Al-Jalil refugee camp where he met
other former Ghoro inhabitants as well as other Palestinian refugees from
various Palestinian villages who had previously been gathered in different
sites around Lebanon.

Abu 'Abbas's entire journey lasted several years, until he finally settled in
Al-Jalil in 1964. When I interviewed him in 2008, he was living in the same
apartment building he had occupied since his arrival from Rashidieh, and
that had once served the French soldiers. Among his most enduring memories from the early days in the camp was a ḥajiz (checkpoint) that the Lebanese
erected at the entrance of the camp to limit entry to only the refugees themselves and those allowed by the Lebanese government and UNRWA. Proudly,
Abu 'Abbas recounted how, in 1968, The Palestine Liberation Organization
(PLO) finally took over the checkpoint. Many problems emerged in the early
days from the assemblage of diverse groups and individuals making up what

---

4   Henceforth, Katā'eb, the Lebanese Phalanges Party, or simply the Phalangists.

became the Al-Jalil refugee community, until finally the deepest divides were at least partially bridged. Even though all of the camp's population was Sunni Muslim, there was a wide economic and cultural gap between what Abu 'Abbas called "those who used *bantalon*" (pants) and "those who used *jallābiyya*" (traditional Arabic one-piece long garment), referring to those who came from the cities and those who came from the countryside, respectively. As a third category, there were nomads – the *bedawy* (beduins) – some of whom tended to circulate throughout the Near East and happened to be settled in Palestine in 1948. Drawing on Abu 'Abbas' testimony, one can argue that Palestinianness had both subjunctive and particular dimensions from the start, and much of the shared Palestinian subjunctive – at least in the refugee camps in Lebanon – took shape through the socialization brought about by the PLO, which consisted not only of discourses, but also of disciplinary practices, including national rituals such as celebrations, rallies, education, festivities, and others. This point is also widely acknowledged in literature about the PLO's Lebanon years.

Many other first-generation Al-Jalil inhabitants mentioned having lived in Ghoro until the 1960s, then joining the group that went to Rashidieh, and finally Al-Jalil. One such person recalled that up to 15 people would initially share same lodging. He also remembered that relations with the Lebanese around him were generally "good" when he settled in Al-Jalil – there were those who were "not nice" and those who were "nice," "depending on the case" – although relations with the Lebanese government were already very problematic.

'Abdallah, yet another elder, this time a resident of Shatila Palestinian refugee camp, also used to live in Ghoro, but instead of Rashidieh, he went to Shatila in search for job opportunities. Because Shatila was located on the southern outskirts of Beirut, demand for cheap seasonal work was always high. He too went to school in Al-Jalil camp, where, at the time of my interview, he still had friends despite having left the area many decades before. Managing to escape with most of his family the 1982 Sabra and Shatila Massacre, which was led by the *Katā'eb* in cooperation with the Israeli army following the departure of the PLO from Lebanon, 'Abdallah moved to Mar Elias, another Palestinian refugee camp located in the southwestern area of Beirut. One of the main reasons leading him to Mar Elias was to join relatives already living there. At the time, he was officially affiliated with *al-Jabha al-Sha'abiyya li-taḥrīr Falasṭyn* (the Popular Front for the Liberation of Palestine [or simply, PFLP]). UNRWA had originally created Mar Elias to accommodate Christian

Palestinian refugees, among whom the abovementioned Marxist group found many supporters. Thus, the PFLP was strong in this camp. According to 'Abdallah, at the time of the Lebanese Civil War, due to the relative ability of Christian Palestinians to emigrate to Europe, America, Canada or Australia, and because many Christian Palestinians assumed Lebanese citizenship, Mar Elias gradually lost its Christian population and replaced it with a new Sunni component that came from destroyed Muslim-majority Palestinian refugee camps, such as Tel Al-Z'atar, Karantina, and Jisr El-Basha. Between 2006 and 2010, there were still a few Christian families living in Mar Elias, although the camp's overwhelming majority was Muslim. The PFLP continued to enjoy large support in the camp, a fact 'Abdallah attributed to both Palestinian political negotiations and the large number of Christian *shuhada* (martyrs) buried in Mar Elias' soil.[5] Due to the turmoil in Shatila, one of 'Abdallah's sons lived his entire childhood in Mar Elias, only to return to Shatila when the camp was rebuilt. 'Abdallah's son also considered himself a communist and took pride in following the same political path as his father. As he and I became good friends, I visited his home in Shatila many times during my fieldwork. Che Guevara posters hung on the walls of his and his brother's room. The figure of the revolutionary prompted discussions about my own background in Latin America, which brought us closer.

The Israeli invasion of Lebanon in 1982 led to PLO defeat and the evacuation of the Palestinian resistance movement from Lebanon to Tunisia, leaving behind militiamen in the refugee camps and a profoundly altered national culture, riddled with standardized PLO symbols and institutions. Although one of the conditions of PLO withdrawal was the guaranteed security of Palestinian refugees in the camps, given the power vacuum left behind by the organization, Lebanese militias proceeded to attack the inadequately protected camps. Above all, the famous "War of the Camps" pitted the main Palestinian factions against the Shi'i social movement/political party AMAL and small Palestinian guerillas, who saw in the conflict an opportunity to reinforce their position *vis-à-vis* the dominant cadres of the PLO. Some camps were particularly targeted for their geographical position or strategic value. The Baalbek area was then dominated by AMAL, which at the time was allied

---

5   In an interview to me in 2007, Dr. Anis Sayigh – a well-known historian, himself a Christian Palestinian refugee and very active in Lebanon despite his old age – attributed the arrangement to a possible compromise between the different religious groups.

with Syria against the PLO, and Al-Jalil's proximity to Syria ensured some support to Palestinian factions allied with Syria, such as *al-Sa'iqa*. According to an Al-Jalil elder, AMAL had little interest in engaging in direct war with Al-Jalil residents, if it could have their allegiance instead. Because of the camp's proximity to Syria, residents had developed close ties with their Syrian neighbors, whose main client in Lebanon at the time was AMAL. Therefore, due both to the camp's political composition and its relative isolation from other camps, the PLO in Al-Jalil was compelled to strike a deal with Syria.

As I was told by Hamza, another Al-Jalil elder, in 1983 Syria already had control over northern Lebanon and the Beqa' Valley (where Baalbek is located), which allowed the Asad regime to influence local Palestinian politics more directly. In April of that year, Fatah units stationed in the Beqa' revolted against 'Arafat's central leadership, establishing the Palestine National Salvation Front (PNSF) in Damascus. Also in 1983, another split in Fatah commanded by Abu Musa gave birth to the Fatah al-Intifada and its socialist ideology. Syria then supported the attacks of Palestinian groups such as the PNSF, al-Sa'eqa, and Fatah Al-Intifada against the Nahr Al-Bared and Beddawi camps in northern Lebanon, forcing 'Arafat's expulsion from his last stronghold in Tripoli. Only later, mainly between 1985 and 1987, did AMAL lead the War of the Camps against 'Arafat's PLO. However, there was no fight between AMAL and the PLO in their camp because the camp was not a strategic post, given its small size and its relative isolation from other camps in Lebanon. Other Al-Jalil elders, however, contested Hamza's account of the events, recounting that conflict was averted when PLO loyalists at the time gave up their weapons to AMAL and its proxies in exchange for safeguarding Al-Jalil's peace. At the time of my fieldwork, one of Fatah al-Intifada's most important strongholds in Lebanon's camps was still based in Al-Jalil. It is partially Al-Jalil's location in such a Shi'i stronghold that has allowed it to develop its unique character, explaining, for instance, the relatively strong partisanship of *harakat* (social movements) such as Fatah al-Intifada and the PFLP-General Command.

Al-Jalil's political trajectory was an outlier among Palestinian refugee camps in Lebanon at the time, and such historical developments are among what make it a unique place today. During my fieldwork, decades after these events, Al-Jalil youth were being socialized in an environment in which the majority of the camp supported Hizbollah and Syria, which was not common in other neighboring camps. This socialization hinged upon a series of embodied dispositions, affects, and sensibilities in great part generated by ritualization practices I introduce in *Chapter 3*. In what follows, we shall see

that history took a different route in Dbayeh, a camp located on a hill over-
looking the road linking Beirut to Tripoli near Kaslik and deep in Christian
territory.

c.   Settling in Dbayeh

"I can understand why people don't know about Dbayeh, because in Dbayeh
they are Christians," responded Dr. Anis Sayigh when I mentioned my difficulties in finding someone who had the community's trust and could thus vouch
for me and my work in the camp. Although Dr. Sayigh was not a camp inhabitant, I contacted him due to his vast knowledge about Dbayeh and Palestinians in Lebanon at large, and his close connections with Dbayeh residents. I
chose here to use his real name because he is a public figure known for his
scholarship and political activism, and because he preferred it this way. As
with the above section on Al-Jalil, in which I followed closely individual memory threads, the following succinct oral history traces closely the narratives of
a few individuals, including those of Dr. Sayigh.

Like Dr. Sayigh himself, most Dbayeh refugees originated from a village
on the northwestern Palestinian border with Lebanon called *Al-Bassa*. During my fieldwork, I was told repeatedly that, both because of its proximity to
the Lebanese border and because of its high Christian component, Al-Bassa
had close connections with Lebanon. In Dr. Sayigh's words, "Al-Bassa was the
most Lebanese town in Palestine (...) good and bad traits." "They were so open
to man and woman relations, love affairs, etc." This openness, he stated, was
mainly among the Christians themselves, and there were almost no inter-reli-
gious marriages. Al-Bassa was split by one street, effectively segregating most
Muslims and Christians from each other. According to Dr. Sayigh, however,
like many places in the Middle East, the village was not sectarian, since he understood "sectarianism" as a political attitude rather than religious or communitarian. In other words, the fact that different religious congregations would
choose to live among themselves would sometimes cause tensions, but these
at no time manifested in the political arena, and in Palestine – he claimed
– Muslims and Christians did not fight for political hegemony as they did in
Lebanon.

According to Dr. Sayigh, "at the beginning there were very few of us who
became Lebanese, but then there were more. From their questions you would
know. Such as: what is your religion?" Thus, "becoming Lebanese" for him was
a question of cultural attitude rather than simply taking up citizenship, and

"becoming Lebanese" could entail embodying a disposition toward sectarianism. "Christians in Palestine tended to be more educated[6] and had more money," he told me. The majority of the Christian population was living in or around the biggest cities and the most important centers of trade and industry. Furthermore, a high percentage of them also worked in liberal professions such as law and medicine. Most of these educated Palestinians went to study in Lebanon. The alternative was going to Damascus to study, but since Lebanon was an important center for Christians, the Christian Palestinian community had firmer ties with Lebanon than with Syria, and the tendency after 1948 was to go to Lebanon. Still, according to him, even those who did not study in Lebanon would have probably engaged in some form of trade with Lebanese merchants or would travel there to sell and buy goods on their own. Finally, there were those who, despite having none of these ties, would still frequently choose Lebanon as a holiday destination. However, Dr. Sayigh also added that a significant number of Christians living in northern Palestine were peasants cultivating land for local or absentee landlords. The *fellaḥyn* (peasants) were excluded from these ties with Lebanon as they were not interested in education, did not engage in trade, and could not afford to travel for vacation. Dr. Sayigh's remarks notwithstanding, if one takes into consideration that many of Palestine's landlords were absentee landowners, that many of them lived in Beirut, and that during the late Ottoman Empire many parts of northern Palestine were under the jurisdiction of the Sanjak of Beirut (Khalidi 1997), even the Christian fellaḥyn can be thought of as having a distant historical connection with Lebanon.

As Dr. Sayigh pointed out, these economic and education ties, and the general cultural affinity of Christianity, motivated Christians fleeing Palestine after 1948 to set out for Lebanon. Most of them came from Haifa, Jaffa, Tiberias, Jerusalem, or from the northern countryside of Galilee. Regardless of their cities of origin, since at the beginning "they thought, they would return to Palestine," wealthy ones, who had no need for tents and rations, did not register with UNRWA. In addition, the Lebanese government had its own plan to deal with the refugees. Initially, President Camille Chamoun offered citizenship to any Palestinian Christian who came to Lebanon. The Lebanese president was "very sectarian," and the plan was to increase the number of Christians in the country in order to maintain the *status quo* in which Christians (mainly Maronites) were the hegemonic political power in Lebanon. However,

---

6   He meant here strictly that Christians tended to have more access to education.

"it [Citizenship] was just for the Christians," added Dr. Sayigh. In practice, Christian refugees knew about this plan since priests often informed them in church after mass. In fact, most Palestinian Christians did not even come into Lebanon as refugees, and the wealthy and connected ones could also obtain citizenship in Western countries, such as the United States, Canada, or in Europe.

Thus, an important consequence of the 1948 war was the vanishing of a large number of Palestinian Christians from official numbers and history, since, having taken up other citizenships, they started to figure in books, journalist pieces, and official data as something other than Palestinian. Disappointed, Dr. Sayigh pointed out that, after the Nakba, more and more Christian Palestinians were cast to the shadows, so much so that few people today know that, prior to 1948, the Palestinian Christian community was thriving in number and in economic, political, religious, and social matters. He also lamented that as early as the 1930s, part of the Christian Palestinian community was already aligned with the Zionists, and between 1936 and 1939 the national movement killed many of them and expelled others from Palestine. "I have to be very careful when I talk about that," he added, "perhaps 1000 people. I don't want to say that the Christians sold their souls to the Zionists." After Hajj Amin Al-Huseini went to live in Germany following British persecution, many of these exiled Christians went back to Palestine.

Incidentally, it is important to acknowledge evidence for the existence of certain sectarian tensions, despite Dr. Sayigh's best efforts to deny the fact. Throughout my fieldwork, the denial of even a hint of sectarianism among Palestinians was a common narrative among activists and political figures, whose attitude toward the subject reflected much of the ideals propagated by the PLO and other social and political movements, especially during the *ayam al-thawra* ("days of the revolution," as the Palestinians in Lebanon tended to call the period when the PLO was headquartered in Lebanon). Given Dr. Sayigh's extensive understanding of the topic, it would be clearly wrong to interpret this denial as stemming from lack of knowledge. Given his reputation as a scholar and as a human being, it would be also wrong to suppose he and so many other Palestinians were simply lying. Rather, I understand this recourse to denying the existence of that which is undesirable in their eyes (and in my eyes, as well), as a dispositive or technique of collective cultivation akin to those Hirschkind and Mahmood describe elsewhere about self-cultivation and the cultivation of religious values (Hirschkind 2011; 2006; 2001; Mahmood 2005).

According to Dbayeh's elders, however, not every Christian Palestinian in the camp took Lebanese citizenship. The most important reasons for this were the following: a) many believed they would soon return to Palestine; b) others simply refused to take Lebanese citizenship based on the notion that they would be "selling out" their Palestinianness; c) a few ideologists and politically conscious individuals had already realized and convinced others that, by accepting citizenship, they would be surrendering a key asset. For, the refugee status was a prerequisite for a future return to Palestine and for any claims to compensation for lost property; d) finally, among those Palestinian Christians who sought Lebanese citizenship, some discovered they were ineligible, as obtaining the necessary documentation in practice required the payment of a relatively small sum to the Lebanese government. Although I did not learn exactly why this payment was necessary, I was told that in a few cases it prevented poorer Palestinians from becoming Lebanese citizens, either for simply not having the sum, or for not knowing how to proceed with the process. As a result, many of those who ended up in the camps were peasants or the least financially and socially privileged.[7] For Dr. Sayigh, "those who bought [citizenship] did it so they could travel. There were no passports then. It was more for the passports than for the citizenship."

Dr. Anis Sayigh's father was among the group who, according to Chamoun's rules, was entitled to Lebanese citizenship. When we talked, he highlighted that his father was from the Golan Heights, but his family had often relocated within the Levant, between what are now Palestine, Israel, Lebanon, and Syria[8] (Sayigh 2015). In 1948, his father became a refugee just like others of non-Palestinian origin who happened to be living in Palestine at that time. Once Dr. Sayigh's father reached Lebanon, he built a Protestant church in Dbayeh – the North Church, which at the time of my research was in the hands of the Lebanese – even though he did not live as a refugee in the camp. With the help of a *wasta* (middleman; fixer), Dr. Sayigh's father was guaranteed Lebanese citizenship for his whole family without having to pay a fee to Chamoun.

The fact that most Christian Palestinians were offered citizenship is well documented, but Dr. Sayigh brought to my attention a much less known de-

---

7   A few Christians who became Lebanese citizens did not do so through a payment to Chamoun.

8   His brother, the well-known Palestinian economist and activist Yusif Sayigh, lived for a few years also in Iraq (Sayigh 2015).

tail: Palestinian Shi'a were ostensibly also offered Lebanese citizenship immediately upon entering Lebanon during *al-Nakba*. The argument was a cultural one, based on the assumption that all Shi'a in that area were Lebanese. Very little is known about this even today, and it could not be verified. Yet, I have heard it also as a local popular story among the elderly in Dbayeh and among some other Christian Palestinian elders. It does reflect the complexity of how older generations of Palestinian Christians tended to perceive their arrival, establishment, and place in Lebanon in relation to other Palestinian religious groups. Nevertheless, from the point of view of Dbayeh's elderly in general, as opposed to that of Dr. Sayigh, Christian Palestinians were offered Lebanese citizenship not only as a political privilege serving as a tool for the Lebanese president at the time, but often also as a positive cultural acknowledgement of their common Christian identity. Be it just popular myth or historical fact, I could not learn much about Palestinians who were Shi'a before moving to Lebanon. A common counter-narrative is that there were no Shi'a in northern Palestine, as opposed to the south of Lebanon. Therefore, the Palestinian Shi'a case was often mobilized by Christian Palestinians to show that Christians were not the only ones who benefitted from Lebanese citizenship, but seldom mobilized by Sunni Palestinians so as to reinforce the privilege argument.

As Dr. Sayigh explained, it was commonly known that the very south of Lebanon comprised a Shi'a majority with a significant Christian population. The French and the British set the borders between southern Lebanon and northern Palestine after they had drawn the territories designated for their mandates in Lebanon and Palestine. Given that the areas constituted a social and political continuum rather than a divide, the Shi'a also inhabited northern Palestine, although Palestine is not commonly considered to have had a Shi'a population. If Dr. Sayigh and the other Dbayeh elders who confirmed his account are correct, then there was an unspoken and deeply cultural assumption after the creation of Israel that to be Shi'a in that part of the world was *ipso facto* to be Lebanese.[9] These Palestinian Shi'a who supposedly assumed

---

9   This cultural assumption was created mainly as a result of the border dispute between the French and British mandates after World War I and confirmed by several documents of the time, as noted, for example, by Asher Kaufman: *"Henri Gouraud, the first High Commissioner of the French Mandate in Lebanon, directed the French officer in charge of negotiating the border in the Paulet-Newcombe Boundary Commission to try to include all the Shi'i villages within the borders of Lebanon, on the grounds that they were a natural part of it. Gouraud added that if he proved unable to include them all, it was preferable to leave several*

Lebanese citizenship were all from *Kura Saba'* (The Seven Villages – today located in northern Israel), and according to Dr. Sayigh's memory, they were
actually between about 21 and 23 villages. When asked if he would agree with
the assumption that all Shi'a in Palestine were in fact Lebanese, Dr. Sayigh
told me that he thinks "they [the government] were right. They were Palestinians and Lebanese at the same time."

Abu George, a *Jīl Al-Nakba* elder from Al-Bassa, told me how he arrived in
Dbayeh. Following the 1948 events in Palestine, he initially settled in Rashidieh among other Palestinian refugees, Muslims and Christians, from cities
and villages alike. Only after about three years did he move to *Dbayeh Al-Taḥet*
(Lower Dbayeh). As far as he could recollect, his motivation to move to Dbayeh
was to "avoid problems," but he preferred not to elaborate on this topic. Other
Jīl Al-Nakba Dbayeh residents, on other occasions, explained to me that a number of Christian Palestinians went from Rashidieh to Dbayeh at the invitation
of a Lebanese priest. According to their accounts, the reasons behind the invitation were mainly to keep the Christian Palestinian community safe by placing it under Christian protection and bringing it closer to Christian territory.
The monks of a monastery[10] in Dbayeh then set up a tent camp in close proximity to their own land, and only in 1956 did UNRWA take the camp under its
mandate with the help of the Pontifical Mission of Palestine, founded by the
Vatican to help Catholic Palestinian refugees.

Initially, the land around Dbayeh was still largely uninhabited, but as
Christian Lebanese businesspeople began developing the area for agricultural
production, Palestinians could find seasonal work there. Although not part of
the elders' accounts, according to the anthropologist Rosemary Sayigh (1994),
it is widely known that a common practice among Lebanese Christians and
Muslims in Beirut and elsewhere before 1967 was to hire Palestinians for work,
as they were willing to accept half the pay the Shi'a expected.[11]

To Abu George, what made the Lebanese invitation even more attractive
were the following: Christian Palestinians, at least in Al-Bassa, had already
demonstrated a preference for living among other Christians while still in
Palestine; the appeal of living under the guidance of a priest; and finally, the

---

*villages within the boundary of the British Mandate so that one or two Shi'i villages would not
remain isolated on the other side of the border"* (Kaufman 2006: 688).

10   This monastery is later referenced in this book as the Maronite Mar Yusif al-Burj
Monastery.

11   The Shi'a were the poorest Lebanese social group at that time.

opportunity to earn a living rather than rely solely on charity and favor. Considering the circumstances, most heeded the call to relocate to Dbayeh, where
they were joined by relatives and Christian Palestinians from other villages.
Therefore, as was the case with many other refugees from varying places in
Palestine, inhabitants of Al-Bassa tended to maintain their village and family bonds upon arriving in Lebanon, and the refugee camp structure tended
to reflect village belonging. Only in this case, al-Bassa Christian and Muslim communities were severed by elements characterized not only, or mainly,
by conscious choices, but also greatly by restrictions imposed by a historical
situation engendered by the Lebanese context. In other words, as Christian
Palestinians repeatedly informed me, they did not choose to be apart from
their Muslim neighbors due to sectarian attitudes or theology. In moving
to Lebanon, religion influenced these refugees' choices in far more complex
ways. Regardless of their motivation, Abu George confirmed that "here [in
Dbayeh], since the beginning, there were just Christians." A number of other
Palestinian Christians settled in Jisr Al-Basha and Mar Elias, motivated by village and family belonging, which was of great importance both in Palestine
and in Lebanon. UNRWA took up management of the gathering of Palestinians in Dbayeh only in 1956, renting the space for 99 years and converting it
into a Christian Palestinian refugee camp along with Mar Elias, while Jisr
Al-Basha also contained a Muslim component.

In 1975, after the beginning of the Lebanese Civil war, Dbayeh was attacked and largely evacuated in the same wave of violence that destroyed Tel
Al-Zaatar and Karantina. After the end of the civil war, previous residents returned to the camp. This time, although the majority of them were Palestinian
Christians, Lebanese and Palestinians from other religious backgrounds also
settled there. Abu George remembered the harsh conditions in which they
lived in the beginning. After abandoning the tents, they moved into wooden
houses with roofs made of zinc where there were no private bathrooms – only
what he called *mushtaraky* (shared). After many years and following the camp's
first conflict, they finally moved to *Dbayeh Al-Fawq* (Upper Dbayeh), as they had
been preparing the land for settlement. Because of this conflict, Abu George
points out, not everybody in Dbayeh "is from 1948," or even Palestinian at all.
In his words, it was *kullun ghurub* ("all strangers," as in Lebanese Christians)
that came to live in the camp because it was "safe" during the Lebanese Civil
War.

As Dbayeh's elderly told me, there were conflicts between Dbayeh's Palestinians and the Lebanese army as early as 1973. In addition, as soon as the

Lebanese Civil War broke out in 1975, the Palestinian refugee camps located in East Beirut (an area dominated by the Phalangists and other Christian militias) came under siege. Yasser Arafat, then chairman of the PLO, could not maintain his position in the northeastern suburbs of Beirut, and in the process of this struggle all camps in this region were either wiped out, or partially destroyed and occupied. Incidentally, Jihane Sfeir (2008) notes that the massacres of Tel Al-Z'atar and Karantina became infamous, but other less prominent camps fell in the same way, such as the Christian majority camp of Jisr El-Basha. The only camp that remained standing in the area was Dbayeh, and the reasons for that are due both to the camp's unique character and its early takeover by Phalangist militiamen.[12]

One of Dbayeh's elders insisted that the camp was actually the spearhead of an intelligence effort that also involved the camps of Jisr El-Basha, and Karantina, while others would agree that while the camp was never a fertile ground for PLO militiamen, it witnessed PLO intelligence efforts, given its advanced position in enemy territory. However, most agreed that as soon as the Lebanese Civil War erupted, there were simply no conditions for the PLO to maintain its headquarters north of Beirut, given that the area was a Phalangist stronghold. By 1976, after the destruction of Jisr El-Basha, Karantina and Tel Al-Z'atar, every line of communication was cut off, and Dbayeh inhabitants were left at the Phalangists' mercy. Although initially not as accusatory as others in the Christian camp, when talking about this issue Abu George simply mentioned that some Lebanese went to live in Dbayeh in 1976 "because of the Katā'eb."

Some in Dbayeh defended the idea that an early commitment existed between the camp's refugee community and the Christian community around, such that the fight for the Palestinian cause should not pit camp inhabitants against their Christian neighbors. While some Dbayeh elders attributed this attitude to an early religious identification with the local community (despite the heavy stigmatization of being Palestinian), others claimed that it would have been simply impossible to act differently in the highly Christian dominated area of Dbayeh without putting families' lives and livelihoods at risk. Conversely, Muslim inhabitants of other Palestinian refugee camps frequently

---

12   Some of whom would later form "al-Quwwāt al-Lubnānīya" (Lebanese Forces) and ally with Tel-Aviv in many of their operations inside Lebanon, as for example the "Sabra and Shatila Massacre" – operated by the Lebanese Christian group with Israeli logistic support.

told me that Dbayeh's residents were simply not "active in the Palestinian cause," while many in Dbayeh blamed the PLO instead for never having played an active role in the area because of its Christian inhabitants, thereby leaving them to be repeatedly attacked and subjugated.

As Abu George recounted, there were mainly four conflicts in Dbayeh that shaped the camp's life and relations with the Lebanese. The first occurred in 1973, the second in 1975, followed by the Israeli Invasion in 1982, and finally the conflict in 1990 after the Taif Agreement, which marked the official end of the civil war.

The 1973 conflict transpired between the Palestinians in Dbayeh and the Lebanese army, which mounted a checkpoint along the highway below the camp and demanded that everyone going up the hill to the camp show an identity card. All those identified as Palestinian would be stopped and interrogated. Many were able to avoid problems at first, though, because they could pass for Lebanese. On the identity cards of many who obtained Lebanese nationality, "Palestinian" was omitted, since they were born in Lebanon. Abu George concluded that for these Palestinians, "one could only know it if [they] speak about it, or from the accent. But many know how to emulate the Lebanese accent, as many were born here." A number of Palestinians stopped at the checkpoint were beaten, and many others jailed. The few remaining PLO militants in Dbayeh fought the Lebanese army with their Kalashnikovs. As a result, the relationship between Dbayeh residents and the surrounding Lebanese Christians deteriorated even further.

With the triggering of the Civil War by the infamous 'Ayn Al-Rumene bus incident,[13] Dbayeh came under siege from January 7 to January 14, 1976. In a Phalangist effort to control the camp, fighting erupted between the Phalange Party, al-Aḥrār[14] (free men; from ḥurriyya, meaning freedom), and the Palestinians. There was little resistance because, as Abu George indicated, the camp was "small" and did not contain many "PLO people." In the aftermath of the siege, Katā'eb militias finally occupied the camp by force and installed about five offices at different points in the camp. As Abu George recalls, many Katā'eb militants occupied Palestinians' houses, seized their money, and coerced them to fill and carry sandbags to their front positions in East Beirut.

---

13   The Lebanese opened fire on a bus carrying a number of Palestinians in 'Ayn Al-Rumene neighborhood of Beirut. This event is widely considered to mark the formal beginning of the Lebanese Civil War.

14   As I understood it, anyone that did not represent a political party or army.

As he told me, nobody tried to stop the massacre because such violence was not prohibited. *Ma kan fy dawleh!* ("There was no state!"). The camp remained under Phalangist control until the end of the war or, as some in the camp claimed, until "today."

Near the end of the war, the Lebanese army, led by General Michel Aoun, started its "War of Liberation," which was intended to eradicate all Lebanese militias as a precondition for the transition from Aoun's military rule to the establishment of a civil Lebanese government. One of the Army's main battles was with the *Katā'eb*, which refused to cede its positions, accusing Aoun of abuse of power. To Dbayeh's misfortune, the *Katā'eb* territory bordered that of Aoun precisely at the campsite, and because the *Katā'eb* still held offices in militarily strategic positions in Dbayeh, the Lebanese Army shelled Dbayeh in 1990. According to Abu George, this time, the Palestinian refugees were not the cause of the conflict, but rather caught in the crossfire. According to UN-RWA data, in 1990 alone, following the army's success, a quarter of Dbayeh was turned to rubble (UNRWA 2010). Abu George spoke to me about these matters in his own residence and in a low voice, as, according to him, many of the Lebanese who sought shelter from the war and who came with the *Katā'eb* were his next-door neighbors. After the conflict, Dbayeh was largely evacuated, and its Palestinian refugees took up residence in many different countries, notably, the United States and Canada. Following the rebuilding of the camp in the late 1990s and early 2000s, most of these refugees living abroad were forced to return, as they were commonly denied citizenship or residency in other countries. Many of them were already widowed elderly men.

Therefore, unlike the experience in other camps, for Dbayeh residents the most important and immediate effect of the PLO's coming to Lebanon was a final severing of their connections with the rest of the Palestinian refugee camps. This resulted in a sometimes voluntary and sometimes forced openness to the context around them under pressure from *Katā'eb* militiamen and Lebanese Christian social institutions, such as NGO's, schools, churches, and hospitals. Thus, by the time the PLO started building its institutions in Lebanon's Palestinian refugee camps, and with them the dispositions, affects, and sensibilities that would later motivate camp inhabitants to fight united under the PLO banner, Dbayeh was already cut off from the other camps in Lebanon due to multiple reasons. First, it is indeed plausible that, for the PLO, Dbayeh was not strategically worth the investment, given the camp's small population and its location deep within enemy territory.

Moreover, since we know that few were those in Dbayeh who actively resisted the Phalangists with weapons – at a minimum because they did not have the necessary weapons – we can assume that identification with the Christian Lebanese must have played a role at least in allowing residents to minimize the effects of the occupation. At the time of my fieldwork, Dbayeh youth had been socialized in such a way as to avoid conflict with the surrounding Lebanese population, given that survival depended largely on their benevolence. Their parents, along with the hostile environment outside their houses – even within the camp itself – taught them to assimilate as much as possible, including adjusting their accent, their political expressions, social behavior, and even mannerisms and interests. If parents were afraid and wanted above else the wellbeing of their children, among the young there was a widespread will to conceal the stigma of being Palestinian and become like the Lebanese to be accepted by those around them. As a result, without necessarily concealing their Palestinianness completely, most would in one way or another articulate their genealogical heritage with their local present in Lebanon. With this disciplinary socialization, especially among Dbayeh Palestinian residents who had Lebanese citizenship, many understood that although Palestinian, they were not hostile like "the others" because they were different, and this difference was Christianity. While few rejected Lebaneseness more emphatically, others went as far as to even reject their Palestinianness completely, denying to me that they had ever been Palestinian, as I illustrate later in this book.

*

These two broad and concise oral histories demonstrate that, from the inhabitants' perspectives, the histories of their camps were unique, albeit sharing similar narratives of *Al-Nakba*. Dbayeh locals did not understand their camp's uniqueness as a direct result of divergent religious affiliations. Rather, the homogenous Christian composition of the camp was a consequence of Lebanese efforts. A pivotal role was played by the Lebanese priest who recruited a select Christian sample of refugees from Rashidieh in south Lebanon, which incidentally was the same camp from where many left to finally settle in Al-Jalil.

It is a fact that, as Dr. Sayigh puts it, Christians, and Muslims tended to live and marry among themselves in Palestinian villages such as Al-Bassa. However, that Christians in Al-Bassa lived in different quarters did not necessarily mean they preferred to avoid Muslims in other areas of social life.

The fact that religion is a determining factor for identity construction among Christian Palestinians is not a novelty inaugurated by their arrival in Lebanon as refugees. Rather, as I suggested above and will substantiate in what follows, much of the way that some Dbayeh Palestinians today, especially the younger generations, blur their Palestinianness by affiliation with Christianity, is a result of their tentative accommodation to the Lebanese surroundings.

Finally, it is also important to note that practices of belonging in Dbayeh, both identitarian and relating to social organization, did not depend exclusively on practical considerations, for such considerations themselves were generally embedded in a broader idiom of dispositions, affects, and sensibilities evoked, for instance, by collective and personal memory, as shown above, and social practices, as I will show in what follows.

Chapter 3: Ritual Tempo in Al-Jalil

a. From Beirut to Al-Jalil

Upon arriving at the Beirut International Airport in 2007 for what would be the longest stretch of my field research, I picked up my bags and headed straight to *Jisr al-Matar*[1] (Airport Bridge), where I took one of the many vans circulating between Beirut and Baalbek. *Jisr al-Matar* was a crossroads in Beirut that reflected the larger Lebanese territorial junctions. Located right next to Shatila Palestinian refugee camp, this transportation landing took advantage of a local crossway to divide the territory among those going to the south and southeast of the county. There were precise van locations for those wishing to go to any city. If van routes could not accommodate a passenger's desired destination, at least one form of transport could carry the passenger to the next local junction, where a vehicle to the final destination could be found. *Jisr al-Matar* was among the largest of the Lebanese road hubs. Another one, also in Beirut, was *Dawra*, which took passengers from Beirut to Mount Lebanon (including Dbayeh) and to the north and northeast of the country. Around such places, street commerce always flourished. Cigarettes, coffee, fast food, and little trinkets were the most common objects offered, along with van rides.

The first main intersection on the road was Chtaura, a busy crossroads between Lebanon and Syria. Although it was relatively far from the border, the frantic movement of people, things, and money reminded visitors that this was a type of border town. Besides its transit of those coming from Damascus

---

1   Throughout this book, localities and names known outside of the Near East will be transliterated as they are commonly written, while unknown places and names will be transliterated according to the transliteration system provided in the annex (full transliteration for written sources accompanied by the original in Arabic, and phonetic transliteration for vernacular Palestinian and Lebanese terms).

to Beirut, Chtaura also served as a complex internal border. It was a main crossroads between Sunni, Shi'a, and Christian majority areas and different political domains. From my van, I witnessed through the window a diversity of people. Frequently on the route from Beirut to Baalbek, there would be a van change in Chtaura, because drivers operated within their own territories, which reflected their confessional and/or political belonging and the tendency of different territories to be associated with one or the other of these, despite some diversity. Everyone passed through Chtaura, though.

From inside the crowded van, I admired the landscape of the Beqaa, a fertile valley located in the east of Lebanon, between Mount Lebanon and Anti-Lebanon ranges, the latter marking the eastern border with Syria. On that particular trip, the same van went all the way from *Jisr al-Maṭar* to Baalbek. Not long after Chtaura, we passed through Zahlé, known for its wine and *'araq*.[2] Zahlé was the demographic center of the valley and was inhabited by a large majority of Christians, especially Maronites and Armenians.

As we moved further into the countryside, still on the outskirts of Zahlé, Sunni political and religious symbols started to emerge, such as posters of Hariri, mosques, and people doing their ṣalawāt (the 5 daily prayers in Islam, plural for ṣalāh, or ṣalāt, prayer) wherever was convenient. Further along, the mosque-riddled landscape persisted, while the focus of the posters on the walls, particularly evocative of politics and religion, changed. We were now in Shi'a majority territory close to the large town of Baalbek, one of the most important strongholds of Hezbollah. This area was also rich in posters and other symbolic elements heavily inspired by religion and politics, but the Shi'a triad, "Allah – Muhammad – Ali," together with martyrs and leaders of Hezbollah, Amal, and smaller allies became more prominent. As we approached Baalbek, I was struck by one monument in particular. At the center of a public square stood, as a war trophy, an actual war tank on a tall concrete pillar surrounded by Hezbollah paraphernalia. The posters and flags suggested a relationship between the victory leading to the tank's capture, and the will and power of God. Those without linguistic and cultural proficiency may not notice this seemingly subtle transition in social landscape. My own Arabic was poor then and improved as I lived in the region, but it was already sufficient to communicate the basics and to allow me to read the signs. Moreover, I already had enough understanding of the Middle East and Islam to recognize the symbols, leaders, and messages. However subtle the change, there was no mid-

---

2   Levantine traditional anise flavored alcoholic drink.

dle ground. There was nothing in-between Sunni and Shi'i Islam, or between Christianity and Islam, or so one was supposed to think by looking at the symbolic arrangements. As I would learn later, nuances and shades between these orthodoxies did exist, but they could hardly ever be presented as such. The territories themselves, which seemed to be completely homogenous to the foreign onlooker, were in fact far more heterogeneous. Nevertheless, the somewhat diverse political and religious practices and everyday engagement with life did not efface the blunt polarization according to which so much of daily life was organized, and which individuals and groups felt compelled to follow.

At some point a young man sat beside me in the van and asked me where I was going with all of my luggage. I told him I was going to Al-Jalil refugee camp. He wanted to know what I intended to do there. I told him a friend was waiting for me, and I was also going to live in the camp for a while, both due to my research and to volunteer with a local association called *Markaz li-Ḥuqūq al-Insān* (Center for Human Rights).[3] He asked who was my friend, and I explained he was someone from Shatila who now lived in Al-Jalil and worked at the *Markaz*. I also provided his name and a brief description and told him I did not know exactly where to exit the van, as my instructions were to arrive close to Baalbek and then ask the driver to drop me off at the *mukhayyam* (camp). "He will know which camp, there is just one there," my Shatila friend had assured me prior to my arrival in Lebanon. However, as we approached Baalbek, I asked the van driver about the *mukhayyam*, and he asked, "which camp?" "The Palestinian camp," I answered. He laughed, "the Palestinian one, eh? What do you want there?"

The dialogue that followed, in my broken Arabic and the driver's broken English, lasted for quite some time, at least in my mind. Others in the van started interceding and making comments. They all assumed I was one more foreign tourist, like the many backpackers that visit Baalbek for its stunning and internationally known Roman ruins. I rejected any notion that I wanted to stay in the city instead of the camp. It was not that the driver did not know the location of Al-Jalil camp. Rather, he could not understand why a foreigner like me with all his luggage, and who probably didn't seem very tough, would want to go to the Palestinian refugee camp instead of his beautiful city. There were a few mocking comments about me and about the Palestinians before

---

3   I chose to change the name of the institution here, although keeping it related to its objectives, to avoid exposing individuals who might prefer anonymity.

the young man I was sitting next to finally confessed to me in a low voice, in English, that he was from Al-Jalil. Thus, the first thing I learned even before arriving at the camp, was that along with cooperation (as noted in the previous chapter), there was also tension between the camp and its surroundings.

We made our way from one end of the country to another aboard that van, across the mountains and across many different Lebanese social microcosms, but the whole trip only lasted about two hours. After all, despite the immense social diversity and deep divisions, Lebanon is a very small country. Probably within a mile from the main entrance to Baalbek, the young man addressed the driver in a loud, assertive but polite voice: *Nazilna bil-mukhayyam* (drop us off in the camp). Finally, at the entrance of Al-Jalil refugee camp, while I was searching for my money and before I could protest, he had already paid for us both and carried down the biggest of my bags. The young man asked me to wait near a Palestinian *ḥājiz* (checkpoint), where men with their Kalashnikovs and military gear stood seemingly entertained by my presence, while he entered to summon my friend. After about five minutes, the two men arrived together, signaling to inform whoever needed to know that I was finally home.

b.   The Camp

According to UNRWA, today there are 8,806 Palestine refugees registered in the total area of 42,300 square meters of Al-Jalil (UNRWA n.d.). Interconnected concrete buildings formed a wall separating the camp from the outskirts of Baalbek. Larger buildings that once served as French barracks still stood at the center of such walls, buried underneath additional stories built by the residents to accommodate the ever-growing camp population. This configuration left just enough space for an asphalted street to cut across the wall and the center of the camp. The main street was shaped as a square, with an appendix opening to the outside world. It was slightly wider than one 1970s Mercedes 230[4] at its narrowest, and a little wider than two such cars at its widest. Narrow alleys connected the margins of the camp to its center in inconsistent fashion, enclosing men and women who chatted at the doorsteps

---

4   The most popular car in Lebanon at its time, the Mercedes 230 and others of its generation were still beloved and very popular in the country during my fieldwork, making up much of the taxi fleet.

of their houses and young men gathered to smoke *argile*. However, such numbers and boundaries can be deceiving. During my stay in Al-Jalil, many locals told me that about sixty percent of all Al-Jalil's populace (*Ahl Al-Jalil*) live today in Scandinavia or Germany, and I myself met some as they flocked to the camp during summer to reconnect with their families and friends. In 2014, I also engaged in fieldwork in Aarhus, Denmark, where a large number of these refugees from al-Jalil lived. For this reason, Al-Jalil was known in other Palestinian refugee camps in Lebanon as the "Denmark Camp." However, as I learned during this fieldtrip, the majority of these refugees, along with Syrians, Somalis, Iraqis, and Kurds from across the Middle East, were also segregated from the rest of the country, even if the walls encircling them in Denmark were not made of concrete.

There were no trees or other plants in Al-Jalil, only concrete. In terms of infrastructure, the camp was in itself a small city, for it had: stores for food, house cleaning and hygiene products, medicine, gas, and the necessities of daily life; political offices (*maktab al-siyasiyya*, plural, *makātib al-siyasiyya*); NGO and charitable organization centers (*markaz*, plural *marākaz*; or *jam'aiyya*, plural, *jam'ayāt*); a mosque; an UNRWA school; the UNRWA administrative office; and its own taxi drivers – some of which operated illegally but were tolerated by Baalbek authorities, provided they kept to their own territory – linking the camp to the outside word. Public gathering spaces almost always faced the main street. Among the stores, there were at least two pharmacies, four or five food markets, two manakish[5] bakeries, a falafel sandwich shop, a *qahwe* (coffee shop), a second *qahwe* that also offered *argile*,[6] an internet games room with six computers, a room with a pool table and a football table, four or more barbershops, a trendy CD store, and a general store where one could buy anything from frying pans to blankets. Besides these shops, a cooking gas store, a garage shop, an internet café, another barbershop, and a cell phone shop all stood facing the road to Baalbek.

Al-Jalil boasted twelve political parties or "movements" (*harakāt al-siyāsiyya*; singlular *haraka al-siyāsiyya*[7]) at the time, most of which had their

---

5   Near Eastern (mostly Lebanese) traditional pastry

6   This shop was opened after my arrival in Al-Jalil by two refugee brothers from Nahr El-Bared who found shelter in Al-Jalil after the destruction of their camp in 2007 by the Lebanese Army. Their shop closed before I left due to community pressure claiming that the store was promoting bad behavior among the youth.

7   Or *tanẓimāt* (organizations; singular, *tanẓim*) as they were also called

own offices there. Among these groups, the most important were Fatah, Fatah al-Intifada, PFLP, Hamas,[8] and Islamic Jihad (not in any particular order of importance). Moreover, the UNRWA's administrative office was only one among the many other offices of charitable organizations, cultural centers, and NGOs, such as the *Markaz li-Ḥuqūq al-Insān* (henceforth, just *Markaz*), *Al-Najda Al-Ijtimaʿiyya, Beit Aṭfāl Al-Ṣumūd*, and Caritas. It is important to note that other groups were also active in Al-Jalil, even if they did not have offices of their own. These groups tended to consist mostly of children, and they could either be fairly independent, as in the case of one *dabke* group and a musical band, or associated with an association or socio-political movement, as in the case of another *dabke* group, the boy scouts, and a football team.

While the shops provided services for the community and economic sustenance for their owners, the political offices, the centers, and other associations and NGOs performed, above all, a social function. Being active in such organizations entailed a certain status, as did owning a pharmacy, a barbershop, or an *argile* store. Barbershops and the *argile* shop were very important gathering places for the youth, for example. Thus, owning such an establishment generally led to an accumulation of social capital, along with economic benefits.[9] Status cannot be understood in terms of a hierarchical form of social organization, as generally people were respected above all for their contribution to the community.

As previously indicated, the main entrance to the camp was guarded by a checkpoint. This checkpoint was built next to one of Fatah's offices located to the right of the camp's entrance. To the left of this checkpoint was the *zāwya* (corner), a spot clear of buildings, regularly used as a gathering place for speeches, demonstrations, strikes, celebrations, and other public collective expressions. The UNRWA office was located just behind this *zāwya*, and thus always loomed large when event speakers were photographed and filmed by local organizations. In this way, the UNRWA office was a symbolic connection to the world at large, and particularly to world powers. While UNRWA was thus often attacked for its incompetence, self-serving goals, and/or institutional arrogance (for thinking it knew what was best for refugees before

---

8   Hamas' office was inaugurated during my fieldwork.

9   Although the *argile* shop was morally ambiguous from the broadest perspective in the camp, it was quite popular with a significant part of the youth. It was among this youth that the owners of the shop gained social capital.

consulting them), speeches addressing the USA or Israel would also often be held in front of the UNRWA headquarters.

c.   Ritual Tempo

Posters and flags marked the camps, even more so than in their surround-ings. Among many others, the variety of posters included the following im-ages, all against a black background: portraits of martyrs with prayers; pic-tures of Shaykh Ahmad Yassin along with Qur'anic verses; Arafat's portrait; a particular political symbol made of crossed Kalashnikovs, a grenade, and the pre-1948 map of Palestine; another symbol containing the pre-1948 map of Palestine, the Dome of the Rock, Kalashnikovs and the dictum "God is the Greatest" in Arabic. Each of the abovementioned stores and institutions had such posters on their walls. While the most overtly political or religious of these places would display their own symbols or those they supported, others would simply hang on their walls whatever was available. Whenever a poster was affixed, such as, for example, one of a dear Palestinian martyr who had given his or her life to al-Qaḍiyya al-Falasṭyniyya (the Palestinian Cause), few would dare take it down, since, in this case, a martyr was deserving of God's blessings, whatever "the cause" may mean to one or another resident. People strongly felt they had a social responsibility which extended beyond the in-dividual, that they shared a common history and predicament, and that they needed to keep together to change their situation. This, in turn, put empha-sis, but also stress, on social norms, collective action, and processes of identity construction. The national "we" in Al-Jalil was more important than in most other places I was aware of, which also meant that disputes about "us" tended to be more severe.[10] Furthermore, inasmuch as "we" is always multiple and contextual, their refugee condition, or that which brought them together to this camp to live shared predicaments and to experience similar events, oc-cupied much of their hearts and minds, and was firmly tied, as it were, to nationhood.

In this way, daily social interaction in Al-Jalil was marked by ubiquitous symbols of Palestinianness, such as the Palestinian flag, the images of the fighter and the martyr, the key, the map of pre-1948 Palestine, and others. While the Palestinian flag and the map evoked the continuity of the nation

---

10   I was never part of this collectively, although I was mostly seen as an aggregate, some-times an ally, and very often with suspicion, as I develop in *Chapters 1 and 7*.

in Palestine and in exile, the fighter, the martyr, and the key evoked the process by which the community engaged in searching for the utopian union. Referents were mobilized and took shape inside the offices, public gathering places, social organizations, and creative minds of individuals, and were reproduced and dispersed throughout the community via group networks and public performances constitutive of what I call the *ritual tempo* of the community.

Al-Jalil camp had a very defined and frequent set of public practices and discourses, ranging from simple day-to-day social interactions to a vernacular repertoire and a calendar of events. It had a certain rhythm of life, a tempo, that mobilized referents, dispositions, affects, and sensitivities that, in turn, socialized and disciplined members of the community into a set of values, practices and behaviors, providing frameworks for understanding and engaging the world, greatly influencing the organization of memory, history, and geopolitics, and demarcating the boundaries of the community vis-à-vis others.

I understand my own concept of ritual tempo as building upon what Rosemary Sayigh called "the tempo of daily life" in *Too Many Enemies*:

With the expansion of PRM [Palestinian Resistance Movement] programs, the tempo of daily life in the camps changed, becoming charged with commemorations and celebrations: international days such as 1 May and 8 March. All these were occasions for speeches by Resistance leaders, displays of handicrafts, performances of plays, songs, and dances. Such events became part of and helped people to absorb, the continual attacks and losses. 'We mourn and marry on the same day' is the way one young PRM cadre expressed this new popular culture of resistance. (Sayigh 1994: 104)

Like Sayigh, I am interested in public performances such as commemorations and celebrations (*iḥtifalāt*), rallies and demonstrations (*masirāt; muẓāharāt*), strikes (*iḍrabāt*) and other collective public performances as means for expressing social belonging. My development of the concept is therefore geared towards a more explicit understanding of such practices as part of a ritualization process. This, in turn, helps to account for disciplinary and socialization practices entailed in this ritualization process, and their connection with social organization and interaction between different groups inside Al-Jalil. To begin this account, I will describe some of the most overt celebratory expressions of Palestinian identity in Al-Jalil.

d.   Yawm al-Nakba

The day before the 2007 local commemoration of *Yawm al-Nakba* (*Nakba* Day) was slated to take place, locals instructed me to bring along my photo camera. On the day of the event, the first image I saw as I stepped out of the *Markaz* (where I was volunteering as an English teacher for children and staff), was a child wearing a cap with a Brazilian flag holding a plastic Palestinian flag. As he spotted me, he posed for a picture, as most children in the camp would. *Ṣawurny! Ṣawurny!* ("Take my picture! Take my picture!"), he insisted. Children participated in all such public events in Al-Jalil just as much as adults . Not only were their numbers soaring, making their presence a reflection of local demographics, but they were also usually enthusiastic about the prospect of a "party," especially if they could somehow play a role in it. More importantly, however, adults saw the socialization of children in such events as central to the continuity of their efforts towards their national cause. It was part of their education, just as much as going to school and learning from their parents' examples.

A children's band dressed in blue shirts and white scarves beat their drums in a steady pace. They were some of Al-Jalil's boy scouts. Palestinian flags were everywhere: on walls, in the windows of houses, on the hoods of the few parked cars, engraved on the front pockets of the boy scouts' shirts, and brandished by the rallying crowd. Closely following the drummers' march, a single boy, who must have been 8 or 9 years old at most, ceremoniously waved a Palestinian flag taller than himself. Another boy was dressed in military clothes not easily identified with any particular faction. He was succeeded by a group of 8 or 9 children carrying together the biggest of the flags. They were dressed in black and white t-shirts displaying the pattern that became a fa-mous Palestinian symbol by virtue of Yasser Arafat's scarf.[11] The t-shirts were plain with no writing on them, and the only clear sign of a political party was

---

11   Before Arafat (and until today for a minority of Palestinians) the different patterns and colors in the traditional Palestinian and near Eastern scarves (*kufyāt*) in general were sometimes a sign of one's *ḥamūla* (Palestinian traditional clannish organization based on extended family belonging – see (Atran: 1986). The symbol was thus re-appropri-ated by the PLO leader as a national signifier of peasanthood and thus attachment to the historic pre-1967 Palestinian borders. Although many Palestinians understand that Arafat's *kūfiyya* symbolism extends well beyond Fatah, the symbol is also still strongly attached to Fatah.

worn by a child wrapped in a big yellow Fatah flag, with Arafat's head and arms displayed on his back.

The rest of the crowd followed the largest flag carrying posters and other symbols like amulets and keys. The amulets had slogans emphasizing the connection of Jerusalem to Palestinianness, and the keys symbolized the "opening" of Jerusalem for Palestinians. Other posters contained phrases such as "No alternative to the Right of Return,"[12] "We reclaim our promised return to Nahr El-Barid – The Association of Social Support,"[13] "No to the *tawṭīn* [becoming a local citizen]. Yes, to The Return,"[14] "Sanction the Human and Social Rights to the Palestinian refugees. Support the truth about the Right of Return. The Association of Social Support,"[15] and "No to the negotiation. No to the abdication,"[16] among others. Plain black flags were also waved, signaling mourning for the martyrs and for the loss of land. In a very rare instance, one of the children even carried a Lebanese flag.[17] Also on display were balloons in the colors of the Palestinian flag with variations of the mottos above, like "yes to the return," "no to the *tawṭīn*," or simply "Palestine." Along with the political and nationalist slogans, people also voiced Islamic inspired lines – such as God's will (*irāda Allah*), God's retribution (through, for instance, *Allah al-Shakūr*, or God is the most grateful, which is one of God's names in Islam), God's grace ('*aṭā' Allah*) – all linked to the overall notion of a fate (*al-qadr*, or as is *maktūb*, meaning "it is written"), but also suggesting that this destiny is contingent upon one's actions. When such slogans are interwoven with national themes, as encountered in the context of *yawm al-Nakba* celebrations, the subjective is no longer an individual, but a collective, i.e., the Palestinians, or even a country/nation, Palestine. It is important to note that this identification of collective subjects and even land as bound to God's destiny has been common in Islamic theology from the outset and expressed in

---

12   لا تبديل الحق العودة

13   نلطلب بعودة الى نهر البارد. جمعية النجدة الاجتمعية

14   لا للتوطين. نعم للعودة.

15   اقرار الحقوق الإنسانية والاجتماعية لا لجئين. دعم حقيقة لحق العودة. جمعية النجدة الاجتماعية.

16   The negotiation and the abdication here is associated with the Oslo peace process initiated by Arafat that did not mention the Right of Return. The original in Arabic was:
لا للتفاوض. لا للتنازيل

17   Instances when Lebanese symbols would be displayed in Al-Jalil were very rare, and this time it partially meant that Palestinians and Lebanese believed in the same ideal: Palestinians in Lebanon should not remain in Lebanon, but return to Palestine.

concepts such as *Dār al-Ḥarb/Dār al-Salām* (Land of War/Land of Peace),[18] *ahl al-bait* (the Prophet's bloodline), and others. Associations such as these were present in virtually all events I witnessed in Al-Jalil and widely expressed as part of local vernacular politics, as I describe throughout this chapter.

The socially engaged youth of the camp coordinated the children and participated in the event by recording the rally with their point-and-shoot cameras or cell phones. They would then show and exchange the footage among themselves, and post videos on the internet, making them available for Palestinian and non-Palestinians abroad. I was also given such tasks since I worked as a volunteer in the *Markaz*. At these events, a group of children always fought over the possession of a megaphone, which this time was managed by an adult woman in a short black *ḥijāb* (headscarf) and very colorful tight clothes. Some of the girls also wore headscarves, but most of the younger ones did not.

Throughout the parade, which was restricted to the main street of the camp, two girls – one wearing a headscarf, the other not – carried a paper containing song lyrics. They quietly rehearsed their song the entire time while the parade completed one full turn around the camp's main street, reaching once again the *zāwya*, the initial starting point. It was there that the two girls finally sang their song, which spoke about the beauty of Palestine and Palestinian suffering, invoked God's grace and pleaded for mercy. This was a very important moment for the girls, and they were visibly emotional, as were their relatives and some others around them. The event ended with one of the older boys delivering a speech about Palestine and the Palestinians, in tune with the song and the rest of the celebration. Another boy held the megaphone for the speaker, and a third one, the smallest of them all, stood in front of the crowd fixated on the older speaker in utter admiration. While the song was meant to be touching and moving – a moment of deep connection to Palestine and introspective mourning – the final speech was meant to mobilize the residents' dissatisfactions around the Palestinian cause. Subsequently, the crowd dispersed, and participants went about their own affairs, many with a reassured sense of belonging and motivation to carry on.

Yawm al-Nakba (*Nakba* Day) was but one among many other national/civic holydays celebrated in the Palestinian refugee camps in Lebanon. As with *Nakba* day, there was also Land Day, Jerusalem Day, Deir Yassin remembrance celebrations, and many others – not all of them holydays, but still part of the same national calendar. Most of these celebrated a specific chapter in the

---

18   Referring to the lands where to practice Islam is respectively unsafe and safe.

recent history of Palestine associated with the struggle culminating in the creation of Israel and the subsequent Palestinian refuge. Other commemorations also closely followed the Palestinian national calendar, as I will show in this chapter. Some were more specific to a political party, but still of national significance, such as the founding of the PLO, or the martyrdom of Shaikh Ahmad Yassin. These commemorations, being primarily national, political, ethnic or religious, usually took the form of remembrance rites important for their mnemonic, disciplinary, and motivational potential.

The date was May 15 and therefore *Yawm al-Nakba* for Palestinians and *Yom Ha'atzmaut* (Independence Day) for most Israelis. The year was 2008, which added drama to the event as it marked 60 years since the initial date. Palestinian citizens of Israel can commemorate one or the other, or even both on certain occasions – since, at least for a minority, celebrating "the catastrophe" does not necessarily entail the desire to dismantle the Israeli state. For most Palestinians, and for all Palestinians living in Al-Jalil that I knew of, *Nakba* Day was a period of both mourning and rallying against the Israeli state.

In Al-Jalil, they mourned the loss of the land and with it the loss of tradition. During *Nakba* Day they reminisced more than usual about their relatives' houses, businesses, displacement, and quotidian routines. They recalled their villages, the neighbors, the animals and plants, and the fertility of the land. They also remembered the cities, with their streets, shops, neighborhoods, and places of reference such as the most important squares and mosques. Most of the participants had never been to Palestine, but they had been socialized into these memories. Of course, the oldest generation was generally the only one to have seen Palestine firsthand, but these memories were no less vibrant in the minds of younger generations. Sometimes, these second-hand memories could be even more inspiring, as the experienced reality was supplanted by sheer imagination and will. I rarely met a Palestinian in Al-Jalil who spoke negatively about the dryness of the land, the lack of jobs, exploitation by landlords, the food, the culture, or about anything that came from Palestine. Even on the rare occasions when criticism was voiced, it was offset by more pleasant memories of the great days in Palestine before the *Nakba*.

Sadly, few witnesses of the *Jīl al-Nakba* were still alive in 2008, but I was privileged enough to have had hours of interaction with some of these men and women. My own experience confirms Rosemary Sayigh's observation (2007) that men generally talk more about politics and women provide more vivid descriptions of daily life. It was not that men were less interested in ordinary events and women not interested in political matters. Women also pulled their weight, for example, including children in performances such as the ones described above, especially since many of them were involved in managing children's educational activities. In Al-Jalil, however, without it necessarily being a general rule, there was a sense that politics was a male domain while private matters pertained more to women's affairs. Depending on the topic of our conversation, they would recommend that I talk to this or that person of the opposite sex in order to obtain a more detailed picture of what I wished to learn. However, education in the camp was no small task, especially given the importance of Palestinianness to the younger generation, showing the path toward the cause, and demonstrating the perseverance and steadfastness needed to embody the community's values, and therefore to live with dignity. This was so much so, that on this particular event marking the 60th official anniversary of their loss, the parade consisted mainly of children under 14 years old. Among the most striking aspects to me was the conspicuous absence of older men. Apart from some personal memorials, the rally itself was staged to express a more cultural than political idiom, and the initiative for the parade came especially from informal voluntary associations and other informal groups of people, like those in the associations signing the posters described earlier. By contrast, there were many young men, most of whom helped to organize the children, although some simply followed the parade through the main street of the camp. The majority of adults present were women, and their authority seemed to supersede that of the young men. These women were not sent by men to perform the task; rather, they proudly sponsored the event themselves.

Younger and older men and women alike would always have plenty to say about Palestine. Typically, in events such as this one marking the anniversary of the *Nakba*, a powerful socialization and education system was put into motion. Much of this was consciously and strategically organized by party leaders, but much also came from NGO and local voluntary association representatives, and from lay people. Overall, those actively engaged in these events sincerely believed that they were taking necessary steps to achieve *'adl* (justice, also understood as God's justice)[19] in Palestine, which in turn was intrinsically tied to ideas of God's will and destiny. While not all Al-Jalil residents were particularly pious, the disciplinary practices involved in celebrations such as *Nakba* Day mobilized these religious referents as values

---

19   *'Adl* is also one of the names of God in Islam.

engendering and reinforcing what Michel Foucault defines as *regimes of truth*, which residents embodied beyond piety. According to Foucault,

> Truth is to be understood as a system of ordered procedures for the production, regulation, distribution, circulation, and operation of statements. Truth is linked in a circular relation with systems of power which it induces, and which extend it. A 'regime of truth'. This regime is not merely ideological or superstructural. (Foucault 1980: 133)

Foucault conceives regimes of truth as processes and mechanisms producing that which is considered to be true in a given context. As I understand it, celebrations such as *Yawm al-Nakba* are among the most important mechanisms producing the regimes of truth shared in Al-Jalil. In fact, I was not the only one to think so, as the local leaders and most active members of the community of refugees constantly pointed out the importance of such events, often surrounding them with an aura of sacrosanctity. In Al-Jalil, seeking the truth was often considered a duty. It is not that all these Palestinians necessarily equated their understanding of the *Nakba* with a Divine duty. Instead, for many of them, a sense of humanitarian justice was usually associated with how they understood their national past, their present predicament, and the need to resist the forces identified as having put past and present in motion. Thus, religion was intertwined with nationalism by way of a local sense of duty that was both infused and often even confused with the divine. Consequently, celebrations like *Nakba* Day, and others I will present in what follows, powerfully assembled and mobilized a wide range of actors, including women and men, children and adults, and both more and less religiously observant subjects, instilling a sense of belonging and motivating thought, feeling, and action.

e.   The 2008 Pro-Gaza Demonstration

Events such as those associated with *Yawm al-Nakba* have been frequent in Palestinian history, and each one of them has the potential to be transformed into a memory of struggle, just as every fallen Palestinian has the potential to become a national martyr. As these events become part of the Palestinian collective memory, commemorating them is not simply a strategy deployed by Palestinian leaders to disseminate ideology and assemble partisans, but also a popular rite, efficacious in dealing with suffering and in attributing meaning to being Palestinian. The 2008 Israeli invasion of Gaza to combat Hamas had from the start the potential to become a similar commemorative event, as were the first two Intifadas. Just as in 1976, when Palestinian refugee camps across Lebanon held *muẓāharāt* (demonstrations) against land expropriations in Galilee, in 2008 Al-Jalil inhabitants mounted a large *muẓāhara* (demonstration; singular) in support of Gazans, rather than commemorate a past event.

In 2008, Gaza was already controlled by Hamas, and the party was caught in a political deadlock with Fatah regarding the administration of the Occupied Territories. During the demonstration, however, the first image I saw was that of a little boy dressed in a military uniform, struggling to hoist a Fatah flag twice his size. With the flagpole on his belly, he pressed his lip in an expression of effort and proudly refused any help offered. Only the father had his hand gently placed over the boy's shoulders, pressing the little figure against his own body in support. Irrespective of the extent to which one *ḥaraka* supported or disapproved of the other, celebrations, rallies, festivities, demonstrations, and other events of this kind were also venues for public expression. In this case, besides the parties' leadership in organizing the event, people brought their own rally materials from home, their own ideas, feelings, and motivations. Men, women, and children attended this event, every one of them displaying a particular collection of nationalist and/or religious paraphernalia. Flags hung throughout the camp, as well as posters representing one or another political faction or simply displaying general popular support.

Along with local offices of other Palestinian parties in Al-Jalil, Fatah also sponsored the event. The rally was avowedly in support of the Gazan people rather than of Hamas. Perhaps part of Fatah's leadership was satisfied with the military weakening of Hamas, which it blamed for the disaster befalling Gaza and its people. Nevertheless, Fatah still had to maintain and enact support for a single and cohesive Palestine, an ideal it has helped foster since the late 1960s, or otherwise lose legitimacy. Moreover, Al-Jalil inhabitants were in general genuinely horrified by the events and demanded from their own leadership (and the world) some type of action.

A few residents, though, took the opportunity to show their support for Hamas or simply their discontent with Fatah and the Palestinian Authority (PA). One sign read "No to the Judaization of Jerusalem. Popular Front for the Liberation of Palestine - General Command."[20] This was only one such sign among many others by this political group. Another example declared: "No to the *tawṭīn* (Lebanese naturalization). Yes, to the Right of Return to Palestine.

---

20   لا لتهويد القدس. الجبهة شعبية القائدة العامة.

Popular Front for the Liberation of Palestine - General Command."[21] Although these signs did not directly criticize Fatah itself, their very presence and the way in which they were waved by PFLP-GC members and sympathizers were meant to express dissatisfaction and to mobilize residents around their position. The fact that the PFLP-GC was greatly present at the event was no coincidence, as the group was a splinter from the PFLP and founded by an ex-military officer of the Syrian army who believed the PFLP devoted too much time to Marxist philosophizing and not enough on armed struggle. The group was considered pro-Syrian at the time, and it therefore stressed solidarity with Gaza through its links with Hamas. Along with other groups, such as Fatah al-Intifada, the PFLP-GC was the internal response of early PLO groups to Arafat's negotiations with Israel. Arafat generally avoided the issue pertaining to the right of return for refugees in order to reach an agreement with Israel. As a result, many Palestinians in Lebanon tended to feel abandoned by the mainstream faction, no less in Al-Jalil, which, as I already noted, was physically and politically close to Syria.

The camp's proximity to Syria and the fact that its territory was located inside one of the main Hezbollah strongholds in Lebanon (previously Amal's dominion) meant that general support for the Syrian government and political support for some pro-Syrian groups in Al-Jalil were thriving. However, since the War of the Camps in Lebanon (1984-1990), during which Al-Jalil local leaders brokered a deal with Amal and the Syrian government, a bond with Syria was also promoted by embodied dispositions, affects, and sensitivities transmitted no less through the type of practices I describe in this chapter. The young, who were the most exposed to this environment, tended to express these dispositions, affects, and sensibilities more frequently and overtly. For instance, the Syrian government, unlike the Lebanese government during its rule, allowed construction material inside the camp after taking over that region of Lebanon, a fact widely cited not only as a logical argument for Palestinian support of the Syrian government, but also as having forged an emotional bond. This support for Damascus, it is important to note, did not only follow the local brokered military deal cited in the previous chapter, but was already emerging in the camp prior to the war itself. Among young and older generations in the camp, Hezbollah was generally seen as having inherited the role of main resistance against Israel, and, because it was allied with

---

21   لا توطين. نعم لحق العودة إلى الفلسطيني. الجبهة شعبية القائدة العامة.

Syria at the time,[22] than so should be the Palestinians. Very rarely did I meet anyone in Al-Jalil who was deeply critical of Hezbollah. That said, not everyone in Al-Jalil was pro-Syria, and Fatah still enjoyed relatively strong support. The fact that political allegiance to Fatah, as exhibited by some of the residents, could still survive in Al-Jalil, did not necessarily preclude a concomitant thrill over what they perceived as Hezbollah and Damascus victories. As I discuss in more detail in *Chapter 7*, allegiances were a far more complex matter than just standing with one's preferred party or movement.

Back at the pro-Gaza demonstration, a boy scouts group vigorously beat the drums as it paraded through the camp's main street among the growing crowd. One of the local sheikhs handed out small plastic Palestinian flags to everyone, while organizing and motivating the scouts. Women actively chanted nationalist and religious slogans, such as *Allahu Akbar* ("God is the Greatest") and *Al-Falastyn Lina* ("Palestine is ours"). At times the march would come to a standstill, as they waited for an old truck loaded with sound equipment that lagged behind. Atop the truck, men switched places at the microphone. Their speeches stressed the political situation, referring often to Islam for terms and encouragement, thereby aligning the times of the Prophet with the modern Palestinian predicament. The truck was a moving stage, setting the pace of the march.

Following the truck, older men, recognized as leaders and ceremoniously dressed in suits, marched with their arms hooked together forming a human-chain, as the remaining participants paraded behind. Everyone gave way to the mighty chain. At a corner midway through the camp, the convoy stopped before the human chain, and another elegantly dressed man shook the hands of all the elders before joining the line. At one point, when the procession reached the *zāwya* (corner) in front of the camp, one of the Palestinian elders wrapped his arm around the latecomer's arm. The latter man's fist was closed, and he seemed to slightly struggle with his part of the ritual, since he was not one of the locals and therefore not completely accustomed to such a ritual. After all, he was not Palestinian but Lebanese, a representative of Hezbollah, which was officially supporting the event. At the *zāwya*, there were speeches as usual. Several of the local leaders spoke, as did the Hezbollah representative. Local Palestinian institutions were present with their cameras, just like me

---

22   That Hezbollah was not allied to Syria during the Lebanese Civil War, and in fact fought against Amal, only reinforced the support of most Al-Jalil residents to Asad's government, given that the two forces were allied now.

since I had been invited to photograph the event. Some had professional video cameras over their shoulders, and this time even a small group of Hezbollah's television network, Al-Manar, was filming and interviewing participants.

With Hezbollah's support, the event spread beyond the camp for the first and only time during my stay, as it reinforced solidarity and cooperation among Lebanese and Palestinian political factions, in part legitimized by Hezbollah's actions in the 2006 Lebanon War,[23] stated to have been in support of Gaza during the previous siege. The truck left the *zāwya*, took to the street, and roamed around the surroundings outside the camp. Night had already fallen, and lit candles were beautifully placed on the street at the entrance of the camp. Interrupting the traffic on the Beirut-Baalbek road, the candles evoked mourning, rather than the authority imposed by military checkpoints so common in Lebanon. With local Lebanese support, Palestinians stopped traffic, respectfully asking passers-by for a small financial contribution to Gaza. Almost all those who crossed the checkpoint contributed something, filling a few baskets with Lebanese money to be sent to Palestine. However useful the money was, the event was highly symbolic, marking solidarity between the camp residents and those outside.

Touched by the expression of humility and solidarity I had just witnessed, I made my way back to the camp and towards the truck, which had just returned. The crowd around the truck suddenly pushed to the side, while running in my direction with a burning Israeli flag. Many young men around me jumped in to express their anger by vandalizing the flag, while others preferred to avoid the scene. Flag desecration was not a common sight in Al-Jalil's demonstrations, which is why I was taken by surprise, but this was a time of even deeper crisis, and burning a flag was among the few things that some felt they could do to quench their anger and resentment against the massacre in Gaza. Among this flag-burning group, some would direct their anger at Israel, the USA and/or *al-ṣahayūniyya* (Zionism), and some would blend politics, religion and ethnicity, directing their war cries against *al-yahūd* (the Jews). Having never traveled beyond Lebanon, Syria, and Jordan, most of those in the latter group had never interacted with a Jew, and therefore could not understand the difference between the terms Jew and Zionist. Besides mourning and promoting a sense of belonging and solidarity, the flag burning and war cries were a reminder of the power of these events as channels for expression

---

23   This war is known in Arabic as *Ḥarb Tammūz*, or "July War."

and the mobilization of people's affects and sensibilities in whichever form they take.

Similarities between this demonstration and the *Nakba* Day celebration reinforce the value and currency of certain themes and practices within the camp. Vernacular politics with strong Islamic undertones was coupled with a prevalence of nationalist motives in these ritualized practices, even when the participants belonged to secular groups inspired by Marxism or even founded by Christians, such as Fatah or the PFLP, which was still somewhat popular in Al-Jalil. Palestinian nationalism was steeped in Islam as a tradition and as an idiom of everyday life, rather than just mere theology. In this way, even Palestinian Christians from other mixed camps, such as Mar Elias, shared most of these national and quotidian expressions originally of Islamic inspiration, as I will elaborate in *Chapter 6*.

f.   Yawm al-Arḍ

Along with local celebrations inside the Palestinian refugee camps across Lebanon, *Yawm al-Arḍ* (Land Day) was also celebrated in 2007 in a Lebanese convention center in Beirut. This was not a common occurrence, as usually Palestinian celebrations were restricted the refugee camps or smaller Palestinian-friendly spaces such as Ta-Marbuta, Café Yunis or Le Barometre[24] – all left leaning, alternative cafés, the first two located in Hamra, and the last next to the American University of Beirut (AUB), all within the secularized, non-sectarian and alternative intellectual center of Beirut. Residents of all camps joined this celebration, which drew even the largely wealthier Palestinian population residing outside the camps, the Lebanese population sympathetic to the Palestinian cause, and a handful of foreign activists and sympathizers. Therefore, unlike my presentation of the first two rites, I present this Land Day *iḥtifāl* (festivity, celebration) in part to discuss the ways in which and the extent to which such rites may assume meaning outside a camp such as Al-Jalil.

Land Day is the annual celebration of the violent events of March 30, 1976, when Palestinians in Galilee (then already part of Israel) and the Negev desert carried out strikes and political demonstrations against an Israeli government

---

24   Le Barometre's location was supposedly a PLO headquarters during the Lebanese Civil War.

decree that expropriated land with the intention of building new Jewish settlements. In parallel, as is frequently the case, protests were also held in the rest of the Palestinian Occupied Territories and in the Palestinian refugee camps of Lebanon. As a result, a violent clash erupted in Galilee between Palestinians and the Israeli security apparatus led by the IDF. Several Palestinians were shot dead, about one hundred were wounded, and many others imprisoned. Besides the political and human impact of the event in Israel and the Occupied Territories, in the Palestinian camps of Lebanon this became one more day to associate Palestinianness to suffering, to what they called the Palestinian Cause, and to ideals and practices of resistance.

Rather than a parade followed by political speeches, as I learned was common in Al-Jalil from other events of this kind such as the ones described above, the 2007 Beirut Land Day was an event partly organized by enthusiasts of grassroots art themes, for whom the Palestinian drama and common Arabness loomed large. The event was thus organized as a series of art performances meant to showcase and celebrate Palestinian folklore. To the Palestinians, and perhaps especially to the refugees among them, folklore was seen as evidence of the Palestinian rootedness to their land and of their timeless existence as a people before 1948. A mix of unique national foods, dialects, clothing, music, crafts, and others were put on display. Therefore, to most Palestinians present at this event, it was important not only to maintain their "culture" (*thaqafa*), but also to broadcast it to the world at large. In the process, to perform Palestinian culture was imbued with an aura of resistance, and thus, being Palestinian, which in turn meant to somehow also perform the culture off stage, was often understood and presented as a form of resistance. This perspective was at the root of the performers' motivation on that day, as I could observe and was told by some of the proud Al-Jalil residents, who had tirelessly rehearsed to give their best at that moment.

In the spirit of the commonly held belief above, the show was meant to exhibit the rich and, though assaulted, still unblemished Palestinian folklore. The first performer walked onto the stage in silence, displaying a tranquil countenance in front of the relatively large crowd formally sitting in the auditorium. There must have been more than a hundred and fifty people present. He was a flute soloist, but his instrument was special. He played what the Palestinians called a *shibbabe*, or a short duct flute made from reed and open on both sides originally used by shepherds to herd their flocks. That day, however, the performer was playing contemporary and meditative themes to a much more discerning audience. The instrument had already been adapted along the years, being "folklorized" as time went by. As the master played, the public respectfully sat in silence. The audience seemed touched after the *shib-babe* recital. The flutist left the stage for the next part of the show. A young woman came next, bearing no instrument but her own voice. She was dressed in jeans, a fitted black shirt, and preferred to wear her *kufiyya* around her neck, letting her brown curly hair cover part of her face. Supplicating to God and the public, she sang of Palestinian suffering, moving slowly and closing her eyes on each high note, punctuating the drama of the performance. The crowd was very pleased, and many among the men commented on her beauty and on their own yearning for Palestine.

The third performance of the day utterly transformed the solemn *jaww* (social atmosphere) of the event. The lights suddenly turned much brighter and more colorful, as the stage was quickly taken by a group of boys dressed in dark jeans and *kufiyya* patterned white t-shirts, over which hung scarves with the Palestinian flag on one side and their *dabke* group logo on the other. They wore bandanas and necklaces featuring the pre-1948 Palestinian map to match, while a lone boy – not special in any way – carried *Handala*[25] on his chest. The music became louder, while drumbeats and stomping from the boys' feet on the wooden stage dominated the soundscape as they danced the Palestinian *dabke*. At this point, the public, already quite moved by the flute and vocal performances, seemed fully taken by the boys' energy. Like much of contemporary Palestinian *dabke*, their movements were references to their land. The dancers mimed the sowing and reaping of the country's soil, while other movements evoked the olive trees and birds of Palestine, at which point the audience eagerly reacted by clapping their hands and moving their bodies to the beat. The *dabke* then faded into the background, as two of the boys moved forward to center stage to sing a dialogue about the current lives of Palestinians in Palestine and in refuge. As one of the boys left, the other sang a final monologue and finished with a salutation. One of his hands still held the microphone, and the other was raised in divine contemplation, the palm invitingly opened and facing up. As the song stopped, the palm closed into a tight fist, remaining so for the duration of the crowd's thundering applause.

The next performer entered the stage wearing an elegant black robe with detailed golden embroidery. Covering the top of his head was a black and

---

25   A Palestinian character who always carries symbolic messages about the occupation, and is always represented as barefoot, and turning his back to the onlooker, suggesting that he is just one more in a crowd.

white scarf held in place by an *'agāl*[26] (a circle of white rope), as he carried a *mizmār al-iskotlandy*[27] (Scottish bagpipe). Palestinians took the bagpipe from Scottish soldiers stationed in Palestine during the times of the British Mandate, and Palestinian scout troops were the first to play them, at first for the same purpose as the Scotts. The instrument is thus evocative of Palestinian troops before 1948. However, the bagpipe has been repurposed over the decades and turned into part of the Palestinian cultural idiom. Within the Near East, Palestinians are the only ones who play the bagpipes, and therefore this instrument is especially representative of Palestinian uniqueness in relation to its neighbors. As a result, today, for example, a bagpipe performance is an essential part of Christmas celebrations in Bethlehem. No wonder, then, that a bagpipe performer had a special place in the Beirut Land Day celebration, and the man in the black and golden robe did not disappoint the audience, skillfully playing his bagpipe against the background of a large Palestinian flag.

The audience, itself mostly composed of Palestinians young and old, had so far been entertained, but showed special interest when the next performers rushed onto the scene, bringing the *dabke* back with them. They were a mixed gender adult troupe and wore long, colorful Palestinian peasant clothes, evoking the deep relationship between Palestinians and their native land. Like the other performers, all of them wore headscarves, and the men carried small threads of rope in one hand, whirling them to excite the multitude and bridge the stage distance. According to some Al-Jalil residents present, "even some Lebanese" participated in that dance group, inspired by the Palestinian cause and the appeal of the Palestinian *dabke* itself. These members rehearsed in the troupe's headquarters in Burj al-Barajneh Palestinian refugee camp (located in Beirut). Playing well-known themes and dancing together, alternating between two lines and a circle, the group moved with contagious energy, inspiring some in the audience to dance in their seats and cheer loudly. When they finally left the stage, the audience remained highly enthusiastic, maintaining the same atmosphere for the next mixed gender adult *dabke* troupe to enter

---

26   This word has no-Arabic roots, hence the exceptional *g* – pronounced as in "garage" – in my transliteration.

27   Although many Palestinians refer to this instrument simply as *mizmār*, this term in Arabic means any single or double reed wind musical instrument, like the Levantine and Iraqi *mijwiz*.

the scene. In addition to the same thematic scarves, used this time as bandanas, these performers all wore military uniforms, and one man used yet another scarf, tied to his hips, as a belt. The music was loud, the beat strong, and their *dabke* gestures were bold and wide. The military style *dabke* drove the crowd to yet another level of excitement. People rose from their seats, clapping their hands and singing in unison. Some women ululated.

At this point, the last performer took the stage. He entered in silence, alone with his oud. The excited crowd once more sat down and became silent. His oud was aided by the emotional tone of his trembling voice pleading for the lost land in the name of its virtuous people. The audience was once more led to mourn and contemplate. As I understood then, the expressive fluctuation engendered by the structure of the event kept the public interested and emotionally tied to the performances. It would not be entirely accurate to think that the mobilization of symbols and referents by both event organizers and performers were all calculated to produce certain effects in the public. There was certainly intentionality, as the performances were conceived by the performers themselves, and the entire program was curated by the organizers. However, it would be too simplistic to say, for example, that the invocations of land, olive trees, birds, peasants, sowing and reaping, and others, were all drawn from the offices of political parties only to produce obedient subjects, or even to say that the whole event was produced, for example, to mobilize the audience towards an oneiric view of pre-*Nakba* Palestine, a sense of Palestinian cultural and political unity, the need to remain steadfast in the face of predicament, or the legitimacy of the use of military force against Israel. All of these could have emerged or been strengthened as embodied dispositions, affects, and sensitivities. They were not, however, simply commanded by a conscious and manipulative elite to be instilled into an unconscious and naïve crowd.

Upon exiting, relatives and friends were met in front of the convention center by the performers, still dressed in their outfits and most of whom were refugee camp residents. Within the community, they were respected both for their art and as national symbols of what all recognized in one way or another as the Palestinian Cause, regardless of political allegiances. The public left the convention center roused by the quality of the performances, but the effectiveness of the event as a disciplinary practice did not rely exclusively on its success, perceived by either audience or performers. The event's evocation of symbols such as the land, olive trees, birds, peasants, sowing and reaping, and so on, is not unique to Palestinian folklore. Such evocation is in accordance with Liisa Malkki's (1992) general thesis regarding the importance of *botanical metaphors* highlighting rootedness to the earth to invoke and legitimize the connection between a people and their land, which is especially strong among refugees (as the uprooted). The work of disciplinary practices, such as the rites I described above, is thus far more complex, involving different levels of consciousness and intentionality, along with embodied drives and predispositions to not only think, but also perceive, feel, and act. To understand how Palestinian refugees in Lebanon relate to religion and social belonging, what is needed are less geopolitical considerations of the Palestinian question and more archeology of Palestinian knowledge and the social body.

Meanwhile, Land Day was also celebrated in the refugee camps. In al-Jalil, political groups were overtly among the sponsors, and the celebration looked similar to *Nakba* Day. Among the many signs carried or clothes worn by the children, only a few were symbols of party affiliation, and most were in fact sponsored by voluntary associations like *Jam'aiyya al-Najda al-Ijtim'aiyya* (The Association of Social Support) – a local voluntary association composed mainly, if not exclusively, of women engaged in social service and cultural activities in the camp. To call attention to the similarity of the messages between *Nakba* Day and Land Day celebrations in Al-Jalil, among the many posters by *Al-Najda* was one that read as follows: "No concession from our fixed positions; withdrawal of the occupation to June 4 of 1967 borders; an independent country with full sovereignty and Jerusalem as its capital; Return of the refugees to their homes according to Resolution 194. The Association of Social Support."[28] Religiosity, albeit never central to the events, was present in both Land Day celebrations. Nevertheless, in contrast to the festivities in the refugee camps, Beirut's Land Day celebration exhibited a more cultural idiom, while being no less political. Since celebrations were generally restricted to the camps' perimeter, festivities like this one, in which refugees could meet and get to know Palestinians from other camps[29] were rather infrequent and were especially popular among the youth. Moreover, the event showcased Palestinian

---

28   The original was: لا تنازل عن ثوابتنا. جلاء الاحتلال حتى حدو 4 حزيران 67 ودولة مستقلة كاملة السيادة وعاصمتها القدس صودة اللاجئين إلى ديارهم وفقا للقرار 194. جمعية النجدة الاجتماعية.

29   It is also interesting to note that when Palestinian refugees in Lebanon met other Palestinians, personal introductions usually followed the pattern described by Julie Peteet (1996). That is, subjects were interested in first learning which camp their interlocutors were from (if any), and then which village in Palestine.

culture and artistic talent not only to Palestinian refugees themselves, but to the general public in Beirut. This was a special occasion, and some spoke about it for days in Al-Jalil. No less importantly, participants enjoyed their enhanced personal statuses as well, and others in the camp considered taking part the following year. By way of this event, in a process we could call *folklorization*, a single broad Palestinian popular culture and its tie to the Palestinian nation and the claimed pre-1948 Palestinian borders was naturalized, internalized, showcased as representative of the nation, and life was made meaningful.

g. Mawlid al-Naby

One of my local interlocutors, originally from Shatila, laughingly recounted an incident that happened to him: "Once, Amira came to visit us in Shatila and found me in my shorts, sandals, and tank top. She was horrified and told me to go put some clothes on. I told her, relax, you are not in Al-Jalil." He constantly pointed out that Al-Jalil was morally conservative and pious when compared to "his" camp. Having lived in Al-Jalil for months, I tended to agree with his assessment, until one of the locals told me in English[30]: "Come, it is carnival!"[31] Surprised, I left my lodging in the camp and took to the streets to see with my own eyes. Yet, being Brazilian, my idea of carnival was markedly different from what I encountered, namely, *Mawlid al-Naby* (the Prophet's Birthday). The birth of the prophet was celebrated with the hope that God's justice would free Al-Jalil inhabitants from their supposedly temporary yet concretely protracted existence in the camp and place them in a hoped-for idyllic Palestine. The optimists would say that whatever the enemy destroyed, they would later rebuild.

A sea of flags flew over the camp's sky, once more evoking political and religious motifs. Some exhibited the traditional green of Islam, while others wore party colors. A few had both. Many were the political parties that sent

---

30   Although most of my fieldwork was conducted in Arabic, English was also present, especially when I was teaching the language at the *Markaz*, when I needed clarification on the meaning of words I did not know, and when locals wanted to speak English themselves. Very few in al-Jalil were able to have full conversations in English, but many were keen on trying the language even if just for a salutation or a word or two.

31   I occasionally heard the term in English, used to translate the Arabic word *iḥtifāl* (party, or celebration) for the many occasions on which Al-Jalil's community found to celebrate.

representatives to demonstrate support for the prophet's cause, amalgamating Islam and Palestine. Given that secularism in Al-Jalil did not necessarily preclude faith, even secularist, Marxist factions were represented. Thus, in Al-Jalil, as with the other more openly political and nationalist events above, The Prophet's Birthday was also celebrated amidst religious, political, and nationalist themes.

Ululating and shouting a blend of nationalist and religious slogans, women roused the crowd gathering in the main street of the camp. Participants chanted *la illaha ila Allah* ("There is no God but God"),[32] while circulating around the main streets of the camp, just as Muslims do when circling the Kaaba[33] (*ṭawāf*) during the Hajj or lesser pilgrimages to Mecca. The center of the camp was definitely not venerated as the Kaaba, but the ritual resemblance was evocative of religious symbolism empowering local performances, be they religious or not. The event was sponsored by the local mosque, and as always, children participated by circulating through the crowd and attempting to imitate the adults. This time, the women were in charge of organizing the children on behalf of the mosque representatives. As in the events described above, many children played specific roles, such as carrying flags, chanting certain slogans, or reciting the Quran. They learned much by imitating, and by being reprimanded when behaving out of place. The procedures and techniques of one public event were reminiscent of past ones. As always, most children were keen to participate, and so made their way among the others to find the best spots or simply to provoke their peers. From where they stood, the anniversary of the prophet was at the least a great opportunity to celebrate and eat delicious treats, but also, being virtuous or not, they could gain the admiration of the adults and of the other children.

Mawlid al-Naby was an explicitly religious celebration, whereas *Nakba* Day and the pro-Gaza demonstration had a predominantly political character, while Land Day in Beirut had a prevalently cultural tone. However, like all other celebrations, rallies, strikes,[34] or demonstrations, the characteristic

---

32   Phrase constitutive of the *shahāda*, as explained in the introduction.

33   The cube that is at the center of the *Masjid Al-Ḥarām* mosque in Mecca, venerated in Islam as the most sacred place in Earth. It is to the Kaaba that Muslims turn five times a day to pray.

34   Even though in practice most Al-Jalil camp residents could not go on strike (*iḍrāb*), because they had no jobs with bosses beyond the local internal economy of the camp and one or another service they would (sometimes illegally) provide in Baalbek, they would also mark strikes, whenever other Palestinians did, as demonstration.

blend of religious, political, and nationalistic (or ethnic) themes was also present during religious celebrations such as this one. Furthermore, such religious celebrations took a similar form to the other ones in Al-Jalil, consisting of a parade around the camp that tended to appeal to everyone and allow local organized groups to display their paraphernalia, followed by speeches generally delivered by adult men, as most women and children dissipated from the crowd. In addition, however, unlike the other events presented here, the Prophet's birthday was also celebrated within people's homes, over and above the public social gathering outside. Festive meals were cooked and much of the day was filled with prayers, many of which, public or private, were directed toward the Palestinian collective or the land of Palestine. The Prophet's birthday took on multiple facets: on the more personal level it constituted a time to celebrate Islam, bond with the family, meditate and pray, while on the community level it was also another opportunity to remember Palestine and the struggle.

h.   Quotidian tempo

There were many other ritualized performances in Al-Jalil beyond the regular events, such as the ones described in the above sections. Ritualized celebration or mourning occurred sometimes as often as on a weekly basis, depending on the time of year and the political situation. Most political public performances were restricted to the innermost space of the camp and were only rarely taken to the camp's entrance or to the city streets. However, not all of these celebrations observed such restrictions, as the examples of Land Day at the Lebanese Convention Center and of the pro-Gaza rally in Al-Jalil illustrate. Performances geared to and manifested outside the camp, such as the pro-Gaza demonstration, had the approval of Hezbollah as a sign of mutual understanding and of Palestinian acceptance of their guest status in Lebanon. When such performances of Palestinianness reached an even larger audience, as was the case with Land Day celebrated in Beirut in 2007, they had to count not only on official permission, but also on local sympathy. Partially influenced by the sectarianism (ṭā'ifiyya) instilled by the so-called Lebanese confessional-democracy, Lebanese mobilization of sympathy towards Palestinians, in turn, was frequently bound to ethno-religious politics, beyond pure practical reason.

The day after the abovementioned celebrations of the Prophet's Birthday, the general mood in the camp had not completely changed. Some flags were still up, as they had been before the event. Posters still covered the walls, as they had before. Military marches, odes to Palestine, and chanted prayers continued to radiate from political offices, local associations, shops, and the mobile phones of passers-by. The mosque continued its daily calls to prayer, and the sheikhs continued to invoke Palestine in their sermons. The same held true after the pro-Gaza demonstration, *Nakba* Day, Land Day, and any other given day. Day after day, refugees steadfastly performed Palestinianness in the quotidian through the ritualization of both sacred and mundane aspects of their lives. There were always celebrations ahead, for which one needed to prepare, but quotidian life was in itself often ritualized.

Children went to school, the *Markaz*, or other similar facilities, where they drew pictures that almost always featured Palestinian symbols. Birds, olive trees, rivers, the sun, and everything that represented happy settings were generally framed by Palestinian flags, a key element symbolizing the "re-opening of Jerusalem," the map (with political borders of historical Palestine before 1948), the Dome of the Rock, or other symbols of idealized Palestinianness. Children negotiated their future and present by way of the same symbols, conveying dreams, hope, and despair. They did not draw on or talk about these subjects only at school, but everywhere. Expressions of these themes, formalized into discourse and inscribed into the residents' bodies, were part of the quotidian, and their pervasiveness was only seldom noticed by the refugees as a ritualization of daily life. Since most Al-Jalil residents were in fact children, they tended to mobilize on a daily basis, several times a day; they embodied dispositions, sensibilities and affects like those mobilized during calendric celebrations. The same national themes were repeatedly expressed, discussed, reaffirmed, and contextually mobilized on a daily basis. The iteration of national and religious referents and symbols through disciplinary practices inscribed Palestinianness in the bodies of the residents, which in turn embedded dispositions, sensibilities and affects in the quotidian lives of refugees. Beyond calendric events, the very rhythm, or tempo, of daily life was thus marked by such disciplinary practices, as the invocation of certain discourses or the enactment of embodied practices made up much of the camp's own routine.

Even though not all camp life was ritualized, time itself was often the object of ritualization. More than 60 years of resistance against protracted refuge entailed a general rejection of the present as it was lived in the camp and a ritualized objectification and portrayal of this present as Lena Jayyusi (2007) called a *time-within-time* – which I presented in *Chapter 2* – bound, by

God's will or not, to vanish through the refugees' mythical or actual return to Palestine. Yet, the temporary condition of refugeeness was also simultaneously lived as perennial. Often, the residents' faith in what was identified – much through the refugees' own predicament – as the Palestinian cause was shaken, sometimes along with their religious piety. There was a general sense, even among the most secular residents that, if God existed, then their suffering would be mitigated, either here or in the afterlife; however, hope in the national cause and religious piety were intertwined in more complex ways than just through faith. Belief in God did not necessarily entail believing that they or their children would return to Palestine, but it gave hope. I never met anyone in Al-Jalil who would simply admit to not believing in God, but even to potential unbelievers, I understand that hope is beyond faith as much as it is beyond rational choice. Rallying around the cause was first and foremost an embodied and disciplined general framing for life that could indeed be challenged, as I show particularly in *Chapters 1* and *7*. However, as the very context through which much of the quotidian was framed, "the cause" was entrenched in much of peoples' lives, rather than simply being a matter of rational or conscious choice, or religious zeal. In sum, "belief" or "hope" in the cause were not necessarily tied to the actual conditions of possibility for its outcome. Moreover, as much as hope was also an important element mobilizing the residents' dispositions, affects, and sensibilities, the ritualized practices inscribing Palestinianness into the quotidian did not depend exclusively even on hope, as residents would still rally around whatever each one of them considered to be the Palestinian cause, even if they had no hope of achieving it.

Thus, the total context of ritualization in Al-Jalil, what I call the local *ritual tempo*, was an adaptive structure continuously readjusting people's feelings, thoughts, aspirations, desires, and actions. If "the cause" was polyphonic, as it meant different things to different people, being Palestinian in Al-Jalil could also take different forms and be in fact very diverse. However, Palestinianness still emerged much as an entailment of individual and group grappling with the kinds of forces I have so far presented, disseminated in the ritual tempo of the camp.

Chapter 4: Ritual Tempo in Dbayeh

a. Dbayeh's Invisibility

Before visiting Dbayeh for the first time, I had not met a single Christian Palestinian refugee living in a camp. I knew many Christian Palestinian refugees who lived in Lebanese neighborhoods or abroad. I also knew that the relatively tiny (when compared to other Palestinian refugee camps in Lebanon) Mar Elias,[1] located near the boundaries between east, west and south Beirut, was once a Christian Palestinian majority refugee camp. However, after so many massacres in the other refugee camps, including Tel Al-Zaatar, Qarantina, Sabra & Shatila, Nabatieh, and more, Mar Elias's population soared and changed in character. At the time of my fieldwork, most families in Mar Elias were Muslim, but the camp still contained more Christian families than any of the other eleven Palestinian refugee camps in Lebanon except Dbayeh.

At the time of my fieldwork, Dbayeh's main demographic difference from other refugee camps in Lebanon was that only 0.78% of the camp was Muslim, and all other inhabitants were Christian of different denominations (59.9% Catholic – including Melkites and Roman Catholics – 29.17% Maronite, 8.59% Orthodox, 0.78% Latin, 0.52% Evangelical, and 0.26% Jehovah's Witness) (World Vision 2007). According to UNRWA's published official data, in 2010 there were 4,211 individuals grouped in 67 families registered as Palestine refugees in Dbayeh (UNRWA 2010) living in some of the 464 houses in the camp (World Vision 2007). The actual number of refugees living in the camp, however, was considerably lower, and many of the houses included in the World Vision figure above were actually occupied by Lebanese. Like

---

[1]   This was by far the smallest Palestinian refugee camp in Lebanon, with only 615 people registered with UNRWA, according to UNRWA's official website (UNRWA 2010).

Dbayeh, other Palestinian camps in Lebanon – and Shatila is a good example – also had a high percentage of Lebanese inhabitants. The specific historical reasons leading to Dbayeh's Lebanese population will be explored later in this chapter.

While still living in Al-Jalil, I thought that if only I knew one Christian family living in a Muslim majority camp, then I could gain access to Dbayeh. I took for granted that most members of the Christian Palestinian refugee community in Lebanon would have close ties, as is frequently the case with religious or ethnic minorities in the Middle East. The problem, however, was that not a single Christian lived in Al-Jalil, and I did not know any Christian Palestinians living in the other camps. Moreover, almost none of my friends and interlocutors in Al-Jalil could help. An opportunity to meet someone from Dbayeh arose when I encountered a Palestinian circus troupe, which included members from many different Palestinian refugee camps in the country. They used to train in Burj al-Barajneh refugee camp (near Shatila), and two broth-ers from Al-Jalil were among the performers. I knew these young men well, and from them I learned that the troupe was rehearsing for a refugee camp tour. This was my opportunity, I thought. Also interested in the troupe's work itself, and especially in its inter-camp character, I asked the older of the broth-ers if I could join them in Burj al-Barajneh to get to know the group, take pictures of the performances, and perhaps be introduced to members from Dbayeh, given that I planned to do field research there. He agreed and told me that the troupe itself included a young man and a young woman from Dbayeh. Although my interlocutor did not know them well, he offered to bro-ker the contact, suggesting that, with their help, I might be able to talk to one of the camp leaders about the possibility of researching in Dbayeh.

We left from Al-Jalil early, by van, on the Beirut-Baalbek road, arriving in Burj al-Barajneh two hours later. The brothers usually made the trip twice a week to rehearse with the troupe, staying overnight with relatives in the camp. There was constant movement between the camps, either during formal oc-casions, in which people from different camps could come together as a com-munity, or because of family or business. Dbayeh was somehow exceptional in this matter. There was some traffic from Dbayeh to other camps, especially be-cause UNRWA registered refugees in Dbayeh had to go to Burj al-Barajneh for consultation and treatment at the UNRWA run hospital serving all the camps around Beirut. Dbayeh was also vaguely connected to other camps through relations of kinship. Conversely, Palestinians from other camps rarely visited Dbayeh, setting it very much apart from life in the other camps.

In comparison to Shatila or to what once was Nahr al-Bared, Burj al-Barajneh was not as well equipped to receive foreign researchers, journalists, and social workers. Both Shatila and Nahr al-Bared served as the main Palestinian centers in Beirut and Tripoli respectively. Cultural spaces, however, were common throughout all Palestinian refugee camps in Lebanon. In contrast to Al-Jalil, where *dabke* and other performance groups generally had to obtain a rehearsal space from the local UNRWA school or a political party, the much larger Burj El-Barajneh, with its 16,066 registered residents (UN-RWA 2010), offered plenty of space for cultural programs such as the circus troupe. Again, in contrast with the other camps, Dbayeh neither had cultural space nor any local groups performing cultural activities, except those organized by one of the local churches, including a theater play (*masraḥiyya*) held about twice a year, a chorus group, and some other transient activities generally geared toward children. Dbayeh had no boyscouts or *dabke* groups.

The cultural center where the troupe trained in Burj al-Barajneh was fairly large. To the left of the entrance, there was a one-meter-tall stage, and to the right, a large empty space on concrete floor. An enormous panel painted with Palestinian themes covered the wall to the left of the stage. The panel featured a Palestinian martyr's burial consisting of a procession carrying a body covered with a Palestinian flag. The martyr's head was wrapped in a Palestinian themed scarf with the inscription *shahīd* (martyr). Around the body, there were people carrying another Palestinian flag, a flag of a Palestinian party, and the prophet's green flag. Depicted on the panel were also: tents representing the beginnings of a refugee camp; al-Aqsa Mosque; the Church of the Holy Sepulcher; a fallen Intifada hero with a stone still in hand; olive trees; a *fidāʾiyy* (singular for Fedayeen in Arabic) whose Kalashnikov featured a rose bursting from the gun's muzzle; a running horse partially morphed into a Palestinian flag; teenagers firing their slingshots at an Israeli tank, and burning tires with fire and smoke.

As we entered the cultural center, the younger of the Al-Jalil brothers pointed to the two Dbayeh residents. I sat in the back of the room and watched until practice was over. During the rehearsal, the Dbayeh couple seemed actively included, which encouraged me to approach them. I walked up to a man in his early thirties and introduced myself. We talked for a while before I mentioning I was interested in getting to know Dbayeh. He gave me his phone number and asked me to call him to set up a tour of the camp. Over the following days, I called him many times, and never received a positive answer. The couple of times that he actually answered my calls, he indefinitely postponed the trip. As I realized his reluctance, I tried a different approach. Since I had recently been associated with a Lebanese University based in a village near Dbayeh, I asked for help from the university's internal personnel, who gave me the contact of the Caritas Migration Center.

At that time, I thought this connection was facilitated because both institutions were interested in the theme of migration. The university was interested in the Lebanese *mahjar* (the diaspora)[2] from an academic perspective, while the branch of the Christian NGO Caritas was interested in migrants to Lebanon from a social service perspective. I made several attempts to reach someone willing to talk at Caritas, but responses were slow to come back, and when they came, they were never inviting. For instance, as I had done in Al-Jalil, I offered to teach English in the camp as a volunteer. The general manager, however, insisted on more email communication. I resolved to visit the institution personally, hoping to stand a better chance in a face-to-face conversation.

I made my way to Dbayeh on a bus leaving Beirut from *Dawra* towards the North on the Beirut-Tripoli Road. I was instructed that the camp would be near the Lebanese area with the same name, Dbayeh, just after an Armenian conglomerate close to Antelias. Thus, I informed the driver in a loud voice (just as I would do around Baalbek), *Nazilny bil-mukhayyam, 'aml ma'ruf* ("Drop me off at the camp, please"), to which he gave me a lost look and responded, "where?" I explained that I was heading to the Palestinian refugee camp, to which he answered there was no such thing in the area. Dbayeh still seemed to me almost as much of a myth as it did to Palestinians in Al-Jalil, and I worried that I had taken the wrong bus or had wrong directions. The driver suggested that if indeed I wanted to look for a camp in the area, then Dbayeh had two exits I could take. I chose to leave the bus at the first one. The trip did not last longer than twenty minutes from *Dawra* to the first Dbayeh exit. After asking for directions unsuccessfully there, I walked toward the second exit, where I found a gas station and a school – its name written both in Arabic and in French: *Madrasa Al-Maqdysa Rytā – École Sainte Rita*. I asked about the camp at the gas station, but again no one could help. I also had no luck with passers-by, who were puzzled by me request. A local taxi driver waiting next to the gas station finally called me, asking where I wanted to go. He claimed

---

2   The literal word for diaspora in Arabic is *shatāt*, but *mahjar* conveys both the place of immigration and the community of immigrants themselves.

to live up the hill and know everything around, including where to find the Palestinians. For *Alfen* (2,000.00LL)[3] he took me there.

Going up the will, we crossed the Royal Hotel, a local landmark that contained its own water park, and about four minutes later he dropped me off in front of the Caritas Migration Center Dbayeh office, just past the UNRWA office. The houses did not seem like they sheltered refugees, and the place indeed did not feel like a camp to me. The physical environment of the camp was quite open, as modest houses lined the narrow streets. Unlike al-Jalil, trees stood amidst the concrete. In addition, a fresh breeze from the sea blew at the top of the hill, making the environment much more pleasant than the dusty air around Baalbek. In Lebanon, those who can afford to live in the mountains do so, mainly to avoid the summer heat. It seemed to me that Dbayeh was the Palestinian refugee equivalent of those Lebanese summer residences, and I understood then why most among those Palestinians who knew or had heard about Dbayeh envied its inhabitants. Mar Elias was very well organized and Al-Jalil was by far the cleanest of the camps I had visited, kept so only by its residents, but Dbayeh had unparalleled fresh air and lush vegetation, contributing to its seeming openness.

While both were in sight of the entrance, the door to the small UNRWA office was closed, so I went straight to that of the Caritas office. There, I saw elderly people, some with canes, playing cards and drinking tea, while a couple of young women looked up a little puzzled by my presence. I spoke to one of them explaining who I was and that I had been communicating with their general manager for a while over email. I asked if I could perform any type of volunteer work in the camp. She was evasive, presumably because she did not have the authority to make such decisions. I thanked them both and left. From my initial email interactions with Caritas until then, I was made to understand that I needed Caritas' approval to enter the camp. Interestingly, while never answering my questions directly, the organization never redirected me to or even mentioned the local UNRWA office. I decided to not leave just yet and explore the camp on my own.

In the streets, everyone looked at me. Some gave me warm greetings, others just tried to pass by unnoticed. The elderly would crane their necks to see me until I was totally out of sight. I finally found what seemed to be a café, went in, and ordered an *argile* and tea. The owners brought me both and proceeded to ask questions about who I was and what I was doing there. I

---

3   Approximately 1.5 American dollars at the time

explained everything, and they suggested it would be better if I returned another day and talked to a certain man, I will name here Charbel. The next day, I returned and ordered tea and *argile* again, hoping to meet Charbel. A couple of hours later, the café owners took me downstairs to a pastry shop where Charbel was drinking coffee and smoking a cigarette. He offered me some coffee, and I accepted. After meeting Charbel, I stopped dealing with Caritas, and we spent days talking over coffee, as he wanted to be sure to know my intentions in detail if he was to be responsible for my admission to the camp.

I was told, and later learned for myself with regard to Mar Elias, that Palestinian Christians living in other local refugee camps tended to be adapted to life among their Muslim neighbors. Christian Palestinians living outside the camps in Lebanon or abroad tended to have their Arab social circuits more circumscribed to Christians (especially Palestinian), although frequently they had close ties to Muslim Palestinians too. Dbayeh's Palestinians, however, seemed isolated from other Palestinians in a way that I had never seen before. How and why was this the case? This was one of the first questions I had in mind once I bridged the distance and started to live in Dbayeh. I did not move from one camp to the other all at once, but rather, the process lasted about ten days after my first contact with Charbel. As it turned out, he arranged an apartment for me in the camp. Neither Caritas nor the UNRWA ever objected to my staying in the camp, mostly because Dbayeh was seen as something other than a camp, as I will go on to explain.

From atop Dbayeh, I could see first the enormous and luxurious Hotel Royal, followed by the Beirut/Tripoli highway, and the vastness of the Mediterranean Sea beyond. To the right (north), Nahr al-Kalb was just down the hill. The camp was only twelve kilometers northeast of Beirut, after the town of Antelias – well known in Lebanon for housing the *Armenian Catholicosate of the Great House of Cilicia*. Only one street led to the entrance of the camp, at the top of the hill where both UNRWA and Caritas were located. *Deyr Mār Yūsif Al-Burj* ("Mar Yussif Tower Monastery"), a Greek Catholic (*Melkite*) monastery/church to the left of Caritas, marked the entrance to the camp, which was distinct from its surroundings. Its buildings, small and tightly packed together, formed a rectangle with its longer sides parallel to the sea. Since all its entrances were on the same side, the camp resembled the prongs of a fork, with the houses arranged one next to the other forming lines, and the streets forming the gaps in between. The main road leading to the camp ended in a three-way junction in front of the Caritas office: the first way led out of the camp and down the mountain, the second, to the left, led to the Mar Yussif church. The third, to the right, became one of the streets of the camp, ultimately leading to a dead end. At Mar Yussif church the street curved to face the top of the hill once more, and after springing 3 more streets to the right, it bent to the right, becoming a dead end soon after the last house of the camp. These main streets were called only by their numbers (no.1; no.2; no.3...). Narrow alleys, mostly made of stairs, cut up and down through the main streets, connecting the entire camp. Unlike Al-Jalil, there was no main street or *zāwya* serving as a public square apart from the headquarters of social institutions like the church, UNRWA, and Caritas. The relative lack of community life in Dbayeh when compared to Al-Jalil was evident.

Although virtually entirely Christian, it can be argued that Dbayeh was religiously and nationally more diverse than Al-Jalil due to the different Christian denominations of its residents, and to the Lebanese component. Only 67.41% of the camp's inhabitants were registered Palestinians (or Palestinian/Lebanese double citizens), and 31.34% were Lebanese[4] (World Vision 2007). Although there were some Palestinian Maronites, most of the Maronites were Lebanese, while most Christians of other denominations were Palestinian. According to the locals, most of the registered Palestinians who at the time of my fieldwork identified as Maronites were converted from another denomination in Lebanon. There were also a few Armenians in the camp (Catholic and Orthodox), some of whom lived in Palestine before the creation of Israel, and some of whom moved to the camp due to matrimonial ties with Palestinian families. All the Armenian families had Lebanese citizenship.

b. Ethnicity as a Local Frame

Most Lebanese and Palestinians in Lebanon perceived and engaged with their different nationalities somewhat similarly to how Fredrik Barth (1969) understands *ethnicity*, that is, as a dynamic and contrastive figment of social belonging, in which one group constructs itself in relation to others. As such, it is "a matter of social organization above and beyond questions of empirical cultural differences"; "a matter of self-ascription and ascription by others"; and "cultural features of greatest import" are to be found as "boundary-connected" (ibid: 6). In other words, the differences between being Lebanese and being

---

4   Not including three Syrians, one unregistered Palestinian, and one Iraqi refugee.

Palestinian around Dbayeh (and in Lebanon at large) were represented much as a feature of a "boundary-making mechanism" (ibid: 10) through which both Palestinians and Lebanese constructed and experienced national belonging. However, while Barth highlights the work of consciousness and entrepreneurship, I highlight the inseparability of practical, strategic, and conscious reason on one side, and informal, embodied, unconscious dispositions, affects and sensibilities on the other. In other words, being Lebanese or Palestinian in Dbayeh was not only a matter of conscious choice, but nor was it a nonnegotiable reality, even if generally naturalized as such by locals.

The differentiation between ethnicity and race in *fuṣḥa* ("Modern Standard Arabic") is not so clear, and terms such as *'irq* and *'unṣur* or *'unṣuriyya* are used to express both ideas. While the latter two were used to express prejudice (as in "racial"), the former was virtually never used anywhere in Lebanon during my fieldwork to express racial identity. *Arabness* was usually expressed simply by the term "Arab" itself. However, ethnicity was also commonly expressed in Al-Jalil, Dbayeh, and in Lebanon in general by way of *qawmiyya* ("nationality"), and also often conflated with religion, depending on the context, as I will develop in what follows. Thus, the attribution of naturalized qualities through national identification constantly highlighted the difference between Palestinians and Lebanese, where this difference was thought of as an ethnic inherent distinction.

With the exception of Lebanon, Muslims are the overwhelming majority in the Middle East. Thus, it is common that Muslims there think of Islam as overlapping with nationhood and Arabness. Perhaps due to the role of the PLO during the Lebanese Civil War, around Dbayeh, where the Lebanese population is almost completely Christian, Palestinians were also commonly represented as Muslims, even if virtually all Lebanese Christians consciously know of the Palestinian Christian population and of the importance of Palestinian Christian symbols such as the Church of the Holy Sepulcher, Jerusalem, and others. This sacred Christian Palestine was usually relegated to the past to the detriment of the mundane present, allowing Christian Palestinians in the present to be understood, if anything, as an exception to what Palestine currently represented to them. As I suggested in the previous chapter, this association was also strong in Al-Jalil, where – to illustrate even more emphatically – a resident once told me that "in the beginning there were Palestinians and Christians in Al-Jalil," when referring to Palestinian Muslims and Palestinian Christians. This slip was not commonly heard there, but it is illustrative of the extent to which, in Lebanon, the association is often present in the minds and hearts of Palestinians themselves.

As religion, ethnicity, and nationhood often overlapped, so did corresponding ethnic attributes. For example, Christian Palestinians were not often thought of as part of armed militias, in association with religious extremism, as refugees, and so on. This, in turn, helps explain Dbayeh's invisibility (as presented above) in the eyes of the Lebanese living so close to the refugee camp itself. Yet, as I develop in what follows, this is merely another factor in an intricate process of social belonging in which nationhood, ethnicity, and religion are often intertwined, and which Dbayeh's invisibility illustrates.

Moreover, when, in a given context, these terms (religion, national and ethnic belonging, political positioning, and others) were shown to not overlap, Palestinians and Lebanese alike often found it difficult to make sense of the subject's identity, and thus to align and to position themselves in relation to it. Taking one element as a signifier for one's ultimate belonging was a common local way of negotiating such a difficult classification. For instance, one was often taken as ultimately Palestinian, or Christian, or politically pro-Aoun, or a refugee, in positive or negative ways, depending on the context. In this way, motivated by embodied dispositions, affects, and sensibilities as much as by practical reason, Dbayeh's Christian Palestinians could be thus contextually perceived more decisively as Christians or Palestinians, or less decidedly as both. At times, ambiguity had "positive" effects for Dbayeh's Palestinians, and at other times it did not.

The hierarchization of belonging categories of Christian Palestinians in Lebanon – more or less instrumental depending on the case and context – was often a part of people's process of making sense of themselves and others. The classified subject(s) would typically still hold a more or less uncertain place in the minds of those engaged in the act of classification. That is, they could never be entirely trusted, for their group affiliations made for divided loyalties. It was through this lens of divided loyalties that many Muslim Palestinian refugees and Lebanese alike saw the Palestinian Christians of Dbayeh. It was common to hear in Lebanon phrases such as "in the end everyone goes back to their own roots." Irrespective of how much one pledged allegiance to one or another group, he/she was at times still expected to act according to his/her own "true" belonging, being that whichever the classifier suspected. This search for the "true" locus of belonging usually exceeded simple practical reasoning. However, there was no "true" belonging for Christian Palestinian refugees in Lebanon. They also engaged in difficult self-classifications such as mentioned above, and only partially following practical reason. Different subjects hierarchized their belonging differently and contextually, and while generally much importance was ascribed to one's national and religious belonging, expressions were diverse and variable to a degree.

Departing from such a conceptualization of ethnicity can shed light on the matter. Since ethnicity might be easily conflated with nationalism and/or religion, it would be unwise to single out any one of these categories as the ultimate source of a subject's belonging. This can explain the relative infrequency of interreligious marriage in Lebanon – among Palestinians in Lebanon the situation was no different – when compared, for example, to the Americas or Europe. Furthermore, the way in which most Lebanese tended to be politically aligned with a representative of their own sect was also telling of the importance of ethnicity. The Lebanese state's confessional democratic system tended to greatly reinforce this ethnicity, since some of the most basic rights and duties of citizens (like those of ownership, inheritance, and marriage) were defined by the political organs of their own religious sect, rather than by the Lebanese state in general (Saadeh 1993). Such a confessional system thus defined and constrained the proper official place for social belonging, first by not allowing for the possibility of secular marriage itself, and second by strictly regulating secular matrimony entered into abroad. Interreligious marriage was therefore rare in Lebanon, and Palestinian refugees formed a type of addendum to the country's confessions, given that, by definition, they were not citizens and as such did not legally fit the established classifications of either Sunni Muslims or Christians in Lebanon.

At the time of my residence in the refugee camps, the Lebanese constitution defined the rights and duties of the Palestinian community in a distinct manner, in many cases differently even from other migrating communities like the Syrians, Filipinos, Sudanese, and Sri Lankans. Palestinians were legally considered a group set apart even from other Arabs due to their stateless status and the politics of reciprocity. Thus, on a societal level, despite the initial positive attitude the Lebanese exhibited toward refugees, most Lebanese Christians, but also many Shi'a and Sunnis, conflated Palestinians with the actions of the PLO, whose alleged attempts at assuming control over Lebanon were perceived as having precipitated the Lebanese Civil War and both Israeli invasions (1978 and 1982). Most in Lebanon then perceived being Palestinian as an almost inescapable index of political attitude that was usually inarticulately and largely unconsciously attributed to inherent ethnicity.

The sectarian communities were themselves historically fragmented. During my fieldwork, the Lebanese Christian communities – particularly the Maronites – were as divided as they had been during the civil war and perhaps even increasingly polarized. Other sects were also highly politically divided in the past. For example, a Sunni might have supported Pan-Arabism (like the *Murabitun*), favored Lebaneseness, and supported the PLO, or many other political positions. Among the Druze, many supported the Jumblats, while a minority supported Talal Arslan. Likewise, the Shi'a were divided between Amal and Hezbollah after the second Israeli invasion, a division that was respectively associated with an anti- or pro-PLO stance, and therefore for and against Palestinian presence in Lebanon respectively, since Hezbollah had helped the major Palestinian factions in their fight against Amal during the war of the camps.

Because the Christians lost most of their bargaining power with the Taif Agreement that ended the Civil War, between 2006 and 2010 (and largely until today) the political arena was greatly polarized between the Sunni supporters of Hariri (and anti-Syrian interference in Lebanon) of the March 14 block, and the Shi'a supporters of Hezbollah (and pro-Syrian interference via financial and political backing) of the March 8 block. There were Sunni supporting March 8 and Shi'a supporting March 14 as well, but these were relatively rare. The Christian community was more wholly divided into factions on one or the other side of this divide. It is thus possible to claim that for the Christian Lebanese population, political belonging was not equated with religion and/or ethnicity, as on both sides, Christians joined forces with different Muslim groups. Furthermore, no matter which side was taken, the majority of Lebanese continued to see both Muslim and Christian Palestinians alike as they had done during the civil war, that is, as an unwelcome enemy, even when paying lip service to "the Palestinian cause" as an "Arab" or "Muslim cause." As a result, the Christian Lebanese around Dbayeh still saw the Christian Palestinian camp inhabitants as either a threat or an unpleasant and undesired presence that was to be avoided and preferably washed away.

Only a few secularist parties, like the Lebanese Communist Party composed of Christians and Muslims, still rallied in support of the Palestinians in Lebanon, but their numbers did not represent any threat to the overall balance of power, and hardly had any effect in the streets. Besides, these parties were scarce on the outskirts of Dbayeh, the only Lebanese piece of land where Dbayeh's presence was noticeable. There were always both Palestinian and Lebanese subjects that escaped an all-encompassing rationality that categorized all orders of people within an ultimate typology of ethnic belonging, but they tended to be rarer in more homogenous areas such as Baalbek and Metn,[5] since interpersonal contact between subjects situated in different categories were less frequent, allowing for stereotypes to remain unchallenged. Many Lebanese, and especially the Christians among them, saw themselves as distinct from other Arabs, and political belonging was frequently taken more as the natural consequence of an individual's religious belonging as indexed through the sect than as a choice. In contrast, the Lebanese primarily viewed Palestinians in Lebanon as an undifferentiated mass, and only secondarily as Christian or Sunni, or as aligned with Fatah or Hamas or any other party. Thus, as Barth theorized (1969), the ethnic label still survives, even when the ethnic divide is bridged by individuals or groups willing to do so. Sectarianism in Lebanon operated in such manner, and so did the Lebanese-Palestinian divide. They were never absolute, yet still powerfully operative.

Lebanese essentializing of Palestinians as a national/ethnic unit reflected the reality of the Palestinian political situation in Lebanon, since all Palestinians, aside from the few who were citizens, were barred from formal political participation. They could not vote, their opinions were rarely listened to and often not publicly articulated, and they were officially treated as foreigners with few civil rights, if any. For the Lebanese, therefore, the Palestinians' internal differences did not matter as much as their general exclusion. This attitude was reinforced by the principled refusal by the majority of Palestinians – both the public[6] and the political intelligentsia – to lobby for Lebanese citizenship. The predominant Shi'a and Christian parties in Lebanon supported this position out of fear that active participation of the mainly Sunni Palestinians in Lebanese politics would upset the country's precarious balance of power.

The Lebanese propensity to identify Palestinians by an ethnic national indexing, coupled with a widespread sense among the Lebanese that the Palestinians were troublemakers responsible for most of the nation's problems, had a powerful effect on the refugees, reinforcing their sense of foreignness and exclusion, and greatly enhancing their own views of their political and eco-

---

5   The Lebanese region just north of Beirut where Dbayeh is located
6   This does not mean that most Palestinian refugees did not covet Lebanese citizenship. Instead, it only reflects the prevailing gap between desiring it and publicly rallying around the issue as a political objective or civic right, as I will present in due course.

nomic[7] modes of belonging as embodied ethnic trait. In Al-Jalil, the Lebanese disposition towards Palestinians caused the refugees to over-state their Palestinianness; in Dbayeh, the same disposition led the refugees, especially the younger generation, to try to blend in and efface their Palestinianness. The aesthetic rules and tendencies of social relations in Dbayeh, coupled with the marking of calendar time with Christian rather than Palestinian themes, accentuated that blurring tendency, as will be demonstrated in the following sections of this chapter.

Due to their refugee condition, but also reinforced by the ethnic divides in Lebanon and the way Palestinians fit the overall ethnic landscape, Palestinian refugees in Lebanon tended to experience being Palestinian as their ultimate category of belonging. That is, their need to make sense of their presence, status, and daily lives in Lebanon collectively and above all as Palestinians. Thus, among Palestinians in general, Palestinianness and the polyphonic concept of *the Palestinian cause* also worked as a political equivalent to sectarian belonging, bringing some closer to the imagined community and pushing some away from it. Since the Lebanese also tended to see Palestinians as a distinct ethnic group, Palestinianness cut across religious, political, and economic belongings, although Dbayeh inhabitants tended to live these categories ("Christian" and "Palestinian") in ways allowing for greater levels of ambiguity than in Al-Jalil. Dbayeh was exceptional in this regard: firstly, because some refugees in Dbayeh were among the only Palestinian refugees to have citizenship in Lebanon – apart from Palestinian women married to Lebanese men of the same sect – and, secondly, because the Palestinian Cause had a more distant and complex place in the camp's quotidian life, as I will present in what follows.

c.   The muwāṭiniyyn

World Vision data indicates a number of Lebanese living in Dbayeh. Most of these were Lebanese from the surrounding area who mostly came during the civil war for several reasons: some sought "protection" (according to a Lebanese perspective); some came with the Phalange militias to take over the camp and remained as of the time of my fieldwork; some came following the camp's evacuation in 1991, after the Lebanese army shelled the camp

---

7   As in, for instance, when Palestinians think of themselves as "peasants" (Swedenburg 1990; Sayigh 2008).

(their motivation was a belief that, since UNRWA had provided the camp to Palestinians, no one living inside its borders would have to pay rent); and, finally, some were of Palestinian origin (*aśl Falasṭyny*) but had Lebanese citizenship (*jensiyya Lubnāniyya*). They appear in the World Vision assessment as simply "Palestinians." This last group comprised one of the major categories in the camp, and since all Palestinian Christians were offered citizenship in the 1950s,[8] the question of how some were naturalized is less important than why others were not. According to the camp's elderly community, Palestinians in Dbayeh without Lebanese citizenship (a significant part of the population) did not have it either because their ancestors refused it, or simply because they could not afford it, as a relatively small sum was needed to issue the proper documentation, which also entailed a bureaucratic process that many could not navigate.

The local term for naturalization was the general Palestinian one, *tawṭyn* (to take on citizenship; to become a citizen). Since to obtain Lebanese citizenship one had to renounce the right to Palestinian citizenship, *tawṭyn* was the formal process of a subject's "conversion"[9] into a Lebanese. In Dbayeh, nationally converted citizens were called *muwāṭan*,[10] which meant Lebanese citizens, given that no refugee had Palestinian citizenship. The term *muwāṭan* was also expressed as "Lebanese with Palestinian origins" (*Lubnāny aśl Falasṭyny* for men and *Lubnānya aśl Falasṭyniyya* for women).

Despite the proximity of devastating past wars, relations among non-Lebanese Palestinian refugees, Palestinian *muwāṭiniyyn*, and Lebanese living in Dbayeh were not particularly tense, at least on the surface. First of all, relations between non-*muwāṭiniyyn* Palestinians[11] and *muwāṭiniyyn* Palestinians

---

8   As with the Armenians, the major difference being that since the 1970s all Armenians are officially Lebanese citizens, while a few Christian Palestinians are still officially refugees and mostly located in Dbayeh.

9   This is my own term. Palestinians and Lebanese most commonly expressed the concept through the term *ṣyr* (to be/to become).

10   Both *tawṭyn* and *muwāṭan* refer to the word *watan*, meaning in its colloquial usage by Lebanese and Palestinians "nation." The plural of *muwāṭan* is *muwāṭiniyyn*.

11   I cannot use the term "Palestinian citizens" to refer to all Palestinian refugees who did not go under *tawṭyn* and therefore did not become *muwāṭiniyyn*. In the wake of the Oslo Process, Palestinians living in the Occupied Territories have had their right to a Palestinian citizenship recognized internationally, but the Palestinian Authority did not offer citizenship for the refugees living abroad, such as Dbayeh or Al-Jalil camp residents.

were very good and depended on individual and group affinity, even if the divide was always implicit in their relationships. There was also a sense of inferiority permeating non-*muwāṭiniyyn* Palestinians in Dbayeh, which was not as significant for Palestinians living in other camps who took on a different citizenship,[12] such as in Al-Jalil, where Palestinianness was much more celebrated. As a counterpart to this dynamics, *muwāṭiniyyn* Palestinians in Dbayeh tended to see themselves at an advantage, and at times preferred to stress their Lebaneseness over their Palestinianness, even amongst other Palestinians. For example, some *muwāṭiniyyn* Palestinians preferred to call the camp *dey'a* (or *kūra*; meaning "the village"), just like Palestinians and Lebanese alike call their villages of origin. This did not depend only on strategic uses of double belonging, as sometimes they felt compelled to display one or the other, due not only to external pressures, but also due to self-imposed reasons. Thus, double belonging as Palestinian and Lebanese did not constitute two entirely different identities, but most of the time a single composite not only contingent on strategy, but also deeply rooted in feelings and emotions. In other words, the extent to which subjects would emphasize Lebanesese-ness or Palestinianness was contextual and depended on practical reason as much as on embodied affects, sensibilities, and dispositions.

The relations between the *muwāṭiniyyn* Palestinians and the Lebanese were also informed by what they both perceived to be ethnic differences, despite the fact that many *muwāṭiniyyn* Palestinians were born and raised in Lebanon and felt sometimes culturally closer to the local population than to other Palestinians. This closeness was articulated in a variety of ways, ranging from their accent, behavior, and social practices, to their interests and self-identification. The scars of recent conflicts and political views about Lebanon and Palestine were ever present, however, and could resurface easily, depending on the situation. For instance, a few of the *muwāṭiniyyn* Palestinians I met in Dbayeh were soldiers in the Lebanese army. This was a common strategy for social and economic ascendance among poor Lebanese in general, but it also demonstrates a certain level of identification with the Lebanese nation among the refugees.[13] Joseph, a young *muwāṭan* Palestinian from Dbayeh who was a soldier in the Lebanese army, told me that despite his identifying as a Lebanese

---

12   Usually, Scandinavian or German in the case of refugees from Al-Jalil. Those would typically not live in the camp, but only return to visit fairly rarely.

13   In Al-Jalil, in principle the few *muwāṭiniyyn* could join the army, but to my knowledge, none did.

citizen, his *muwāṭan* Palestinian background was recorded in his army documentation and marked forever within the institution, possibly leading to his loyalty being questioned and thereby jeopardizing any ambitions of advancement. The identification of Dbayeh *muwāṭiniyyn* as also Palestinian was further evident in their choice to remain in the camp rather than live elsewhere in Lebanon, justified by most as a result of the strong personal bonds they had with their family and neighbors, Palestinians or not. However, this choice was just as often at least secondarily justified by economic concerns. As far as I understood, no *muwāṭiniyyn* Palestinian participated in the war against the Palestinians, since both the Lebanese and the Palestinians in general strictly enforced the boundaries between Palestinianness and Lebaneseness during the war.

Finally, relations between non-*aṣl Falasṭyny* Lebanese and the non-*muwāṭiniyyn* Palestinians in Dbayeh were also marked by the same tensions found in the relations between the other categories. On one hand, many non-*muwāṭiniyyn* Palestinians expressed resentment toward their Lebanese neighbors, blaming them for their predicament, citing incidents in which their property had been seized, a family member killed, or they were driven into forced labor by a Lebanese neighbor. On the other hand, many non-*muwāṭiniyyn* Palestinians in Dbayeh also described one or another specific Lebanese in Dbayeh as a "good man," citing their helpfulness in difficult situations, and thereby painting a more nuanced picture. In turn, the Lebanese living in Dbayeh played down accusations, usually by stating that "the past is past" and that things had been different then. As an illustration of the general underlying tensions, Ayub, a non-*muwāṭan* Palestinian, told me that after about two decades of living together, all these groups developed close ties with each other. In his words, "today we marry their women, and they marry ours; they buy in my shop, and I pay visits to them." Although these practices existed in reality, one could never be certain of how much tension had accumulated below the surface. The issue was generally avoided and rarely, if ever, brought up publicly. As a *muwāṭan* Palestinian once told me, "for decades we had to learn to share the camp (...) now, everything is fine, but if there is a new war nobody knows and cannot know what will happen."[14] Thus, the past was generally tentatively blurred or buried in the public sphere due to the fear of stirring up conflict and out of a desire to move forward.

---

14   This dialogue was written in English in my fieldwork diary.

d.   Further Divisions

Dbayeh stores all faced one of the five main streets. The camp had one *foren*[15] (literally, oven, in this context, a pastry shop), one *ṣāj*[16] shop, a butcher's shop, a sandwich/*argile* shop, as many as four or five food markets, two general stores, a shoe shop, and a couple of other smaller stores. In addition, there was only one barber shop, and one café located across the street of the camp's border and later owned by a man I will call Butrus, who for a while during my field research owned the restaurant located in *Nahr El-Kalb*,[17] less than 2 miles away from the base of the hill where Dbayeh is located. As in Al-Jalil, relatives and friends tended to frequent stores according to their level of social and physical proximity with the owners, whenever they had a choice. The barber-shop also served as a gathering place for the youth but was not as integral to daily life and social interactions as barbershops were in Al-Jalil. The sand-wich/*argile* shop was also very important, especially since it featured the only public computer with internet access in the camp.[18] Customers close enough to the owner did not always pay for its use, but others were required to pay a very small fee. While older Lebanese and Palestinian men alike (on aver-age above their fifties) frequented the café, Palestinians rarely frequented the restaurant in Nahr Al-Kalb, which opened and then closed its doors during my stay in the camp. The division of space mirrored the generational conflict, which was much more pervasive than in Al-Jalil. This conflict developed in part as members of the older generation in Dbayeh were still deeply attached

---

15   A shop that sold pastries and provided the service of baking dishes made with dough, pre-prepared by the women living in the camp or around, or dough made by the owner of the establishment.

16   Near Eastern flatbread baked over a convex metal surface

17   Nahr El-Kalb is the Arabic name for the short ancient Lycus or Eleutherus River that once served as the border between Egyptian and Hittite land. The place where the river meets the highway is the site for monuments raised by Ramses II, Marcus Aurelius, and more recent conquerors. It also harbors a monument commemorating the Lebanese independence.

18   When I returned to Dbayeh in 2009, the place had been totally transformed into a cybercafé with about 10 computers. While it still maintained its pool table in another room where only youngsters would gather, the kitchen was permanently closed. The owner of the shop also sold corn and *fūl* (beans, Lebanese style) in the street in front of the café.

to their Palestinianness, while many of the younger generations disguised, blurred, or even entirely effaced their Palestinian roots.

Non-*aṣl Falastyny* Lebanese, *muwāṭiniyyn* Palestinians, and non-*muwāṭiniyyn* Palestinians dwelled everywhere in the camp, and no one space was reserved for a particular group. However, another deep divide pervaded Dbayeh: kinship and neighborhood ties. If one were to look at the totality of the camp from above, one could divide the rectangle representing the whole into four neighborhoods. These neighborhoods not only revealed kinship ties – collateral, by descent, and by marriage alliances alike – but also spatially represented parties that disputed resources, especially water distribution. Thus, in addition to the continuum between Palestinian and Lebanese, political divides, and kinship ties, neighborhood alliances also inscribed different subjects into different allegiance groups in the eyes of the locals. Again, these divisions often tended to overlap, but not always.

Dbayeh youth also walked around the camp in groups, though usually much smaller ones and without displaying their ties with as much intensity as the youth of Al-Jalil. Above all, visible spaces were much more fragmented between one neighborhood and another, which were demarcated by the streets. When taking me to interview some elders on the upper streets, Charbel told me that it had been about three years since the last time he walked down those streets. This would be impossible in Al-Jalil. Nonetheless, he still waved to most people peering from their windows and verandas.

Along with the stores, the Caritas, and the UNRWA offices, the camp included: two churches; a Little Sisters of Nazareth house[19] – a branch of the Catholic Near East Welfare Association (CNEWA), which is in turn an agency of the Holy See; an office for World Vision Lebanon; a "clinic" or health post, only open for a few hours a couple of days a week; the Joint Christian Committee for Social Services in Lebanon, and a couple of other NGOs. Apart from the foreign nuns of the Little Sisters, employees were usually Christian Lebanese. None of them were Palestinian, although some of them employed Palestinians in the lower ranks of their staff. These organizations tended to find it easier to hire someone from within the local community to pass on their own educational agenda. In that regard, some Palestinians complained

---

19   The Little Sisters of Nazareth had nuns stationed in Beirut since 1971. After the war started, however, they moved to Jordan in 1976, and upon returning to Lebanon in 1978, the Pontifical Mission provided the living quarters in Dbayeh that they occupy today.

that the services provided were not made for Palestinians, and that most of the beneficiaries were in fact "Lebanese" (a category that, as we saw, could include, or be completely composed of the *muwāṭiniyyn* Palestinians).

Contrary to Al-Jalil, where authority over the camp was heavily disputed among the UNRWA appointees, the many socio-political movements/parties, traditional leaders, and to a lesser extent, NGO or association presidents, Dbayeh seemed to be firmly ruled by the Lebanese. The same Palestinians who would complain about the charitable work in Dbayeh also complained that the manager of the local UNRWA office was a Muslim non-resident of Dbayeh – contrary to the organization's stipulation that the manager of a camp should always be a local refugee. Nevertheless, the actual manager of the camp was not UNRWA. The *de facto* manager of the camp was Caritas Lebanon Migration Center, at least according to many Palestinians living in Dbayeh.[20]

As opposed to Al-Jalil, there were no political organizations inside the camp whatsoever, neither Palestinian nor Lebanese. However, graffiti covered the walls of houses around the camp, and especially near its southern border with the Lebanese surroundings, marking the territorial dominance of the *Katā'eb* (Phalangists) or the *Quwāt al-Lubnāniyya* (Lebanese Forces, or L.F). The residents voiced political preferences in terms of Lebanese politics, and almost never in terms of the Palestinian ones. A sizable part of the camp supported "General Aoun," a Maronite Christian known for his recent alliance with Hezbollah and for ordering the army shelling of the camp in the 1990 conflict. Having experienced the destruction, these Palestinians nonetheless tended to see Aoun as an ally who came to liberate the camp from the hands of the Phalangists. However, some also supported the Lebanese Forces (L.F.), which had split from the *Katā'eb* prior to the party's militia invasion of Dbayeh. These two groups were seen as completely distinct from one another in Dbayeh as in Lebanon, but not among almost all other Palestinian refugees. During my entire stay in Dbayeh, I saw only three posters in support of Aoun, and no poster whatsoever for any other politician. However, I used to see a sixteen-year-old boy brandishing an LF flag on the moped he used for work to deliver all kinds of goods to the area surrounding the camp. Once, upon encountering him at the local L.F. office located just up from the gas station at the base of the hill, he told me that he worked for the party.

---

20   As explained in the introductory section of this chapter, I had to ask authorization from Caritas (and not UNRWA) to be able to conduct field research in Dbayeh.

Due to the local political *modus operandi*, it was common even among those against the Phalangists or the L.F. to try to maintain at least one *wasṭa* (intermediary; fixer) in one of these parties to be able to deal with official state matters, emergency situations, or simply for access to certain privileges that might improve daily life. This state of affairs merely reflected a general preference for interpersonal relations over formal and institutional ties in Lebanon[21] - which informed not only Lebanese politics, but also Lebanese and Palestinian quotidian life in the country. Drawing on the observations above, it is possible to argue that, since politics in Dbayeh was expressed through support for one or another Lebanese party, this alone would have been enough for Al-Jalil residents – and those of any other Palestinian refugee camp in Lebanon – to claim that Dbayeh refugees had become Lebanese.

e.   Ritual tempo in Dbayeh

Drawing on the insights gathered during my field trip there and recounted so far in this chapter, what I call the ritual tempo in Dbayeh was significantly different from that of Al-Jalil. First and most importantly, it did not revolve around the public articulation of a certain explicit Palestinianness. Precisely the opposite was true: Palestinian identity was mostly constructed and articulated in private, so as to eschew the resurgence of old conflicts with the local population. The open celebration of Palestinianness was in general relegated to the private sphere, especially for those who – like me – had close ties with Palestinians from other camps. Second, social life in Dbayeh was much more dispersed than it was in Al-Jalil as a result of a number of factors. These included: the different categories of belonging (non-*muwāṭiniyyn* Palestinians, *muwāṭiniyyn* Palestinians, and non-*aṣl Falasṭyny* Lebanese); the diffuse physical environment of the camp; the absence of the Palestinian institutions brought by the PLO and the corresponding political vernacular expressed in support of Lebanese politicians; the priority of local kinship and neighborhood disputes over manifestations of political and ethnic identity; and the residents'

---

21   Again – just like anywhere else in Lebanon – there were also those in Dbayeh who refused such bonds with anyone that was not from a specific category of belonging deemed among the most respectable ones for these subjects. However, in Dbayeh, ideologies such as any political or nationalistic ones tended to lose much of their appeal in the eyes of the locals, who generally regarded local community gains, losses, and other local and personal issues as much more important than any greater cause.

attachment to Christian values and perceptions of themselves as Christians and therefore different from other Palestinian refugees, which related to an effacement of the Palestinian national character as an identity marker, and to its substitution with a desire to mingle with their Lebanese neighbors. Third, and most striking to the observer, Dbayeh's ritual tempo was subtle, slow, much less formalized, and often marked by hypo-expression of identity, especially when compared to the fast-paced, formalized, and hyper-expressed ritual tempo of Al-Jalil. This, however, does not mean that there were no public celebrations in Dbayeh as well.

f. Church Ceremonies

Contrary to all other refugee camps, in Dbayeh, there were never demonstrations, rallies, strikes, or any other organized mass public manifestations of political belonging defined by either ethnicity or the national order of things. Moreover, apart from weddings, birthdays, and funerals, there were practically no public ceremonies and celebrations, and the few that occurred were held inside the two churches and involved only invited guests.

Along with the Maronite Monastery of Mar Yussif at the entrance of the camp, which owns the 84 *dunums* (84.000 square meters) of the camp, Dbayeh also accommodates another church: *Kanysa mār jāūrjys li-l-rūm al-malkiyyn al-kāthūlyk al-mukhayyam* (Church of St. George for the Roman Catholic Melkite – The camp).[22] However, in the words of a local Palestinian resident, the Melkite church was less popular than Mar Yussif, and the only public ceremonies it held were the regular Christian services (masses, prayers, funerals, etc.). Between 2006 and 2010, this church was frequented mostly by Lebanese living in one of the neighboring villages outside the camp. Mar Yussif was effectively the most common site for religious rituals and celebrations, in spite of the large number of Palestinian Melkites in the camp, given that the Christians of Al-Bassa were overwhelmingly Melkites. There has been at least another church in Dbayeh, the Roman Catholic church of the Pontifical Mission,

---

22   I took the full name, containing the suffix *"al-mukhayyam"* (the camp) from a poster of a local itinerant religious festival mentioning all visited localities, hence the need to further qualify the church. Since this suffix is not commonly added, I kept the suffix separated in my translation. Besides, it is also worth noticing that "the camp" was mentioned in such a poster not because it is a known entity, but probably because the festival had the support of the international organization, the *Catholic Near East Welfare Association*, which is in turn active in supporting Dbayeh's refugees.

which Dr. Anis Sayigh's father helped to build in 1974 (see *Chapter 2*). However, it was destroyed during the civil war. Despite the wishes of some local Palestinians, the priest was a Lebanese nonresident of the camp, who made his formal appearance in the church only about twice a week.[23] Therefore, the church was geared to appeal to the interests of the whole mixed parish, and not the particular interests of the Palestinians.[24]

As a consequence, in Dbayeh, the calendar of celebrations and other organized events of mass participation were exclusively dependent on the Christian calendar and did not involve ethnic or national themes. However, social references springing from these motives were still constitutive of daily life in Dbayeh, and especially through the pivotal socializing role the *muwāṭiniyyn* played in the camp. Furthermore, organized mass participation events that highlighted social belonging and did not coincide with the foreseeable local calendars did not occur during my field trip, with the exception of one event that I will describe in what follows. As in Al-Jalil, marriages, funerals, births, anniversaries, and other more personal celebrations often provided motivation for social gatherings. In Dbayeh, such celebrations represented the extent of social occasions, alongside church led events and a small number of tentative meetings to establish a social work association.[25] In addition, due to local divisions, they tended to occur in smaller enclosed spaces, such as the church itself or private houses, and in attendance of just a few Dbayeh residents

Celebrations tended to be much less public in Dbayeh because there was not as much social common ground for celebration as there was in Al-Jalil, and because events such as marriages were typically family matters. I was formally invited to a few weddings in Al-Jalil. For some of them, part of the marriage ceremony was conducted in the mosque, followed by more private festivities held in community centers. The party was never held at the mosque. I also attended a wedding in Mar Elias in Beirut, where the same happened. However, in Dbayeh marriages were a private matter, and I was actually never invited to one. For instance, when a local friend's sister was married, I learned about her wedding only upon inquiring about the reason for the fireworks

---

23   This was also the case with health agents and the UNRWA administrator (although the latter was a Muslim Palestinian nonresident of the camp).

24   The conflict over the given church being a place for Palestinians to voice their own demands and desires will be more fully developed in the next chapter.

25   This theme will be developed in conjunction with the role of the church in the next chapter of this book.

display in the area, since as far as I was aware, there were no major political events that night. Someone informed me of the marriage, and when I walked down two streets (I used to live on the fourth street up the camp), I could hear loud and happy chatter coming from my friend's parent's house. On the following day, when I congratulated him for his sister's marriage, he excused himself saying that, since it was his sister's marriage, he was not permitted personal guests.

In Al-Jalil, I hardly needed an invitation to go and listen to the sheikh's speech about the couple and the union, which was also almost always charged with national and religious themes and the way in which the couple related to them. However, since the local ritual tempo of Dbayeh was much more reserved and did not revolve so much around the public celebration of an overarching community theme, the local social fragmentation made events such as marriages much more private and personal than they were in other camps in general. While formal ceremonies were frequently held outside the camp, only the closer relatives and friends were invited for the ensuing party. On the day of my friend's sister's wedding, I had already suspected that someone was getting married due to comments I overheard. However, since I took for granted that marriage ceremonies would be as public as those in Al-Jalil, I initially assumed that this wedding ceremony could not possibly take place within the camp.

In fact, marriage ceremonies outside the camp were fairly common during my field research in Dbayeh, as many Palestinians who could work did so in villages and towns around the camp such as Antelias or Jal Al-Dib. If they were *muwāṭan*, chances were that they would wed a Lebanese partner. Such an outcome was highly desirable among the younger generations in the camp, since it could resolve or at least help mitigate their refugee status. Which is not to say that such marital unions were purely pragmatic; they naturally also entailed sincere romantic bonds between the parties. Unfortunately, women had a much higher likelihood of finding such unions. This was because Lebanese women and their families tended to avoid what was often considered a hypogamic marriage with a Palestinian refugee man. In a culture where rights and much more, including citizenship, are passed on to the next generation through the male lineage, a union between a Lebanese man and a Palestinian woman was far less inconvenient than the reverse. Due to Lebanon's patriarchal descent rule, only women could gain Lebanese citizenship and thus become *muwāṭanat* (feminine plural of citizens), while in the much rarer cases of non-*muwāṭiniyyn* Palestinian men marrying Lebanese women, the man would still be considered Palestinian along with his descendants.[26]

In a rare intersectarian instance, a Palestinian woman from Dbayeh with no Lebanese citizenship married a wealthy (for Dbayeh standards at least) Muslim from Tyr in south Lebanon. She moved from the camp to south Lebanon and converted to Islam. It was not clear to me how much the conversion was motivated by her and her children's rights and obligations versus a spontaneous change in her beliefs. If she had remained Christian, she and her children could not inherit anything from her Muslim husband (Saʿadeh 1993) and being Palestinian would only complicate matters further. Her conversion to Islam was manifested in, for example, not allowing any man, even kin, to kiss her children on the cheek, as was common practice among Christian Lebanese, stating that such behavior was religiously interdicted (*ḥarām*). Neither she nor her daughters wore a *ḥijāb* (headscarf), but her brothers – still Christian – reinforced the respectful treatment of their Muslim nieces.

The Tyr case aside, such international (or interethnic) alliances were very rare in the Palestinian refugee camps in Lebanon, and whenever they did occur, the couple would as a matter of course live outside the camp. In fact, an entire area along the highway near Al-Jalil (i.e., from the camp towards Zahlé) was also known to be demographically Palestinian, although symbolically and politically within Lebanese territory. In addition to the many Palestinians who moved there due to the lack of space inside the camp or in search of a more comfortable financial situation,[27] those who married local residents of Baalbek generally found refuge in this neutral place as well.

In Dbayeh, the borders of the camp did not define community as much as they did in Al-Jalil. For example, when considering wedding guests, different subjects would typically invite family and friends from outside the camp, but not invite many of the camp's inhabitants. Closeness to one's heart (*qaryb ʿal-qalb*, as it was commonly expressed to me) was the main criterion for such

---

26   This was partially why it was much rarer (although not impossible) to find a Palestinian man married to a Lebanese woman.

27   This was the case, for instance, for those many who had relatives living in northern Europe, such as Sweden or Denmark. Some local political offices and one of the sheikhs estimated that about 50% of all registered camp residents were living in northern Europe, as these countries were known to be friendly towards Palestinians, having offered citizenship to many refugees and funded social work inside the camps.

decisions. Equally important, however, what defined the number of guests was usually the financial situation of the couple's families. While wedding celebrations traditionally and ideally included hundreds of guests, in practice this number had to be greatly reduced to a few dozen, naturally leading to a selection process among the camp's residents. In contrast, this selection was not as pronounced in Al-Jalil, where marriage ceremonies would typically be held in open spaces accessible to all, even when outside the camp.

In Al-Jalil, the mosque and other institutions would help finance weddings (or funerals) for those who could not afford them. Conversely, residents told me that there was no such practice in Dbayeh, indicating the relative lack of civic unity in the Christian camp. However, as in Al-Jalil, a man in Dbayeh had to show proof of his stable financial situation and an ability to provide for his future family in order to gain the woman's parents' permission for the marriage. In both camps, one common (formal or informal) requirement was to build a separate residence in the camp, or to make arrangements for such a place outside the camp. More than once, I witnessed men working by day, and by night building another story above their parents' house or elsewhere in the camp alone or with the help of colleagues. They did so either when they already had a bride in mind, or even when they still only dreamed of marriage without yet any particular person in mind.

The talk I had overheard about my friend's sister's wedding was in fact gossip regarding the list of invitees and other details about the event. As one might expect, some people were entrusted with more detail than others about who would be invited or not, and such topics as related to the wedding, the engagement, or the marriage. Although the families of the bride and the groom allegedly wished to keep a low profile about wedding details, purportedly to not offend those not invited, even a foreigner like me was privy to a number of rumors. With only an acceptable command of the language and culture, it was fairly easy even for me to survey information about the wedding, since people normally would have private (and not so private) contests over who could display the most inside information. Besides, the wedding celebration did take place inside the camp at the bride's parents' house with music, *dabke* dancing, and fireworks. The next day, people resumed gossiping about the party, and life went on.

As I left the camp, I became convinced that not only was a certain measure of leaked information about such private events normal, but also it was desired by those at the center of the "secret" (*sir*), such as in the abovementioned wedding celebration. In other words, perhaps the whole sharing and concealing of information can be better understood, at least in part, as a struggle to become closer to the protagonists, and/or to become closer to the center of the event itself. As such, this is a good example of the ritualized social practices that were central to the dynamics of social life in Dbayeh, and that in *Chapter 7* I shall call politico-moral local economies of trust. Such practices were by no means absent in Al-Jalil, but while in Al-Jalil they were part of a much more normative ritualized tempo, in Dbayeh they were almost all there was to a collective ritualization of daily life, evoking and enforcing embodied collective sensibilities, affects, and dispositions to camp residents.

g.   Pilgrimage to "Our" Lady of Lebanon

Family related celebrations held semi-publicly in the camp and widespread subtle ritualized practices of interpersonal relations were almost all there was to the ritual tempo in Dbayeh. However, a few religious events such as Christmas, Easter, and others also dotted the public calendar of the camp. This Christian calendar was, however, by no means restricted to Dbayeh, but also shared with the Lebanese surroundings. A major collective event of this sort was the Pilgrimage to Harissa, which had been a common topic of discussion for at least a week by the time May 2008 came around, a month known in Lebanon as *al-Shahar al-Maryamy* (The Virgin Mary's Month). I recall one day in particular when we were all talking about it, including Charbel, two young men in their thirties, a man in his seventies, some children running around, and me, along with whoever else went down the stairs to order something from Charbel's *pastry shop*. Even passersby made comments about the event from the street level down to us in the *pastry shop*.

Harissa is the name of a village in Mount Lebanon located on a mountain top east of Jounieh and about 12.5 miles north of Beirut. It was one of Mount Lebanon's most important tourist attractions, and visitors could reach the top of the mountain either by means of a 2,130-foot-tall *téléferique* (cable car) located in Jounieh, or by car following the paved road on the western face of the mountain. Harissa was named after the 15-ton statue of the Virgin Mary,[28] which was also locally known as *Sayda Lubnān* (Arabic), *Notre Dame du Liban* (French), and Our Lady of Lebanon. It was located atop the mountain near the tiny Virgin Mary Cathedral. Many Lebanese, both Christian and Muslim,

---

28   Harissa was inaugurated in 1908, is made of bronze, and painted in white. Until today, it is under the auspices of the Maronite church.

believed that a teardrop fell from the statue's eye during the Lebanese Civil War. A dark vertical line descending from its eye was taken as proof of this miracle and a clear sign of the Virgin Mary's disapproval of the war.

On the day we were discussing the pilgrimage at Charbel's *pastry shop*, the group told me that all Christian denominations alike participated in the event. No one was really sure, however, since all of those present were Catholic, like most Palestinians in the camp. They were also not sure if the statue and cathedral were Roman Catholic, Melkite, or Maronite, which did not seem to matter much in their eyes.[29] Of most importance was that the Pope[30] himself once visited the site. When most of them expressed a desire to join the pilgrimage by walking from Dbayeh to the statue, I declared that wished to join them. No one questioned my intentions, but some of them did question my actual willingness (and even capacity) for such physical effort. After all, it would take many hours of walking to reach our destination. Looking around me, I judged that I was not in the worst of physical fitness among us all, and I confirmed my willingness. It was then agreed that we would all meet at night and leave together from the camp. I arranged to meet one of the young men at the *pastry shop*, since I did not know the location of the house where the others were gathering. The group expressed a wish to spend the night at the pilgrimage site itself, at which point Charbel regretted that while he wished to join us, he could not leave his shop, as he had to open early in the morning.

Later that night, I returned to Charbel's shop, where the man who was to accompany me was already waiting with a friend. They were all wearing their best clothes and advised me to go back home (two streets above) and do the same. Once I came back to the shop, we finally moved on to the meeting point. There, the two men and I met a woman in her early forties taking care of one child, while her other child, a boy of about thirteen, curiously asked me questions. We all waited for one more person before leaving, and I wondered out loud what had happened to the others who had expressed interest earlier that day, not to mention other camp residents in general. I was told that, while some would go alone and meet us on the way or at the top, most of the others would not be joining us, since they had to work the next day.

---

29   I later learned that the shrine belongs to the Maronite patriarchate.

30   Jean Paul II visited Harissa on May 10, 1997. Dbayeh Palestinians and Christian Lebanese alike commonly reported to me that it was already a pilgrimage site before Jean Paul II's visit, but that the site's popularity drastically increased after.

I thought that most residents would make the trip another time, since there was no agreed upon day for the pilgrimage and people would continuously visit the site, walking up and down the path to Harissa, throughout The Virgin Mary's Month. However, it was also true that most people who would go on pilgrimage would do so at the beginning of the month, especially on the first day as we were doing. Hence, for one reason or another, the Dbayeh inhabitants participating in the pilgrimage were few in number when considering the camp's demography as a whole. I asked the woman whether there were other pilgrimages, and she said there was Jerusalem, but that Palestinians (meaning those living in Lebanon) could not join. That was all she could remember. Therefore, Harissa was the only pilgrimage most Dbayeh refugees would generally undertake.

When the last person finally joined our little group, we set out, cutting through the concrete stairways of Dbayeh's narrow, meandering alleys. Shortly thereafter, we arrived in front of a pile of trash that marked one of the official boundaries of the camp at the back of a Lebanese sports club. Some in the group commented in disgust at how the Lebanese discarded their trash at the boundaries of the camp, explaining that this practice revealed a general disrespect for the camp's Palestinians. Soon after, however, they were smiling again. The pilgrimage, as experienced by the local Palestinian refugees, was at least as much a happy occasion to come together and celebrate as it was a time of penitence. It was not a time, however, for socio-political critique, as such an event would have been in Al-Jalil.

After a short walk, during which we casually chatted about many things, we reached the gas station at the base of the hill and then headed north along the Beirut-Tripoli highway. We seemed to be the only ones resembling a group on a pilgrimage. The rare other pedestrians we encountered were those in the most urban areas, walking along the opposite side on the highway's coastal lane, and carrying plastic supermarket bags or other hand luggage suggesting they were not participating in the event. That said, however, perhaps we did not much resemble pilgrims either, but a group of friends going to a party instead. Little by little, I started seeing small groups of individuals coming out of cars and public buses. Then, as we walked across the Nahr El-Kalb monument site at the mouth of a highway tunnel, the number of pilgrims dramatically increased. As people gathered, it finally felt to me that we were in fact on a pilgrimage. Both older and younger people joined in, but mostly young adults walked alongside us.

In Al-Jalil, children or youth played an important role in public performances, which was understandable not only given the usually high number of
children in Palestinian refugee camps in Lebanon,[31] but especially due to the
perceived need to pave the future path of "the Palestinian Cause" towards "the
Return." Thus, in celebrations of national events such as Nakba Day or Land
Day, children played a central part. Likewise, in the pilgrimage to Harissa,
an even larger number of young people participated for different reasons.
First, I noticed older people only joined the procession closer to the statue
site, as the physical challenge of the long walk was an impediment to many.
Those who could not complete the walk starting from Nahr al-Kalb or further away, were usually dropped off near the statue where they could take
the final steps of their pilgrimage. The most important aspect of the pilgrimage was to challenge one's will and physical limitations in a sign of penitence
and respect. Second, as we walked along, I realized that, for the youth, this
was also an opportunity to bond and have fun, as most who had agreed to
join were not in fact eager to be challenged out of their comfort zones and
showed signs of weariness right away. Thus, it could be argued that, although
many of the camp's residents were considered "religious," and while organized Christianity along with embodied affects, sensibilities, and dispositions
greatly influenced by religion did in fact impact much of the camp's routine,
most of Dbayeh's residents should not be considered particularly pious. While
the same could be said about many in Al-Jalil, the overall conformity to religious principles of behavior and expectations concerning the observation of
religious rituals and tenets was much stricter there. In this way, the group I
joined for the Harissa pilgrimage was only partly motivated by piety, while
also motivated by habit, social expectation, prospects for social gathering,
management of community social standing, and others, all inextricably linked
with each other. The remainder of this story helps to substantiate this argument.

At a certain point, one of the young men looked at me and asked if I was
tired and if I preferred to take one of the buses that delivered people to the
highway leading up to Harissa. I assured him I was fine, but, looking at the
unhappy faces of the younger ones among us, I asked in turn if he preferred
to take a bus. He answered no, but that the others should probably do so. I
agreed, as another young man laughed teasingly at a tired boy. Throughout

---

31   Dbayeh was again exceptional in this sense, given that only about 49% of the popula-
      tion were children or young adults (World Vision 2007).

the walk, this boy had been a source of amusement for our group, especially since he had to find where to relieve himself along the margin of the highway in the middle of the way. While the others tried their best to be respectful and maintain an aura of sacredness about the procession, even they did not quite manage at that moment, bursting into giggles as they pointed and made faces at the boy, only to regret it later. This cycle of mundane mockery and regret recurred throughout our pilgrimage.

Close to Jounieh, we all stopped for refreshments at a small market. I bought water and went outside to wait for the others who came out and sat on the curb. While the boy had a juice bottle, the adults opted for beer to quench their thirst. This pause was also an opportunity to light cigarettes, despite the visible lack of breath of some and particularly of the young woman, whose nose, forehead, and neck were covered in sweat. I asked whether it was perhaps contradictory to smoke and drink while on pilgrimage. They found my point about smoking curious and answered that smoking did not represent a problem. As for drinking, one or another beer was normal, they explained, but they certainly had no intention of becoming drunk, especially because there was still a long way to go.

About 4 hours later, having joked and chatted all along the way, but also having repeatedly evoked the sacredness of the ritual, we finally reached the base of the mount leading towards the Virgin Marry statue, and took a cheap bus to reach the top. However, there was some fear of being seen in the bus and consequently not being taken seriously. The pilgrimage would not produce the desired effect this way. Somehow, the efficacy of the pilgrimage and the likelihood of being seen by others on a bus – rather than taking the bus whether or not anyone would see it – was at times entangled in the group's talk. So, we all agreed to remain on the bus only until the last curve before the statue, and to approach Harissa walking.

On this final stretch, as we walked up the hill, there were many tents and improvised huts selling food, refreshments, and souvenirs. Many stands were also giving away food and other items for free. These non-commercial stands were all subsidized by Christian Lebanese political parties, mainly the *Katā'eb*, the L.F., and the Free Patriotic Movement of Michel Aoun. They handed out water bottles, pastries, and other refreshments, as well as party t-shirts and caps. Upon seeing such a scene, I remembered that on the day before, I had worked hard to help Charbel produce hundreds of pastries to be distributed at Harissa. The work, he said, was commissioned by a politician. He did not, however, reveal the politician's name, and so I avoided asking. After all, had he been working for Aoun, whom he openly supported, he would have had no shame in telling me about it. Instead, he confessed about the pastry order in a hushed voice, indicating he would not have accepted it if he did not need the revenue.

On the hill, young people also gathered around their cars communicating agitatedly among themselves, some with their car trunks open to help spread the sound of political hymns playing on their radios in a bid to be louder than the others. I was especially struck by a military march for Samir Geagea's LF, which sounded stronger than any Palestinian hymn I had heard while living in Al-Jalil. This display was nothing less than impressive and even surprising to me, given the supposedly religious character of the pilgrimage. Similar to Palestinian political hymns, the LF recording featured a men's chorus singing nationalist mottos in deep guttural voices, while marching drums set a rallying tone. None in our group directly approached such politically charged areas. If in Dbayeh religious rituals were generally not coupled with political activism as they were in Al-Jalil, the pilgrimage to Harissa in this Lebanese setting certainly was.

At the top of the mountain, I began to see more Muslims, who were easy to spot due to the veiled women. I then realized that the political attitude I had been witnessing was territorial in character. Given the status of the Virgin Mary in Islam, and that the area was a common tourist attraction, many Muslim pilgrims also participated that night. Muslim men and veiled and unveiled Muslim women made their supplications and prayers at the same statue where the huge Christian-majority multitude was gathering.

On top of the hill but outside the fenced area demarcating the sanctuary, composed of the statue and a couple of churches and shrines, the youth set up their tents where they intended to spend the night. Others, including a small number of travelers from places such as Syria and Jordan, camped as well. Inside the fenced area, thousands of people filled the sanctuary. The basilica alone fit about four thousand, and people came and went in all directions inside and outside the many buildings and around the central plaza. The modern basilica was built next to the Harissa Cathedral in the 1970s by the Maronite patriarchate[32] to receive the pilgrims, but the most imposing building of them all was the Melkite Basilica of St. Paul. To the Dbayeh pilgrims, however, the most important building, besides the statue, was the Apostolic Nun-

---

32   Located a few miles below the site

ciature.[33] To me, this preference, coupled with the fact that among the Palestinian refugees in Dbayeh the Maronite monastery was more popular than the Melkite church, signaled that many of the camp's Palestinian refugees did not put much stock into following the theology and religious network of their own Christian denomination. Besides these observations, there were also other instances confirming my assessment. For example, some of the Melkite residents belonged to the Maronite monastery children's chorus, while others enrolled their children in the Maronite school bellow the camp. Practical reasons, such as convenience, seemed to be among the most important factors driving this trend, but community life – both within the camp and in relation to its surroundings – strongly influenced the practice of engaging different churches and Christian denominations.

At the entrance of the sanctuary, we met other Dbayeh Palestinians who had made the pilgrimage, some of whom had taken a bus or car straight to the top. They were not many, and most roamed around to meet people while accomplishing their few pilgrimage obligations, which consisted of lighting a candle for each prayer, as well as walking to the sanctuary or at least visiting its sacred sites. Following the lead of my group, I bought some candles at the store next to the cathedral and lit them while praying. I myself was also not a particularly pious person, nor did I especially adhere to the tenets of my Roman Catholic upbringing, but so was the case with the others in my group, after all.

To my surprise, we began our return to Dbayeh not long after reaching the top of Harissa. I reminded the others that we had intended to spend the night at the site, but they explained that they were tired – the young woman added that she had to wake up early to work in Jal El-Dib, where she was a house cleaner for a Lebanese family. I began to wonder if they would have even made the trip, had it not been for my repeated nudging and inquiry into their commitment to the event. While I will probably never know, what matters here is to note the way in which the group had to live up to expectations only minimally so as to reaffirm their Christianity, and, with it, their character. Even if this time they went through with the pilgrimage only because of my prodding, I understand that had it been that of anyone else in the camp or its surroundings, the result would have been the same. This, in turn, illustrates how subjects, while not necessarily individually committed to this and other such rites in Dbayeh, collectively they were. We walked halfway down the hill

---

33   Papal embassy

and embarked on a bus back to the gas station at the bottom of Dbayeh. Wishing everybody a good night, I knew that on the next day we would be telling tales of that year's pilgrimage, reaping the social but also internalized personal rewards for having done it. After all, they were pilgrims not just in the eyes of the others, but also in their own eyes.

Following my experience in the previous camp, I expected to find in the Harissa pilgrimage the equivalent to all those rituals that had set the tempo of daily life in Al-Jalil. I found instead that, when compared with Al-Jalil, Dbayeh's lack of an ideological commitment to a cause and its lack of a vibrant community life were also reflected in its relative absence of common ritual life. It seemed that there were not many shared messages, rules, and utopias set forth in Dbayeh. There was no evidence of a single people striving towards a common goal, as I had found in Al-Jalil. Instead, Dbayeh residents in general were struggling in an entirely different way. While the younger generations, partially represented in the Harissa pilgrimage, tried to assimilate as much as possible, the elderly strove to keep a safe distance from everything that represented the outside, including both the Palestinians from other camps and the surrounding Lebanese population.[34]

Finally, just as in Jalil, religion permeated every single social institution in Dbayeh and tended to hold sway over both the discourse and the actions of local Palestinians. Once more similar to Al-Jalil, religion was not always a binding and imperative manual of behavior, but more of a general moral compass for social and personal actions. In other words, people often did not behave precisely according to what they read in their divine books, or what they heard from their clerics. Rather, these orthodoxies evoked dispositions, affects, and sensibilities as they intermingled with other traditions, practices, and discourses found in the context of each camp. Therefore, it was not that Dbayeh Palestinians were less religious than Al-Jalil ones. In general, they were less pious than many in Al-Jalil, and followed less closely religious, ethnic, national or even political imperatives. This, in turn, accounted for the lack of communal goals relative to Al-Jalil, greatly contributing to the fragmentation of the local social fabric and concomitantly opening it to the surrounding community – our Lady of Lebanon being thus also theirs. However, the consequent lack of public ritual life in the camp, especially turned inwards but also in general, did not prevent religiosity in Dbayeh to continue to inform the refugees' quotidian routine and their understanding of themselves just

---

34   This is in accordance with the theme of suspicion developed in *Chapter 1*.

as much as it did in Al-Jalil. So far, I had not yet seen Dbayeh acting as a community, but I had not yet seen it all.

h.   The Funeral and the Groom

One afternoon, I was walking around Dbayeh when I noticed people running from one place to another in a panic. The sight of an old lady standing, covering her open mouth with one hand, and supporting her elbow with the other was enough for anyone to realize that a tragedy had occurred. I was told that Suleyman, a 31-year-old young man from the camp, had been accidently electrocuted while taking a shower. As the day went on, someone would continuously appear carrying news about the incident. First, we were told the details of the accident, then of plans to take him to the hospital, and after that, we were informed that the victim was *en route* to the hospital. People were eager to hear news updates, and the atmosphere in the camp was tense – so much so, that I thought Suleyman, the victim, may have had especially strong ties to my section of the camp, though he lived far from it. After a while without news, we were finally told that he had died. I was faced with the tragic death of a young *muwāṭan* who died in an accident. He was not an especially prominent member of the community, but the commotion after the shock of the incident mobilized everyone. At the time of my fieldwork, this was as big as news would get in the camp, and it was the only time I saw the entire camp coming together and acting as a community.

Immediately upon hearing of his death, I went to see some neighbors who were close to the victim. Like everyone else in the camp, apparently, they already knew of the incident. Tragic information traveled remarkably fast. Fifteen minutes later, I went home to change into better clothes. Along the way, almost all pedestrians either asked if I already knew what had happened, or greeted me sharing the tragedy, taking for granted that I had already heard about it. Shortly thereafter, I went to the deceased's house, accompanying my neighbors who were intimate with the victim. His mother was beyond consoling, and others cried copiously at the sight of her state.

A couple of hours after the confirmed death, Muslim women arrived by taxi. It was not the first time I had seen Muslim women visiting the camp, as occasionally they came in small groups of two or three to visit relatives. It was much more unusual to see Muslim men. Muslims in general were a rare sight in Dbayeh, and the event I was witnessing brought many more than usual. As

Suleyman's mother recognized one of the Muslim women exiting the car, she rushed toward the veiled lady, bursting into tears upon contact.

One boy approached me pointing to a photoshopped poster that featured a picture of the deceased posing in front of a flowered garden with his arms crossed. The poster hung from a utility pole, and the inscription at the bottom read: *Lan nansāk abadan*[35] (we will never forget you). As I looked around, I noticed others like it everywhere.

Suleyman's parent's house had set up an improvised mourning room in the small yard and garage with many chairs and a canopy covering the entire place. Judging by the number of chairs, it was likely that many had been brought by relatives and neighbors, who would have helped the family prepare the space. The body was still in the hospital, but many people came and went and trays with refreshments and cigarettes were passed around, especially to the elders occupying the chairs. Young men stood embracing and leaning on each other for support as they cried loudly.

The next morning, some people stood outside the camp at the corner of the Royal Hotel, awaiting the body to arrive from the hospital. Strangely, for me, in contrast to the previous day's mourning, the mood was celebratory as the sound of a *derbake, daff*,[36] and singing filled the air. The music sounded like *dabke* to me. As I made myself available to help with whatever was needed, I waited up on the hill for about 30 minutes along with a few friends from the camp. We finally spotted the motorcade. The cars honked, and each was decorated with a silky white ribbon tied from front to rear or from one side to the other. The majority of Suleyman's closer relatives did not wear black. When the car containing the body reached the corner of the street, a group of twenty-five to thirty women in black came down the camp yelling and wailing. Although wearing black, they all held white flowers in their hands. Fireworks cracked as the coffin was lifted from the car. A friend who had been driving one of the procession cars came to me with a key in hand and entrusted me to park it in a designated area next to Suleyman's parents' house, as he was busy with other preparations. I did this quickly, so that I could go back and watch the rest of the ceremony.

On foot, the procession now made its way to Suleyman's house. There, the coffin was laid open in the mourning room that had been arranged the day before, and many of the same people now occupied similar spots. Mourners

---

35   لن ننساك أبدا
36   Two percussion instruments typical in the Levant

approached and looked through the top of the coffin, some braking down in tears. A group of women moved to the site and stood around the coffin, they then danced, each in her own place, singing a serenade to the deceased. The women bent their knees and swung their heads from side to side. Carrying white flowers in their hands, they simultaneously swung their arms from side to side and front to back, extending the white flowers to the coffin. The sight resembled the spread of smoke from burning incense in a priest's swinging censer during mass.

After a few hours, the coffin was once more paraded in the streets through half the camp as it made its way to the church in an indirect route. A group of about six men, all relatives, and close friends of the deceased, led the parade carrying the coffin. Some of the carriers switched roles at times, as they became too emotionally affected to bear the weight of the coffin, or even remain standing. As they marched inside the camp, fireworks cracked at every corner. Certain people were responsible for lighting them at strategic points signaling the procession's passage. The sounds of the *derbake*, *daff*, ululation, singing, weeping, and howling accompanied the fireworks.

The men shook the coffin by alternately bending their knees and arms, while beating it with the palms of their hands. I worried the coffin would turn or even break, but this never happened, and I seemed to be the only one concerned. People, some wearing black and some not, cried and threw rice into the streets from their houses as the marching group passed by. Others threw rice from the margins of the streets, while a few timidly and reluctantly tried to approach Suleyman's body for a last look. Besides those who participated by standing in the streets or hanging from the windows, doors, and verandas of their houses, I estimated around at least four hundred people following the procession.

At first, I did not understand the reason for the prominent use of the color white, the throwing of rice, the serenade, the *dabke*, and other such elements that did not fit with a traditional Christian funeral, as I knew it. I was aware that, traditionally, village funerals in Palestine tended to be celebrated with dancing and not bound by black,[37] but Suleyman's funeral was exceptionally white and more festive than what I had previously known. I thought perhaps Christian Palestinian and/or Christian Lebanese funerals were different like this, as the only funeral I had attended in Al-Jalil looked much more like

---

37   I had heard accounts of marriages celebrated as such in Lebanese villages as well.

the ones I was used to seeing in Brazil, Europe, the USA, or elsewhere. I remembered another funeral I once witnessed in Shatila, in which there was also dancing and a procession while the coffin was covered with a Palestinian flag, and then there was the symbolic burial of George Habash in that camp as well, as I described earlier in this book. In the Shatila cases, however, funerals were thus commemorated because the deceased was to be treated as a *shahyd* (martyr), for whom there should be celebration along with mourning.

While Suleyman belonged to the Lebanese army, he was not exactly a martyr. Later I realized this was indeed a special funeral, but for entirely different reasons. Suleyman may not have been a martyr, but it also was not his time to die. Looking back, the men seemed to have lost control over their emotions at the remembrance of Suleyman more so than the women, contrary to stereotypes. This revealed a certain depth in male-to-male friendships in Dbayeh (also valid for Al-Jalil). A single young woman, however, at one point fainted and had to be taken away by car. She, I later learned, was Suleyman's fiancé to whom he was soon to be married. As lamented by some of those present, "Suleyman was too young to die." It was "not right" for "the parents to bury their son." In fact, he was supposed to marry, and instead he died. Given the circumstances, his funeral was to be celebrated as much as possible according to what those present thought it should have been: a marriage.

As soon as Suleyman's body arrived inside Mar Yussif church, the *dabke* stopped. The coffin was then placed near the altar, while people filled the rest of the church sitting on the benches and leaning against the walls. A pair of Lebanese military trousers was placed on top of the coffin, signaling his army credentials. One young man in Lebanese army gear cried alone in a corner, and a Lebanese army officer with his cap and full chevron blue uniform greeted everyone. As he even greeted me, I realized he did not know many people at that funeral, however he warmly embraced the deceased's brother. A woman, looking a bit lost, chattered about the "*shab* Falastyny" (the Palestinian young man) while pointing to Suleyman. During the procession and especially at the church, many Lebanese were present from inside and outside the camp. Likewise, many Palestinians attended, a few also from outside the camp. An old Muslim woman in front of the altar silently examined the statues of the saints and their positions, while another one leaning on the wall near the door at the other end of the church prayed. Another Muslim woman sat amidst the rest of the congregation, where I was, in the middle of the church, asking a pair of Christian women next to her about eating the *host*, or sacramental bread symbolizing the body of Christ. After listening to their answer, she made an expression of distaste. She then asked another question that I could not hear, the answer to which provoked the same reaction from the elderly Muslim woman. The two Christian women accompanying her did not seem to mind, however, and delicately accommodated the stranger. At some point, a man complained that "they" (Dbayeh residents) would go down to Rashidyeh, Shatila or Burj El-Barajneh on such occasions as this, but that the reverse was not true.

Although everyone was already at the church, the actual ceremony did not start until a few hours later. Some around me therefore suggested we leave for a while. Outside, free water bottles were provided for those who needed them,[38] and there were trays containing about a dozen brands of cigarettes that were rapidly being consumed. A group of Lebanese army soldiers stood at the entrance of the small room next to the church entrance where the cigarettes were being served. In the afternoon, the number of people seemed to have increased, and around thirty soldiers with two different uniforms were present. Most paid their respects and did not linger.

The same women danced around the coffin again, this time circling it, while onlookers inside the church contemplated the ritual. One at a time, the women cried out testimonies and loudly pleaded on behalf of the deceased in the afterlife. From time to time, one woman would substitute the other in their supplications, to avoid silence. At other times, they would all pause only to resume a few moments later. A Muslim elderly woman remained still next to the coffin for the whole duration of the dance. Suddenly, the women stopped and went to their places in the pews. The Lebanese priest of the church was already at the altar, and soon he started his collective prayers, which were much shorter than I expected. Soon, the same young man I once knew as the Dbayeh circus performer in Burj al-Barajneh took to the altar to speak about Suleyman's place in the community. I had already learned then that the performer was very much engaged in the church's activities, including the chorus and one or another sporadic *masrahiyya* (theater play).

When it was time to take the body to its final resting place in the church cemetery, the same group of men who had carried the coffin to the church earlier now took it to the grave. During this process, just outside the church, a well-known Dbayeh resident who was also one of the carriers abandoned the

---

38   As recommended by local friends, I had bought some myself and brought them to the church.

coffin with his arms stretched wide open and his head leaning on his shoulder. His eyes were closed, and his eyebrows sharply contracted. After swirling away from the coffin, he fainted on the floor and was carried away from the scene. The whole movement reminded me of certain Sufi zikr[39] performances, although the person in question was a Melkite Christian. Once again, the rest of the carriers beat the coffin making Suleymans' body dance. When the body reached its final resting place, it was deposited without any more ceremony, except that some did not want to put the body into the grave. The whole ceremony marked expressions of feelings for the deceased in most radical ways. Apart from rare occasions, such as when the priest spoke, there was no calm or silence. Havoc was the rule, not the exception. Instead of manifesting acceptance of death, the whole ritual was marked by the pretense of a marriage ceremony. That is, many participants behaved as though the deceased was still alive, and the lack of formality to finally bury the body was thus in line with the rest of the ritual.

One year after the funeral, posters of Suleyman were still on the utility posts and walls of the camp and in portrait frames in a few Dbayeh living rooms. Only then did I fully appreciate the importance of the poster the boy had shown me on the day of the funeral: "we will never forget you," it read. Dbayeh residents refused to forget Suleyman, especially given the cause of his death and the events that followed it. The poster made in homage to his memory predicted and reinforced this. Among other things, the poster and the ceremony indicated to me that, despite a history of violence and ongoing disputes, divisions, and generalized suspicion, there was still a desire for a shared essence among most residents, Palestinians and Lebanese alike. This was not well represented by the camp's fragmented social institutions and daily interactions, because it mostly did not exist in the quotidian, however it existed as a shared yearning.

The emotionally powerful ritual, triggered by an unexpected tragedy that seemed to turn the ordinary world upside down, served to instill radical order and unity into a deeply divided social universe, if only momentarily and tentatively. However, the ritual would not have been efficacious, or even possible, were it not for a common widespread desired sense of community. As I mentioned earlier, that desire was there at least among the younger Palestinian refugees, but Suleyman's funeral showed me that, to some extent, it was also

---

39   From the classic Arabic ذكر ; meaning remembrance, or recitation. Zikr is the common term designating a richly varied gathering ritual performed by different Sufi orders.

present among the Lebanese inhabitants of the camp. Maybe some of these Lebanese were trying to cope with guilt. Maybe they simply wanted to efface Dbayeh's Palestinians refugeeness as much as they could. Maybe they were imbued that day with a great sense of neighborly solidarity. Maybe Suleyman was perceived differently from other local Palestinian refugees. Whatever the answer, the ritual drew strength and gained momentum from this still very much unarticulated common communal embryo, nowhere to be found in the camp's regular ritual tempo and daily routine.

As I have shown before, in Al-Jalil community life was an all-encompassing situation expressed by a variety of local social institutions and interpersonal relations. Community life in Dbayeh was not so simple or inclusive since the absence of overall grassroots social institutions allowed local divisions to multiply. Nonetheless, Suleyman's funeral demonstrates that a tentative way of giving meaning to suffering through the collective expression of grief generated a shared dimension that united Dbayeh's inhabitants as a community. To a lesser extent, happier occasions such as weddings, as I also described above, tapped into this same desire as well. In the case of Suleyman's funeral, this process passed through a reciprocated effort to integrate all camp inhabitants, and their most important *liaisons*, despite national and ethnic categories. I suggest that this effort, and the form it took in practice, can be seen as another expression of the local economy of trust, as I will discuss in *Chapter 7*.

Since in Dbayeh a broader local collective could not be easily defined through performances and expressions of national belonging, things like local religious funeral rites served as a basis for a collective rooted in neighborhood ties and religion. The collective display of suffering and the common denominator of conceptions of the afterlife effaced differences and provided felt experiences of unity. Beyond practical reason, at least for the Lebanese, the strong local moral imperatives relating to eschatology stemming from people's embodied shared religiosities, rather than from orthodox sacraments, further blurred the main local divides. However, differences between local categories did not disappear. Rather, the collective funeral rite is perhaps better seen as a cathartic collective display of emotional sharing and entrustment, strengthening, and creating further social bonds desired by many – bonds difficult if not impossible to maintain in the fragmented social reality of the quotidian. Finally, Suleyman's *muwāṭan* identity, at the center of the polarized ethnic division between Palestinianness and Lebaneseness, was perhaps the only possible locus for such general catharsis. What brought the Palestinian refugees close to the Lebanese seemed to have been, after all, Suleyman's Lebaneseness.

Part II – Ritual, Time and Resistance

Ritual symbols and meanings are too indeterminate and their schemes too flexible to lend themselves to any simple process of instilling fixed ideas. (Bell 1992: 221)

To acknowledge self-consciousness is to recognize another competence of ritual: That it provides a means through which individuals construct the terms of their membership, establish the meanings of selfhood and society to them, and rehearse their rights to their selves. (Cohen 1993: 79)

Chapter 5: On Ritual, Religion, and Time

The idea that everyday social interactions can be understood as including rituals and/or be subject to ritualization already has a respectable place in anthropological literature. In one way or another, authors such as Emile Durkheim, Max Gluckman, Edmund Leach, Erving Goffman, Stanley Tambiah, Roy Rappaport, Talal Asad and others, have contributed to the theoretical development of this theme for many decades. This section aims to clarify my definition of ritualization, given the polyvocality of the debate and much disagreement in the field.

To review, in *Chapter 2* I first presented an overview of how Palestinians from Al-Jalil and Dbayeh settled in Lebanon and in their camps. Then, *Chapters 3* and *4* discussed social belonging and the organization of each camp, emphasizing their ritual tempo and the way it affects the quotidian. *Chapter 3* introduced Al-Jalil along with the concept of "ritual tempo," which will be developed in depth in this present chapter. *Chapter 4* introduced Dbayeh and problematized the camp's exceptional status, which is generally attributed to its Christian character. Throughout *Part I*, I argued that the ritualization of daily life is a privileged perspective for understanding the main differences between the two camps, which Palestinians and Lebanese alike tended to attribute to religion as a doctrinal system of values (or as theology, as I called it). Thus, *Part I* had the main goal of showing that the influence of religion was not necessarily as homogenous and predictable as one might expect, but also more pervasive, as it was interwoven with every aspect of quotidian life.

Now, in *Part II* I will further develop my approach to ritualization by taking an in depth look at sacralization and its relation to religion and refugeeness. Especially in Al-Jalil, religion was infused with nationalism in ways I shall further explore in what follows. To start, this chapter briefly develops my broad definition of ritualization as independent of religion yet traversed by all traditions (including religious and others) informing a given context, and

that does not exclude, by definition, the quotidian. Then, *Chapter 6* will discuss two main interrelated forces articulating Al-Jalil's ritual tempo: the Palestinian conception of time, already presented in *Chapter 2*, and a widespread
Palestinian conception of resistance. The former of these forces was primarily linked to ideas of national belonging, and the experience of the latter is
intimate to religiosity, as I will demonstrate. Both forces existed to different
extents in both settings, each camp expressing them differently in everyday
life. Furthermore, while Al-Jalil's tendencies followed closely those of the other
Palestinian refugee camps in Lebanon in general, Dbayeh developed a distinct
practice of blending its refugees' Palestinianness with quotidian living. Thus,
Chapter 6 introduces an imperative informing the Palestinian experience of
refugeeness, the concept of *al-ṣumūd*, which I translate to English as at once
resistance and steadfastness. As I will show, although *al-ṣumūd* has roots in
the Islamic tradition, it was secularized by the PLO. At the time of my fieldwork, however, ṣumūd still tended to subtly but pervasively evoke religious
themes, values, and experiences even when the refugees' expressions of it did
not draw inspiration directly from Islamic or Christian eschatologies, that is,
even when it remained largely secularized.

a.   An Anthropology of Knowledge

This book is as much about agency as it is about belonging, and as can be inferred from what I have presented so far, my approach to ritualization stresses
that social order is made through daily life actions, and not only or mainly
on special occasions when the order of things (from a subject's standpoint)
is articulated in discourses or in, for instance, rites of passage. The order of
things, or what we may call the *social order*, is akin to the common principle
behind Barth's (2002) and Asad's (1993) definition of *knowledge* and its relation
to different *traditions*.

Barth proposed the usefulness of utilizing the concept of knowledge to
"demonstrate how already established thoughts, representations, and social
relations to a considerable extent configure and filter our individual human
experience of the world around us and thereby generate culturally diverse
worldviews" (2002: 1). To him, knowledge has three interconnected aspects:
it contains a corpus of substantive assertions and ideas about aspects of the
world, it is substantiated through partial representations, and it is transmitted within instituted social relations. Governing it, are "criteria of validity,"
emerging out of the constraints embedded in the social organization and de-

pendent on "conventions of representation, the network of relations of trust and identification, and instituted authority positions" (ibid: 3). Thus, as opposed to culture, knowledge is situated "relative to events, actions, and social relationships" (ibid: 1) and "can range from an assemblage of disconnected empirical detail to a 'theory of everything'" (ibid: 8).

The present book resonates with Barth's project for an anthropology of knowledge in that it examines how people "construct the world by their knowledge and live by it" (Barth 2002: 10) and develops "a comparative ethnographic analysis on how bodies of knowledge are produced in different persons and populations in the context of the social relations that they sustain" (ibid: 1), and how knowledge "varieties are variously produced, represented, transmitted, and applied" (ibid: 10). It looks to the "the processes that generate these vast bodies of accumulated public knowledge" (ibid: 17), not only as substantive sets of discourses, but also in other forms of expression that do not favor "language over other forms of codification" (ibid: 16). In the same way, Barth saw the "ritual tradition" of the Baktaman he studied as conforming to his concept of knowledge, since it "provided people with a way to understand major aspects of the world, ways to think and feel about the world, and ways to act on it" (ibid: 4); this book focuses on the way residents of Al-Jalil and Dbayeh engaged their quotidian through their different ritual tempi. Through these peculiar ritual tempi, in turn, "Large populations partake in large flows of knowledge within a diverse and multi-sited tradition" (ibid: 6), flows which, in turn, stem from "broader traditions of knowledge, such as (...) Islam" (ibid: 6).

Barth's anthropology of knowledge was only explicitly developed as such after the seminal *An Anthropology of Knowledge* (2002). However, his theoretical framework emerged from extensive research conducted since the mid-1950s, both theoretically and methodologically already evident in *Cosmologies in the Making: A Generative Approach to Cultural Variation in Inner New Guinea* (1987). Alongside Barth, another central figure in the anthropology of knowledge is Talal Asad. His intellectual engagement with the topic came only around the time of his *Anthropology and the Colonial Encounter* (1973), and then more directly at the time of his *Anthropological Conceptions of Religion: Reflections on Geertz* (1983), and his *The Idea of an Anthropology of Islam* (1986). However, his most well-known publication on knowledge is probably *Genealogies of Religion: Discipline and Reasons of Power in Christianity and Islam* (1993). It was in this last book that his more complete approach to knowledge, but also *tradition, religion* and *ritual* feature prominently.

Despite an early engagement with the work of Barth, evident especially in his *Market Model, Class Structure and Consent: A Reconsideration of Swat Political Organisation* (1972), Asad followed a different route, influenced by the work of Foucault. In his 1972 article, which is a critique of Barth's theoretical approach, Asad already questioned Barth's conflation of power and formal authority and other limitations he attributed to Barth's emphasis on "material circumstances" as "controlled by consciousness." Asad suggested instead different "modes of consciousness" affecting power relations besides formal authority alone, which were manifested more subtly than through conscious strategic reasoning (1972: 93). Power, to Asad, is embodied in law, knowledge, disciplinary practices and the human body (Anjum 2007: 660). Knowledge, thus, is intrinsically tied to a Foucauldian understanding of power as not something subjects simply wield, but as relational and actualized through disciplinary practices in which power is exercised through evaluation and teaching. In turn, disputed socially acknowledged institutional and/or interpersonal authority, asymmetrically distributed in a given social context and relative to power relations, regulates evaluation and teaching.

Whereas modern Christianity separated knowledge from belief, Asad treats knowledge as relative to a given context and intertwined with that context's particular regime of power. In this way, religion also must be understood as "a tradition" bound to specific regimes and "history" of power/knowledge, "including a particular understanding of our legitimate past and future" (Asad 1993: 54), which precludes a general anthropological definition of religion. Drawing on Barth and Asad, tradition is the broad frame I use in this book to understand the place of religiosity in everyday life among Muslims and Christians alike. It is at once "a theoretical location for raising questions about authority, time, language use, and embodiment" and "an empirical arrangement in which discursivity and materiality are connected through the minutiae of everyday living" (Asad 2015). In other words, it

consists essentially of discourses that seek to instruct practitioners regarding the correct form and purpose of a given practice that, precisely because it is established, has a history. These discourses relate conceptually to a *past* (when the practice was instituted, and from which the knowledge of its point and proper performance has been transmitted) and *a future* (how the point of that practice can best be secured in the short or long term, or why it should be modified or abandoned), through *a present* (how it is linked to other practices, institutions, and social conditions). (Asad 1986: 20)

As a tradition, Islam, for example, informs practices and discourses in different places in the world, which does not entail that Islam defines every aspect of the lives of Muslims equally everywhere, since "Religious symbols acquire their meaning and efficacy in real life through social and political means and processes in which power, in the form of coercion, discipline, institutions, and knowledge, is intricately involved" (Anjum 2007: 601). The same is valid for Christianity. Moreover, to Asad, "Discourse involved in practice is not the same as that involved in speaking about practice. It is a modern idea that a practitioner cannot know how to live religiously without being able to articulate that knowledge." (1993: 36)

According to Asad, Islam should be approached by anthropologists as a "discursive tradition," connected with the "manipulation of populations" and "resistance" to this manipulation, but also with the "production of appropriate knowledges" and the "formation of moral selves" (Asad 1986: 10). This book has been following Barth's main call for an anthropology of knowledge as delineated above, but with accent on Asad's (and Foucault's before him) understanding of how knowledge is connected to power through embodied disciplinary practices that create affects, dispositions, and sensibilities, which in turn are constitutive of the quotidian in Al-Jalil, Dbayeh , and elsewhere.

According to Asad's perspective and in Charles Hirschkind's words, just as religion, secularism can also be seen as what Talal Asad calls in *Formations of the Secular* "a concept that brings together certain behaviors, knowledges, and sensibilities in modern life" (Asad, apud Hirschkind 2011: 638). A student of Asad, Hirschkind offers insights into what he calls the *sensorium*, partially inspired by Kant's "highly ritualistic" illustration of the dinner party scene. In one particular instance, he says, Kant presents the dinner host with guidelines to engender "civilized sociability" to produce a certain kind of human being, "so as to harmonize the guests' inclination to good living with the inclination to virtue and moral law." Hirschkind reads Kant's rules as a "pedagogical device geared to disciplining the emotions and attitudes of a secular subject" (Hirschkind 2011: 637-638). This is an example of what I call ritualization and the way in which it mobilizes that which Hirschkind calls the *sensorium* as *embodied sensibilities, dispositions, affects,* and *modes of expression* (2011), only I take dispositions to also include modes of expression. Another parallel example to illustrate how dispositions, affects and sensibilities are intertwined with religiosity is given by Hirschkind in his own portrayal of the way in which cassette tape sermons are mobilized in Egypt (2006). According to him, they are another example of a context in which "public speech results not in policy, but in pious dispositions, the embodied sensibilities and modes of expression understood to facilitate the development and practice of Islamic virtues and, therefore, of Islamic ethical comportment" (Hirschkind 2010). Rather than violence or coercion, power here follows a more Foucauldian/Asadian path than it would in Barth's model.

It is true that, as Samuli Schielke puts it, "The traditions of Muslim devotion are important but not sufficient to account for the complex lives my Muslim friends and interlocutors live" and to account for a recent "shift toward moral knowledge and activist commitment" among Muslims in the Middle East (Schielke 2010: 8). However, Schielke aims his criticism toward Talal Asad's most well-known followers, including Charles Hirschkind and Saba Mahmood, suggesting that for these authors to not pay enough attention to "moral knowledge" is to overlook what is actually one of the main theoretical-methodological pillars of the group, since the cultivation and embodiment of moral virtues has been at the center of their main works, such as Hirschkind's *The Ethical Soundscape* (2006) and Mahmood's *Politics of Piety* (2005). Nonetheless, Schielke upholds that the Assadian "research program of piety, ethics and tradition" (Schielke 2010: 5) has also led to the magnification of limitation to the anthropology of Islam by over-emphasizing moral and pious subjectivity and tradition, in this way being "too preoccupied with Islam to make really good sense of what it may mean to be a Muslim" (Schielke 2010: 14). To him, in contraposition,

> to understand the significance of a religious or any other faith in people's lives, it is perhaps more helpful to look at it less specifically as a religion or a tradition and instead take a more fuzzy and open-ended view of it as a grand scheme that is actively imagined and debated by people and that can offer various kinds of direction, meaning and guidance in people's lives. (ibid: 14)

Instead of looking inwards into a tradition then, Schielke suggests starting with "the immediate practice of living a life, the existential concerns and the pragmatic considerations that inform this practice, embedded in but not reduced to the traditions, powers and discourses..." (Schielke 2010: 12). In other words, the focus on the study of piety should turn to the quotidian instead, or what he calls the "messier but richer fields of everyday experiences, personal biographies and complex genealogies" (ibid: 5) – citing Lila Abu-Lughod's anthropology (discussed in the introduction) as a source of inspiration. Yet, to suppose that the realm of everyday life is absent from the Assadian program would be untrue, especially given the weight he himself ascribes to the realm of practice, in which students such as Hirschkind and Mahmood have closely followed. Schielke is correct in pointing out that these authors have relegated anything else that is not Islam (as a tradition) to the background. Neverthe-less – to be fair – a research program focused on Islam as a tradition is just as important as one focused on everyday life, and both can and should reinforce each other, lest we run the risk of losing from sight that, to most people, such things as Islam and Christianity are indeed distinct traditions.

Unlike Asad, Hirschkind, or even Schielke, my main concern here is not "Islam," or even "Muslims," but how social belonging (and Palestinianness in particular) is shaped in the quotidian of two Palestinian refugee camps in Lebanon. Without Assad, my discussion about the extent to which religiosity informs the quotidian and Palestinianness would have been seriously jeop-ardized. To sum up, the flexibility of knowledge as a general frame in which multiple contested traditions are mobilized in daily life allows us to envisage how religion and other facets of human life are embedded in people's behav-iors, actions, thoughts, conceptions, and feelings. Moreover, as suggested by Schielke, by taking heterogeneous traditions such as Islam, Christianity, and Palestinianness as part of a broader comparative frame, we mitigate the risk of essentializing one or the other.

b.   Ritualization and the Quotidian

In practice, engaging the dynamics of ritualization enables us to understand the principles and practices of belonging in Dbayeh and Al-Jalil, along with the relative symbolic space of traditions such as Islam or Christianity. That is, I suggest that each Palestinian refugee camp in Lebanon represents a dif-ferent context, producing a shared subjunctive nexus of space and time very much construed, managed, and transformed through the local ritual tempo. In turn, the local ritual tempo of each camp owes much of its dynamics to broader subjunctives, emanating from different traditions such as, for in-stance, Palestinianness, Islam, or Christianity, and from social constraints such as refugeeness. In other words, this nexus is a ramified social arena, with wider and narrower branches, in which subjects (individuals and groups) both reify and transform the orders of things whereby in-group dynamics and

dynamics between groups are embedded. This process is, therefore, both generative and transformative of social organization and identity.

Earlier anthropologists such as Max Gluckman and Edmund Leach understood that most of the statements we make in our dress codes, manners, and
"most trivial gestures," to use Leach's phrasing, refer to human relationships
and social status. Customs about social interactions are by definition aesthetic
codes that communicate about a supposed, albeit often challenged, order of
people and things. More directly, drawing on a tradition spanning from Jack
Goody (1961) to Catherine Bell (2009, 1997) and Seligman et al (2008), I assume
the concept of ritual as a tool defined differently by different authors to shape
their own analysis. As Seligman et al. state in *Ritual and its Consequences* (2008),
I also understand that ritual is "not some discrete realm of human action and
interaction, set apart and distinct from other forms of human action," but
"a modality of human engagement with the world" (Seligman et al. 2008: x).
Different forms of behavior can be understood through the analytic frame of
ritual because "it is the framing of the actions, not the actions themselves,
that makes them rituals" (ibid: 5). Ritual then is "one possible orientation to
action, rather than as a set of meanings" (ibid: 6), or more substantively, ritual
is a "set of relationships" rather than a "system of meanings," as it is in the
Geertzian tradition (ibid: 34).[1]

Underlying my understanding of knowledge, tradition, ritual, and ritualization, is a concept of *symbols* close to that of Dan Sperber (2007). It is especially on the distributional character of culture found in Sperber's "symbolic
evocation" – essentially, that symbols do not have meaning in themselves, but
that meaning is only evoked contextually – that I draw basic inspiration for
my own concept of *ritualization*. Saying that rituals carry statements about the
general order of things is not the same as saying that all rituals restate a grand
narrative of a presumed social order. At least in the cases I present, there is
no grand-social order even when one is seemingly produced through totaliz-
ing discourses. This social order exists only as what we could call a discursive
orthodoxy, evoked in the heterodoxy of social life in different contexts. That
is, refugees and other Palestinians are greatly engaged in producing "official
versions" of their history and collective selves, and in relating to it as a tradition (in the sense given above). This referencing then localizes subjects within
a collective, and provides framing for social life, albeit being only evocative of

---

1   Seligman et al's main premise is that ritual is conceptually opposed to sincerity, which
     is an assumption that I do not follow in this book.

meaning. As I will also show in *Chapter 7*, even grand narratives like the Nakba, besides providing a shared interpersonal dimension, are evocative of different meanings for different subjects. Therefore, while Palestinian refugees in Al-Jalil and Dbayeh tend to think of Palestinianness as substantive and natural (as an orthodoxy), the contents and shape of this Palestinianness vary according to subject and context.

Max Gluckman's *The Bridge* (1940) already hinted that rituals, as ceremonies, are in practice about and composed of sets of interpersonal relations between different statuses and roles. The event it analyzes is the inauguration of a bridge in Zululand, framing the account through the structure of personal relations. In fact, the main structure of the ceremony itself, Gluckman ponders, reflected the social roles and statuses of colonial Britain and the colonized Zulu. Erving Goffman went one step further to consider conventions of interpersonal behaviors as rituals. In writings such as *Presentations of the Self in Everyday Life* (1959), *Stigma: Notes on the Management of spoiled Identity* (1963), and *Interaction Ritual* (1969), he suggests that in "complex societies," where divisions of labor, groups of interest, religion, ethnicity, politics, profession, etc. are abundant, individuals are always related to many different identities, displaying or hiding each one in their repertoire according to the context (Goffman 1959; 1967). Perhaps Goffman's main contribution to social science then was to focus on "events," their contexts, and their actors' positionality in the analysis of behavior. This meant giving up the search for an underlying abstract social structure to focus on everyday social interactions as the basis of social organization. However, Goffman's perspective focuses on conscious and strategic acts, unlike Hirschkind's *sensorium* (Hirschkind 2001). The main difference is that while Hirschkind's concept may be further used to elucidate different contexts beyond technical acts, such as the ones he analyzed in Egypt, Goffman's concept is much less malleable in structure. Despite this and other limitations to Goffman's theorization of ritual – as in, for example, assuming that the self is made by the sum of its contradicting social roles, assuming that the self is always conscious of the structure of the social situations, and that the self always acts to maximize its input and statuses – his theorization made immense progress in other areas. Especially in ritual, it was clearly demonstrated for the first time that etiquette and other such elements of interpersonal relations defining social statuses and roles could also be understood as rituals, apart from religious rituals and other kinds of ceremonies.

For Stanley Tambiah, rituals not only reflect statuses, as they do for Gluck-man, but they can also alter these statuses. It is precisely this aspect of Tam-biah's theorization of ritual that enriches my own analysis. For Tambiah, ritual behavior cannot be understood apart from the subject's dynamic and contex-tual embeddedness in time, space, and relative positionality. His view was influenced by "Austinian linguistic philosophy," as described by the author himself: "My first monograph in Thailand and many of my essays in Culture, Thought, and Social Action bear witness to Leach's influence, though at the same time I was discovering on my own the possibilities of Austianian lin-guistic philosophy for a performative theory of ritual (Tambiah 2002: xii).

Contrary to Leach, Goffman, and Barth, however, Tambiah's approach was never premised on a rationalist individual maximization of goals perspective. What he retained from Leach was that individuals could alter their statuses in society through rituals. That is, individuals engage rituals not only by follow-ing scripts, but also by negotiating these scripts. Seeking to explain riots in South Asia, Tambiah's approach is a "ritual and cultural semiotics." For him, riots and "associated contexts of collective violence" are "routinized, ritual-ized, and drawn on the public culture's repertoire of presentational forms and practices." Thus, riots should be linked to "the larger world of collective activities in public spaces, involving crowds and rites, music and swordplay, sacred space and sacred time," that is, to a "world often labeled by scholars as 'popular culture'" because "collective activities in public spaces constitute the heart of shared urban experience" (Tambiah 1996: 222 and 223). One promi-nent feature of his "ritual and cultural semiotics" is what he calls the "rou-tinization" and "ritualization" of collective violence as "stereotyped strategies and acts that syntactically and recursively constitute collective events" (ibid: 266). For Tambiah, riots and "associated contexts of collective violence" are "routinized, ritualized, and drawn on the public culture's repertoire of pre-sentationnal forms and practices" (ibid: 222), and thus must be understood in a manner similar to "popular culture." This creates the heuristic space to think about a "ritual tempo" instead of limiting anthropological analyses to ritual instances more contained in time, space, conception, and social reach. As such, Routinization and ritualization have special value for understand-ing political demonstrations and interpersonal interaction that can be largely based on ethnic, national, or religious divides, such as I have described in Al-Jalil. Despite the lack of collective public performances or rioting, celebra-tory or otherwise, Dbayeh also retained some potential for routinized and formalized behavior, as Suleiman's case demonstrates, and some form of rit-

ualization of interpersonal relations, as I will show in *Chapter 7*. It is important to highlight, as Tambiah does, that prestige, legitimacy, authority, power,
and other entitlements and forms of symbolic capital are conferred in rituals
through their performance, which in turn helps explain why honor "indexes"
values, as I will also describe in *Chapter 7*.

Moreover, from Roy Rappaport (2008), I take the need to define ritual
polythetically and less normatively. According to him, not all rituals always
require the same elements in practice, but one should define ritual around
a cluster of features, of which individual renditions may in practice present
only a few. These are: "encoding by other than performers" (Rappaport 2008:
32); "formality (as decorum)" (ibid: 33); "invariance (more or less)," or what we
may call redundancy (ibid: 36); "performance (ritual and other performance
forms)" (ibid: 37); and "formality (vs. physical efficacy or functionality)" (ibid:
46). Moreover, he argues that it would be incorrect to distinguish absolutely
the "formal, stylized or stereotypic" from the "informal or spontaneous." Instead, he proposes a *continuum* between these terms, ranging from slight styl-
ization to more elaborate rituals that require great decorum and/or seem to
be "almost fully specified" (Rappaport 1999: 34). Rituals should be defined not
only to encompass what requires great decorum and seems to be "almost fully
specified," but also to include what is less stylized and less fully specified. In
this way, situations such as teenagers' greetings, which are certainly part of
quotidian life, can also be understood through ritual theory. Thus, formalization of behavior coupled with iterability point to ritualization, as in the
following passage:

> The formalization of acts and utterances, themselves meaningful, and the
> organization of those formalized acts and utterances into more or less in-
> variant sequences, imposes ritual form on the substance of those acts and
> utterances, that is, on their *significata*. (Rappaport 1999: 21)

In this way, even if departing from the Durkheimian tradition, Rappaport
does not see rituals as distinct from quotidian life, even when reproducing
Durkheim's understanding of ritual as sacred, as opposed to mundane quotidian life. Based on this flexibility, and also on Tambiah's understanding of
ritual practices beyond themselves in relation to what he calls "popular culture" (1996), I use the concept of ritualization more as a perspective through
which one can analyze dynamic social phenomena, and less to normatively
define substantive social phenomena to the exclusion of others.

My own definition construes rituals as routinized aestheticized codes for social behavior, contextualized by actors' interpersonal subjectivity and the information communicated. They are in themselves statements about the order of people and things inasmuch as such an order exists only as contested orthodoxy. Rituals accomplish at the very least the simple acknowledgment of that order, to reify, maintain, transform, or dispute it. The fact that rituals, through their performance, are in themselves statements does not mean that the information communicated is not important, for information is embedded in ritual's form. However, it is precisely from performance that ritual derives its efficacy. Following Rappaport (1999), among others, rituals are never pre-conceived blueprints of behavior completely dispossessed of subjects' agencies as if their genesis was their only meaningful moment. As we cannot assume consciousness from all participants at all times – as did Ervin Goffman or Fredrik Barth, for instance – we cannot conceive that the power of rituals is derived solely from the unconscious socialization they entail – as authors such as Claude Lévi-Strauss, Pierre Bourdieu, and French semiologists and linguists tended to, mainly drawing on Saussure's work.

Also, in this way ritual is different from other customs that may not have the same power of reasserting social order. As a result of the performances of ritual, as stated by Catherine Bell (1992), subjects are empowered or disempowered according to their positionality in their varying, and often competing, moral schemes of the world. As Leach (2001) claimed, because of the high level of manipulation and interpretation of moral order(s) that can be involved in rituals, these are not always substantively marked enough to be a coherent and hierarchical set of symbols. Here too, Talal Asad has important thoughts to add. In his words:

> Apt performance involves not symbols to be interpreted but abilities to be acquired according to rules that are sanctioned by those in authority: it presupposes no obscure meanings, but rather the formation of physical and linguistic skills. Rites as apt performances presuppose codes – in the regulative sense as opposed to the semantic – and people who evaluate and teach them. (Asad 1993: 62)

In this sense, ritual is not a set of meanings, nor is it only a set of relationships, as it was for Seligman et al. Rather, it is also a series of acquired social abilities defining the subjects' cultural competence. Thus, bringing the discussion back to Dbayeh and Al-Jalil, ceremonies such as prayers and pilgrimages tended to have more standardized sets of symbols, but everyday social interaction was marked by less socially codified units of communication. Symbols, relations between symbols, meanings, but also embodied dispositions, sensibilities, and affects derived from sets of social referents stemming from contextual engagement, ritual or not, with traditions such as Islam, Christianity, imagined communities such as the Palestinians, and knowledge about and the experience of social processes such as refugeeness. More than accomplishing a task or serving a purpose, rituals are embedded in the vernacular practices of everyday life.

Ritualization, however, is not the same as ritual. In this sense, it is important to note that the concept of *ritualization* has already been used in anthropology in different ways. Max Gluckman, for example, used it to refer to the assignment of ritual roles to individuals in conformity to their secular relations and statuses (Rappaport 2008: 39). Also, Warn Goodenough, Victor Turner, Anthony Wallace, and others suggested that the ability established in the individual to be informed by rituals was acquired in part through rites of passage, and Erik Erikson referred to the "process of preparation" as ritualization (ibid: 111). My own usage differs from these.

Even though Talal Asad does not discuss *ritualization*, he has a similar understanding of the types of processes I subsume under the term, for example, in his discussion about Islam as a "discursive tradition" and how it informs the quotidian lives of Muslims (1993), and in his discussion of secularism (2003). His basic understanding of such processes is Foucauldian, and, as Catherine Bell reminds us, Foucault himself

> ...consistently chooses the nomenclature of 'ritual' to evoke the mechanisms and dynamics of power. He is not, however, concerned to analyze ritual per se or even to generate a description of ritual as an autonomous phenomenon. 'Ritual' is one of the several words he uses to indicate formalized, routinized, and often supervised practices that mold the body. (Bell 2009: 201)

It is to express the same social process described above – of embodiment and contextual mobilization of social referents and embodied disciplined dispositions, affects, and sensitivities – that I use the word ritualization, which I take from Bell (2009, 1997). I prefer ritualization to ritual because the former evokes process and relational dynamics more so than the latter. For instance, according to Bell, ritualization corrects accretions to the term ritual such as *universality, naturalness,* and *an intrinsic structure,* all of which are a consequence of the connection between the term ritual and notions such as *liturgy* and *magic.* Furthermore, ritualization is not entangled with functionalist assumptions of cultural reproduction, since it requires the "external consent of participants while simultaneously tolerating a fair degree of internal resistance" (Bell 2009: 222). That is, it does not work as a top-down mechanism of social control but depends on general commitment and engagement. Finally, it does not transform individuals into a community either, but, according to Bell, it does take "common interests" – or I would prefer common *themes* – "and grounds them in an understanding of the hegemonic order" empowering agents only in "limited" and "highly negotiated ways" (2009: 222-23). Overall,

> ...ritualization generate[s] historical traditions, geographical systems, and levels of professionals. Just as a rite cannot be understood apart from a full spectrum of cultural forms of human action in general, so it must also be seen in the context of other ritualized acts as well. The construction of traditions and subtraditions, the accrual of professional and alternative expertise - all are effected by the play of schemes evoked through ritualization. (Bell 2009: 221)

However, Bell stresses the conscious work of ritualization as seen, for example, in this quotation: "ritualization is a strategic play of power, of domination and resistance, within the arena of the social body" (Bell 2009: 204). In turn, I prefer to deemphasize strategy and play, which suggest consciousness, over the embodied work of disciplined behavior. My own interpretation of Foucault, countering Bell's, leads me to regard the mobilization of social referents (from religious traditions or not) as intrinsic to the dynamics of ritualization as stemming equally from both conscious structuring of social situations and embodied dispositions, sensibilities, and affects in ways that are never completely controlled by the participants.

In the case of Al-Jalil, subjects' acts were all embedded into a ritual tempo which consisted not only of different rituals – all addressing the overall order of things – but was in itself the ritualized pace of daily life. By contrast, daily life in Dbayeh was not as much collectively and overtly ritualized, and the ritual tempo was generally slow and less pervasive than it was in Al-Jalil, at once reflecting and reinforcing the lack of communal life. However, it could also at times peak – as it did in Suleyman's funeral – and manifest as collective expressions of shared predicaments and ideals, which in turn are generative of sociality. This is not a self-regulated functionalist social mechanism to reproduce society, but collective effervescence out of which shared expressions discipline subjects' dispositions, sensibilities, and affects.

Every positioning inside this order is potentially a statement about the overall order, in the sense that this order is dynamic and constantly reshaped through contextualized fragmented interpersonal interactions. Actors may not intend to articulate these statements with such grandiosity (or even articulate them at all), and in fact only rarely do, although Palestinian refugees in Lebanon tend to do so more than in most other places I have seen before. Yet, by affirming or challenging their place in the system of social relations, they are engaging the social context through knowledge composed of dispositions, sensibilities, affects, techniques, and other discourses and practices they learned, and themselves helped to shape through collective expressions, such as the ones I presented especially in *Part I* and interpersonal relations I will present especially in *Chapter 7*.

Furthermore, rituals can be seen as snapshots in broader ritualization processes that can be motivated by subjects' interests and/or empathy as described above. We do not need to import the Durkheimian assumption that rituals are always related to a passage between discrete mundane and sacred worlds. Rather, they lean toward reproducing, managing, transforming, and legitimizing disputed moral orders – in the previously developed sense that such statements need not be grand-narratives of the social order. Therefore, rituals establish the order(s) of things in a constant dynamic process of ritualization, one that is thus highly dependent on iteration so that the "past is made present," "stamps a shape onto the formlessness and chaos of existence" (Seligman et al. 2008: 121, 120), aligning the future with the past.

Like music, ritual exists only in the performance, and so both are social in Rappaport's sense in that "they are not entirely encoded by the performers themselves" (Rappaport *apud* Seligman et al. 2008: 165). As Seligman et al. state, "Even the most fundamental musical repetition – the rhythmic pulse that underlies everything – is not a simple reiteration, as if we were chronometers. Rhythm coordinates; it allows cooperation across boundaries and imposes order on chaos" (Seligman et al. 2008: 169). In this way, there is a connection between time, *tempo*, and ritualization. Following this perspective, while much of contemporary research on ritual reduces it to an "effort toward harmony," its relations to the world are far more complex and improvised, and unarticulated creativity is far more encompassing (ibid: 171).

c.   Ritual Tempo

In *Cronus and Chronos*, Edmund Leach considers two different notions of time, one that evokes the notion of repetition, like measuring time with a metronome, and another that evokes non-repetition, such as when we are aware that every life has a beginning and an end. Treating them both under the rubric of the same concept, he claims, is "religious prejudice" (Leach in Hugh-Jones & Laidlaw 2000: 175). In *Time and False Noses* he reminds us that all over the world people mark their calendars by means of festivals. In this article, he adds to the experience of time one more element. Alongside repetition and aging (entropy), the third way to experience time is the rate at which time passes, which I understand as a fusion of the first two.[2] The most fundamental experience of time would have to do with this third element, which he calls a "pendulum," and would be perceived as a "discontinuity of repeated contrasts" such as "day- night, day – night; hot – cold, hot – cold; wet – dry, wet – dry" (Leach in Hugh-Jones & Laidlaw 2000: 183). His main argument in both articles, however, is that the flow of time is always a human creation since time is not experienced by the senses. It is "ordered" by the "moral persons" (a Durkheimian category) who "participate in the festal rites," these rites being "techniques" for "changing status" from sacred to mundane and vice-versa.[3] In sum, "We talk about measuring time, as if time were a concrete thing waiting to be measured; but in fact we create time by creating intervals of social life. Until we have done this there is no time to be measured" (ibid: 184).

In similar fashion, Rappaport writes, "It would be exaggerating to claim, then, that the sense of time is fully constructed *ex nihilo* by each society; for all normal human beings past infancy must distinguish now from past and future, and pace Edmund Leach (1961), past and future from each other as well. They recognize that some events are periodic and recurrent, while others are not, and perceive some events as to be further in the past or future than others. Although memory, hope, and expectation have no place in the time of the physicist or astronomer they do, to say the least, enter into the

---

2   We could go back to Jakobson here, who stated that the most basic mental operations are metaphor and metonym; all the rest being variations of syntheses of the two. In a similar way, Leach's repetitive and non-repetitive time frames combined would generate "rate," for instance, such as the seasons marking the dual character of time.

3   The thought in this paragraph can be seen as one of Leach's Durkheimian tropes.

temporal experience of the living" (Rappaport 1999: 175). Thus, societies map time through ritual, generating a framework for experiencing everyday life.

With the above understanding of ritual then, I want to highlight Rosemary Sayigh's insightful usage of the *tempo of everyday life* in connection with the types of activities she describes in the Palestinian refugee camps. Life in the camps clearly triggered the appearance of a new sort of social actor: the refugee camp inhabitant. Becoming a refugee both brought about and was brought about by a whole new dynamic of social life. This dynamic is marked not only in everyday social interactions, but also in calendars of events.[4] Celebrations representing time in a singular pendular interval were saturated with the theme of the refugee's new condition in opposition to the idealized past that also was taken to represent the future. These celebrations not only drastically changed the pace of daily life but were also a direct result of it, as they represented collective actions in which subjects actively sought to give meaning to their new condition.[5]

As Palestinians became refugees, they created their own time by creating continuous, repetitive, and pendular intervals of social life. They created their own history, and with it their own social identity. Furthermore, Palestinian refugees in Lebanon tended to mark time as before and after the rupture of the *Nakba*, since this was the event leading to their present condition of refugeeness in first place. Among other things, the *Nakba* is a myth of creation,[6] and a collective one-time negative rite of passage. Just as important, *al-'Awda* (the return to Palestine) is a narrative giving meaning to daily life,[7] and the idea of *al-Ḥaqq al-'Awda* (The Right of Return) is a strong force shaping the dynamics of time, space, and interpersonal relations for most of my refugee interlocutors.

---

4   As an exception, this calendar of events is absent in Dbayeh, as will be developed later.
5   This does not imply that meaning was not continuously created beyond consciousness. That is so not only as in Austin's perlocutionary effects, but also as in Leach's and Rappaport's principle that actions (and happenings) are prior to their explanations. Subjects do not always have total conscious control over the social environments they create, nor are they aware of the significance of their creations.
6   Not in the sense that it is not real, but in the sense that it is a narrative evoked by the collective to make sense of the present.
7   Again, less in Dbayeh, as I will discuss in what follows.

For reasons I will elaborate in the following chapters, these elements are part of the refugee cosmologies[8] (some more influential in Al-Jalil than Dbayeh) and are lived through the performance of daily life. As with any other society in the world, not all these performances are ritualistic, but many of them are. Following Tambiah's suggestion that rituals should not be understood as apart from "popular culture," the local ritual tempi that I described in the first part of this book are comprised of more than just the sum of all the rituals found in Al-Jalil and Dbayeh. They structure the pace of daily life, which is very much marked by the condition of refugeeness, the physical and social environment of the camps, and the way in which these camps fit the contexts that surround them.

Many orders of things – national, religious, political, moral, economic, ethnic – are sometimes almost completely blurred together within the same ritual tempo, and although some individuals try to parse them out, others simply take it for granted that all these orders are one and the same. Although certainly an important element of these ritual tempi, religion is not alone in setting the tone of social life and giving meaning to the quotidian. The ritual tempi per se, where all these elements are embedded and expressed, are the loci from which personal and collective meanings and motivations are reproduced, maintained, and transformed.

d.   Ceremonies and Ritualization in the Palestinian Refugee Camps in Lebanon

While there is much in common between Laleh Khalili's approach and mine, and while my own approach owes much to hers, it is now crucial to highlight important differences. Khalili's perspective on national commemorations seems heavily influenced by Benedict Anderson's (2006), while authors such as Talal Asad, Stanley Tambiah, and Fredrik Barth influence mine. Her emphasis is thus on the symbolization behind commemorations as "mnemonic practices," thus emphasizing that performance reinforces discourse, as can be inferred from the following quotation:

> [I] examine commemoration – *public* performances, rituals, and narratives – because I am concerned not with memories but with 'mnemonic *practices*'

---

8   Cosmology here refers to a possible translation to Immanuel Kant's concept of *Weltan-schauung*.

(Olick 2003), not with images inside people's heads but with the social invocation of past events, persons, places, and symbols in variable social settings.
(2007: 4)

In this book, ritualization deals instead with what Khalili calls "public performances," "rituals," and the performative dimension of discourses embedded in them. Performance here does not simply "invoke" or reiterate discourses, but it is productive of them. To reiterate: while the theoretical frame
of Khalili's *Heroes and Martyrs of Palestine* (2007) does not completely come to
terms with this subjectivity of discourses and the productive quality of ritualization, Khalili often acknowledges the necessity to hold a more nuanced
understanding of the relation between narrative and performance.

Also, as Khalili puts it, "The narrative content is of primary interest to me,
because in articulating a vision of nationhood, commemorative narratives
also proffer possible strategies of cohesion and struggle" (ibid: 5). Even though
Khalili uses the term *nationhood* here, she is first and foremost concerned with
nationalism instead, as noted in the introduction. Furthermore, the focus on
narratives as substantively containing meaning obfuscates the more complex
evocative dynamics of meaning where less normative elements, such as the
Nakba, *al-'Awda*, and the present refugeeness dynamically arranged by subjects in context, are at least as pervasive as top-down discourses created by
political elites in their institutional offices. In other words, while her focus
is on the analysis of discourse and thus on memory and storytelling, mine
is on the performative quality of ritualized social practices, and on how history is contingent while memory is collective yet contextual and subjective.
While the structure of commemoration, to Khalili, is made of substantive
symbols, to me it emerges from the friction inherent to interpersonal interaction. What I aim to show then is not only *that* but *how* these ritualized and
embodied practices, dispositions, sensibilities, and affects surpass nationalist
discourses and are instead embedded in a Palestinian subjunctive alongside
other themes generally considered religious or ethnic, for example. Discourse
does not completely determine action. Although Khalili seems to agree with
this proposition in theory, her account seems too tied to a classical symbolic
(semiologic) understanding of the relationship between discourse and action,
rather than portraying it as a more dynamic ensemble.

Furthermore, Khalili acknowledges that "some forms of commemoration
are borrowed from everyday social and cultural lives of a people and are then
transformed into political events," such as "funeral ceremonies for martyrs"

(ibid: 215). Yet, she only analyzes national commemorations, while my ritualization approach ventures on to more nuanced forms of ritualization and the ritualization of daily life itself, as I will develop further in the remaining chapters.

In addition, one of Khalili's most important insights is that

> Commemoration has not solely emerged out of elite agency. The very performative nature of commemoration that it fundamentally requires an audience – has meant that commemorations have to draw on that audience's values, experiences, memories, sympathies, and beliefs. For commemoration to be popular, for it to resonate with and mobilize Palestinians, it has to say something about *their* past make some meaning to *their* present lives, offer something about *their* future. (ibid: 222)

Yet, concomitantly, she emphasizes "institutional control over commemoration" (ibid: 220) - people merely "leaving their mark on the practices and narratives" (ibid: 222) rather than influencing the process more thoroughly. While this was less the case during the days of the revolution in Lebanon, it has been more so especially after Oslo, when the PLO lost not only control of the refugee camps, but also legitimacy among refugees. As we have seen especially in chapters 3 and 4, these public commemorations were often led not by political parties, but by local associations with loose ties to political forces, and to a certain extent often disputing authority with them.

Finally, to Khalili, "in the absence of a monolithic or universal way of understanding what binds the nation together – shared culture, language, religion, or common origins? – these heroic or tragic narratives map the experiences of nationals within the imaginary space of the nation" (ibid: 226). However, according to what I have presented so far, it would be more accurate to argue that narratives of tragedy and/or heroism do not substitute what is missing from the ideal typical nation. Rather, they fill these categories – culture, religion, ethnicity, territory – which in turn comprise the imaginary of the nation.

e.   Ritual and the Sacred

Since Émile Durkheim, anthropologists in the past thought about rituals as inherently linked to religion. I will depart from the widely influential Durkheimian understanding to present my own. Apart from a small number of Durkheimian concepts, especially by way of Tambiah, I will differentiate my own framework by showing that religion and ritual are not inherently linked with each other, even though they may in practice converge, in the way we have seen in Dbayeh and al-Jalil.

The *sacred* for Durkheim is everything that relates to a dimension "set apart or prohibited." Concomitantly, *religious* is anything related to the sacred, as he states in the very definition put forward in *The Elementary Forms of Religious Life*: "A religion is a unified system of beliefs and practices relative to sacred things, that is to say, things set apart and forbidden – beliefs and practices which unite into one single moral community called a Church, all those who adhere to them" (Durkheim 1954: 47). However, this definition of religion is today widely contested. First, because not everything that is religious is prohibited or set apart from the world, and second, because religion and ritual are two different categories. In his definition, ritual and religion were two sides of the same coin, in which ritual was essentially a form of expression, ordering, and socialization of religious beliefs in practice. Yet, Durkheim's reasoning about this question was not as monolithic it might seem at first glance, and it yielded fruitful insights. In particular, Durkheimian engagement with secular European nationalism carried the possibility of acknowledging the existence of secular rites of the nation, as later developed by his followers (Tsang, Rachel & Woods Eric Taylor 2014: 6-11). Marcel Mauss prominently took on this possibility not only when discussing the nation per se (2002a, 2002b), but also when developing Durkheim's premise to his own understanding of technique as not completely separate from ritual – a point well developed in his *Techniques of the Body* (2006).

According to this perspective, if religion was the primordial origin of social institutions, then the modern secular nation-state played the role of the church, and nationalist ideology would be therefore sacralized as a religion in a derivative form to that of religion itself. In this way, the state would be like a "church," or an institution organized to preserve the sacred and its most important expression, God. For Durkheim, however, in practice God was society itself. Thus, nationalist ideology substituted religious beliefs with logic itself as religious. Thus, military parades and marches, uniforms, national symbols, greetings, and other collective ideological expressions, such as those described in my account of the camp in Al-Jalil, would be examples of national secular rites embodied as techniques. When attached to religion or the nation, ritual had the capacity to alter the consciousness of participants, inducing or intensifying the connection among individuals, who then form a collective body existing beyond the sum of the individual participants. Durkheim (1954) called the condition generated by ritual a *collective effervescence*, and characterized it as a state that occurs when the subjects involved become more receptive to each other and open to suggestions emanating from this collective body thus formed or represented. This effervescence, in turn, generated *social solidarity* (a concept akin to what today we could call identity or social identification), and had the "function" of guaranteeing the group's conformity to norms. Such conformity, in turn, would be guaranteed because collective effervescence generated a sharing of meaning around "sacred objects," thereby creating a "collective consciousness." Today, Durkheimian assumptions, such as that rituals perform a function, that they only guarantee conformity to norms, and that religion is the original social institution, have been largely abandoned by anthropologists. However, his basic insights on the making and maintenance of the collective through rituals still stands.

After Durkheim's *The Elementary Forms of Religious Life*, normalization of the behavior of the masses ceased to be thought of as necessarily pathological and undesirable, as it was for Sigmund Freud (1989). It also ceased to be an argument against democracy, filled with prejudices against the masses, as it was for Gustave Le Bon (2009). The Durkheimian revolution permitted a positive understanding of the "generation of sacred feelings and the representation of collective practices producing and celebrating social solidarity and integration" (Tambiah: 1996, 303). Another important insight of Durkheim was that collective sentiments cannot be expressed except by obeying a certain order that permits movement cooperation and coordination, as with gestures and cries that tend to be rhythmic and regular in musical and dance expressions. Inspired by Durkheim, Tambiah also concludes that sacred symbols are hypostasiated collective ideals, that is, turned into "moral forces." In the same way, Al-Jalil residents implemented national flags, posters, sacred books, keys symbolizing "the Return," The Dome of the Rock, local plants (such as the olive tree), and other references to the nation through collective ritualization such as ceremonies, protests, and processions dynamically re-ordering reality (Tambiah 1996, 306).

With Tambiah, I assume that *collective effervescence* is one of the main forces making ritualization possible. Ritualization then acts as disciplinary practices that socialize group members, maximizing the shared dimension among the collective. This is a continuous and dynamic process in which collectivity is reproduced and recreated at every moment via plural and heterogeneous shared expressions, depending on the context and the subjects involved. Finally, I propose that ritualization only exists in the quotidian, since it entails by definition a routinization and a sacralization effort, conscious or not. In other words, without ritualization there would be no ritual.

Today, even though many of us tend to recognize the limits of the Durkheimian approach to religion and ritual, his insight about the sacred and the profane lives on, more or less adapted, in a number of seminal anthropological works. One of the most important examples is the stream of thought inaugurated by Leach and followed by Stanley Tambiah, which defined ritual mainly as a feature of communication. As early as the 1950s, Leach (2008, 1976, 1966) highlighted the necessity of thinking about the terms sacred and profane as situated on a *continuum* rather than existing as discrete domains. This simple nuance made possible the instrumentalization of the Durkheimian opposition to ritual analysis, without understanding this opposing pair necessarily as reiterating ritual moments hermetically closed and separated. In this way, we can think of ritual as a border maintenance and transformation mechanism between the sacred and the profane, as well as a localization and dislocation of subjects on a *continuum* between the two, always relative to context. In other words, ritual can be thought of as a process, and not necessarily constituting a sphere completely apart from the quotidian as in the original Durkheimian thought. Fredrik Barth was perhaps the best-known anthropologist to rely on Leach's understanding and develop it further.

In this sense, as at least the Al-Jalil case demonstrates and as I will further argue in the following chapter, ritualization is best understood as the inscription of the sacred in the quotidian and as attributive of meaning to mundane life. This sacralization, in turn, involved religious as much as political and ethnic elements all strongly attached to a conception of Palestinianness that was, in part, consciously mobilized and negotiated, and partly an entailment of disciplinary practices incorporated as entailments of socialization, in which previous ritual iterations themselves loomed large. In other words, ritualization and sacralization were implications of the effort, partially conscious and partially embodied, to re-appropriate Palestinianness, to regain control over the lives and destinies of the Palestinian collective. Thus, everyday suffering was at the same time an entailment of *al-Nakba* and the possibility of liberation (*taḥrīr*), as I will explore in more depth in the next chapter. The time of the refuge was liminal. Everyday suffering, inextricably tied to Palestinianness and refugeeness, was then sacralized through the local ritual tempo. However, sacralization and the ritualized expression of Palestinianness were not simply contrasted with a mundane time of the quotidian, especially since after more than 65 years of refugeeness and no hope of settlement on the political horizon, the liminality of the Palestinian protracted refugee was also concomitantly experienced as permanent and intrinsic, as Diana Allen sees it (2014). There existed a paradox according to which the condition of the refugee was experienced as liminal and at the same time permanent. The possibility of change, that is, of making Palestinian collective identity intact once more, was given only through al-'Awda (The Return), which was generally lived as much as an unachievable utopia as the only possible practical solution in which hope could be deposited. In Al-Jalil, as well as in Dbayeh, the sacred did not entail solely religious symbols, and sacralization did not turn the quotidian into a purely religious experience. However, the work of ritualization contributed to the spread of religious values, symbols, practices, and experiences in the quotidian of the refugees. Such religiosity was thus experienced in consonant with values, symbols, and practices springing from other sources, such as nationhood, ethnicity, and politics. Religiosity was therefore a component of the quotidian, sometimes expressed consciously and sometimes surreptitiously embodied in people's feelings, thoughts, and actions. Once more in the words of Asad:

> Ritual in the sense of a sacred performance cannot be the place where religious faith is attained, but the manner in which it is (literally) played out. If we are to understand how this happens, we must examine not only the sacred performance itself but also the entire range of available disciplinary activities, of institutional forms of knowledge and practice, within which dispositions are formed and sustained and through which the possibilities of attaining the truth are marked out - as Augustine clearly saw. (Asad 1993: 50)

In the preceding chapters, I have shown how knowledge pertaining to social belonging was generated and transmitted through the ritual tempo of each camp. So far, I aimed first and foremost to point out the ways in which shared experiences created, maintained, and transformed sociality in the two refugee camps. Next, I will progressively descend to the level of interpersonal relations to look at ritualization in more detail. In the following chapter, I will elucidate the subtle ways in which religiosity is embedded in the everyday life of Palestinian refugees in Lebanon, beyond scripted theology, through the sacralization of the quotidian. Finally, Chapter 7 will tackle ritualization of the quotidian at the level of interpersonal relations, demonstrating how different individuals made sense of and engaged a ritual tempo in different ways.

Chapter 6: *Al-ṣumūd*:
Sacralization and Ritualization of Palestinianness

a. Palestinian Steadfastness as a Mission

In Al-Jalil, the sacralization of Palestinianness was a key component of the ritualization of the quotidian. This chapter contributes to the broad discussion of the possibility of treating religion as a general anthropological category (rather than as brought about by anthropologists' interlocutors), as epitomized by the Clifford Geertz-Talal Asad debate.[1] As we have seen, in both Al-Jalil and Dbayeh religion and nationhood were interwoven and embedded in each other, reinforcing Asad's critique of Geertz' hermeneutical approach. As a result, at least in this case, labeling certain phenomena as simply "religious," isolating and studying them in relation to other such phenomena, is not as constructive as analyzing them in relation to the broader social context. Being a Palestinian refugee in Lebanon, whatever the context, was not only evocative of meaning, but also a moral and existential imperative from which much is derived.

In Al-Jalil and Dbayeh, the Palestinian nation became infused with moral perceptions and values, which in turn often came to be infused with religion. Generally speaking, in the Palestinian refugee camps in Lebanon, *the Palestinian cause* tended to be sacralized and collectively upheld as a mission, thereby contributing to ritualization dynamics in most camps. One of the most common vehicles for this sacralization was the idea of ṣumūd (steadfastness; resistance), which often infused the cause with religious undertones (Schiocchet 2013). Apart from the notion of *al-ṣumūd*, *istashhād* (martyrdom) also tended to sacralize the Palestinian cause and consequently Palestinianness itself. This sacralization, in turn, was firmly tied to the Palestinian

---

1   See especially (Geertz 1973) and (Asad 1993)

time framing processes first presented in *Chapter 2*. While elusive in practice, *ṣumūd* tended to play an important role in the group's processes of belonging. With *ṣumūd*, an Islamic divine attribute,[2] and *ṣāmid* (plural, *ṣāmidyn*), a derived term that denotes the subject who possesses the qualities of *ṣumūd*, many Palestinian refugees indexed the framing of time as Islamic praxis. Through the concept of *ṣumūd*, this chapter discusses the refugee camp environment and its influence on social belonging processes of sacralization and ritualization of the quotidian.

Here, thus, comes yet another point in which my analysis is seemingly similar yet diverges considerably from that of Khalili's *Heroes and Martyrs of Palestine* (2007). Khalili understands *ṣumūd* as a "narrative form" distinct from "heroism" and "suffering" (ibid: 214), whereas I do not think that considering them distinct, even just as ideal types, helps to understand the Palestinian experience of *ṣumūd*. To her, the narrative of suffering "makes suffering itself a virtue, and denies the possibility of agency, mobilization or collective action" (ibid: 224). As I understood from my own fieldwork, however, *ṣumūd* was generally much entangled with suffering and heroism, and even when not relating to *ṣumūd*, suffering could also be a form of agency, albeit one not characterized by resistance, similar to what Saba Mahmood describes in *Politics of Piety* (2005). In practice, however, *ṣumūd* was not just a form of nationalist narrative, but it became an idea prompting dispositions, affects, and sensibilities, more or less embodied in the subjects depending on context and case.

b.   Dbayeh and Al-Jalil in Perspective

Refugees' experiences of religion offer fertile ground for academic investigation, arguably as much as relations between the refugees and extraneous and communitarian religious institutions. However, the former remains relatively unexplored by scholars. In Al-Jalil and Dbayeh, proselytizing religious missions are very rare. Religious institutions mobilize camp residents towards pious behavior instead, encompassing moral conceptions of the self and, more so in Al-Jalil, political activism. This does not mean that religion is lived in the same way by Palestinian refugees everywhere. My own fieldwork experiences among Palestinians in Denmark, Brazil, and Austria, when compared

---

2   In Islam, *Ṣamad*, meaning lord, eternal, or everlasting, is an epithet of God. Both *Ṣamad* and *ṣumūd* derive meaning from the same root "ص" - "م" - "د".

to Lebanon, suggest that the refugee camp plays an important role as a symbolic center of refugee life and in generating and maintaining steadfastness (Schiocchet 2014b). Moreover, engagement with what Oliver Roy (2004) calls "Islamic neo-fundamentalist movements"[3] (such as transnational Salafi networks) was more widespread among Palestinians in Denmark and Lebanon (albeit not in Dbayeh and very little in Al-Jalil). However, such religious groups did not tend to appeal to a largely secularized and demotivated group of Palestinian refugees from Iraq resettled in Brazil, or the older generations of Palestinians living in Austria.

In the Danish case, where Palestinian migrants lived in Gellerupparken – a ghettoized neighborhood of Aarhus – alongside Kurds, Somalis, Iraqis, and other Muslims, Islam was more a part of the language of social belonging than in the other contexts more deeply marked by Palestinian national themes. A large shack in front of the residential compound of Gellerupparken, called Bazar Vest, supplied the community with produce, work, and community life, while two mosques served as spiritual centers. In Aarhus, not only did Palestinians have to share a ghetto-like area with other Muslim minorities, but many among the local Danish population also had a tendency to stigmatize all Muslims, underplaying discrete ethnic or national categories of belonging. By underplaying such differences and concomitantly homogenizing Muslims as a coherent group, the Danish context imposed Islam as a primary category of identification for Palestinians and other Muslim minorities in Denmark. Thus, the local centers of these immigrants' sociality became more associated with religious and economic activities than with folklore or nationhood, thereby favoring second generation immigrants' identification with transnational Islamic movements at the expense of Palestinian national movements.

This process did not occur to the same extent in Austria,[4] where Palestinians mainly arrived in the 1970s, as students rather than refugees, establishing themselves as liberal professionals such as doctors, dentists, and lawyers, and engaging with secular leftist civil society in political, cultural, and social

---

3   To Roy (2004), Islamic neo-fundamentalism is characterized by the intent to purify Islam from politics (such as Al-Qaeda and Daesh), as opposed to political Islam – or the so-called Islamists – which is characterized by the engagement with politics (such as Hezbollah or Hamas).

4   However, the great influx of Afghan and Syrian refugees (among the latter, many Palestinians) in 2015 and to a lesser extent still in 2016, quickly started to change the Austrian context, which became more similar to that of Denmark.

terms. Palestinianness in Austria was thus reinforced by Austrian activists themselves, who had their own understanding of the Palestinian cause and were not interested in religion. This relationship started already during the times of Chancellor Bruno Kreisky, who was – willingly or not - directly responsible for the PLO's legitimization as the sole representative of the Palestinians outside of the Arab world,[5] and opened the path for the shaping of the Palestinian cause as a universal, secular, and mainly socialist agenda among the European Left.

In Brazil, neo-fundamentalism and religious orthodoxy also did not appeal much to the minds of a group of initially 114 Palestinian refugees fleeing Iraq, nor to the older generations of Palestinians who had arrived in Brazil already during the first half of the twentieth century (Schiocchet 2019). Almost all the Palestinian refugees from the group resettled there in 2007 came from the Rwayshed refugee camp in Jordan, where they were initially placed following their persecution in Iraq after the fall of Saddam Hussein in 2003. Almost all these refugees were Muslims, with the exception of one family. Moreover, almost all of them, including the Christian family, tended to praise Hussein as a great secular and popular leader, many having been directly employed in the Iraqi governmental machine run by the Ba'ath party. This connection came about especially because Saddam Hussein himself branded the Palestinian cause his own, rallying against Syria during the Lebanese civil war, and treating the few Palestinians in Iraq with positive distinction. This, in turn, reinforced Palestinianness over religion, especially given that many of the forces opposing Hussein mobilized an Islamic rhetoric. Moreover, prior to their settling in Brazil, there were already strong disagreements within the group that had lived in Rwayshed. In Brazil, interaction was much diminished due to a lack of common space, and consequently the group cannot be said to have formed a community per se. Some were initially drawn to connect to Palestinians who had been living in Brazil for several generations, an encounter first facilitated by the Palestinian Arab Federation of Brazil (FEPAL). These early generations of Palestinians in Brazil arrived mostly between the end of the nineteenth and the first half of the twentieth century, alongside Lebanese and Syrian entrepreneurs.[6] Conflicts erupted between the old and new groups to the extent that, within a couple years, only a handful of the

---

5   Inside the Arab world, the main figure responsible for legitimizing the PLO was Gamal Abdel Nasser.

6   Many in this group were Christians.

Rwayshed refugees remained around the Palestinian cultural and political centers in Brazil, while most of the others were cut off even from humanitarian aid networks. In this way, belonging was not collectively articulated around a refugee camp or any symbolic Palestinian space, but Palestinianness remained a key element to most individuals composing the group.

In Al-Jalil, "Islamist" movements mixing Islamic vernacular expressions with nationalist rhetoric (such as Hamas or the Islamic Jihad) tended to be preferred over "purified" religious identities purged of national content (Roy 2004). I suggest that the camps' historical and geographical context, located in Shi'a dominated territory, under the grip of Lebanese Shi'a movements and the Syrian government but also culturally influenced by their surroundings, was decisive in shaping this tendency in Al-Jalil, as presented in *Chapter 2*. Moreover, as we have seen in *Chapter 4*, Christianity in Dbayeh did tend to frame the language of social belonging as well, albeit not alone, and more by way of social belonging processes than religious piety. Thus, in Denmark, Austria, and Brazil, collective and individual expressions of *ṣumūd* took different shades from those expressed in Al-Jalil, Dbayeh, and the other Palestinian refugee camps in Lebanon. However, virtually all the Palestinian refugees with whom I interacted, whether in Al-Jalil, Dbayeh, Denmark, Austria, Brazil, or elsewhere, in one way or another associated their present suffering with the time framing tendency described in *Chapter 2*. Furthermore, they often framed the act of enduring the present through the concept of *al-ṣumūd*.

Refugees are stripped of citizenship rights. Citizenship is supplanted by dispossession and displacement, making nationhood (or its absence) an imperative shaping the refugee experience.[7] This, in turn, tends to profoundly shape the experience of life in general. Religion, ethnicity, and much else besides, even when not the initial cause of flight, tend to be infused with nationhood and humanness, whether through nationalism and humanitarianism or not. The refugee experience, however, is diverse. Comparing two groups of Hutu refugees in Tanzania, one living in a refugee camp in an urban area and the other living outside the refugee camp, Malkki came to the conclusion that the refugee experience varies even among the Hutu themselves, and that the juridical category *refugee* has serious limitations due to its universalist approach and practical design. As in Malkki's *Purity and Exile* (1995), this chapter shows the plurality of the refugee experience, but also suggests that Palestinianness, albeit plural, should be treated as a single arena of negotiation,

---

7   Or, as Malkki puts it, "the national order of things" (1995).

where widespread tendencies shape social belonging and the refugee experience in various ways. Rather than being approached as unique and random accounts, the case studies presented here are better understood as variations underscored by dominant tendencies of a shared but diverse subjunctive. The peculiar Palestinian tendency to frame time as presented in *Chapter 2* is generally compelling, while different subjects (both individuals and groups) engage it differently according to context. In other words, a critical event (*Nakba*) and a utopian turnout of events (*al-'awda*), disposed in temporal sequence, unite the historical past with a moral mythical future, and locate a highly varied present Palestinian refugee experience within these terms. This present tends to be experienced minimally through a condition of passive resistance and moral commitment to whatever is perceived as "the cause" (*al-qadiyya*), which is often partially expressed through the idiom of *ṣumūd*, as I will develop in the remainder of this chapter. This formula, however, is not to be taken normatively, but only as a widespread tendency in the Palestinian refugee camps in Lebanon, actualized through unique iterations there and beyond, yet generally evocative of the elements described above. Furthermore, the fact that some Palestinians chose to distance themselves from Palestinianness, as I found in some cases both in Denmark and in Dbayeh, does not necessarily mean that Palestinianness is perceived differently by these subjects, only that their self-ascription is focused elsewhere.

c.   Existence as Resistance

In practice as much as in discourse, the broadest understanding of Palestinianness among refugees is embodied by a shared experience of loss and the condition of exile to which they are subjected. Faced with more than six decades of displacement, Palestinian refugees are haunted by fears of the effacement of their properties, rights, lifestyles, and, more importantly, their own identity. Such fears mark their understanding of themselves, which in turn frame their engagement with the world. The fear of self-effacement also leads to an idealization of one's own existence as resistance. Within Palestinian refugee camps in general, being a refugee is one more element reinforcing the equation "existence = resistance" as an attribute of Palestinianness – an equation present in peoples' discourses, rally signs, songs, etc.

The "existence=resistance" equation defines the type of passive resistance that characterizes the idea of *ṣumūd* as opposed to, for example, *muqāwama*, which is a more active (and often armed) form of resistance. Palestinian refugees tend to feel and say they are *maḥrumīn* (dispossessed). Their shared experience of dispossession makes them *maḥrumīn* and at the same time turns their mundane, quotidian routines into acts of resistance. Through language, folklore, and practices such as those described earlier, they insist on their dream of living the plenitude of their Palestinianness – that is, being Palestinian without the attached stigma of the term and the practical impediments that it engenders. The most pressing of these impediments is the refugee condition. Thus, there is an implicit (and sometimes explicit) understanding that living as a refugee automatically entails being *ṣāmid* but does not necessarily entail participation in the *muqāwama*.

All *ṣāmidīn* Palestinians are also considered martyrs of *al-Qadiyya al-Falastyniyya* upon death – not only according to the discourse of the political parties and social movements, but also in popular understanding. However, participation in a martyrdom operation, whether independent or organized by an Islamist or secular political group, generally awards the participant more social capital and thereby adds to his/her Palestinianness. Today, this differentiation has even caused a modification in colloquial Arabic usage, introducing the new term *istishhādy*[8] to refer to a martyr that deliberately seeks martyrdom, as opposed to *shahīd*, a martyr in a more general sense.

d. Al-ṣumūd in Context

Despite the contemporary tendency to inscribe *ṣumūd* into the quotidian through often-embodied Islamic praxis,[9] the concept also has a more "secular" history, as evidenced by the PLO's usage of the term. This emphasizes that to live as a refugee and to insist on being solely Palestinian, for example, through celebrating Palestinian food or dance, is already an important form of resistance against the perceived imperialist objectives of Israel. However, even among the Palestinian Christians or Marxists I met, for whom Islam did not define the terms of their vernacular politics, *ṣumūd* conceptions were still influenced by the sacredness that the term holds in Islam. This is partially because even the PLO's framing of the Palestinian cause, which popularized the general usage of the term *ṣumūd* in Palestinian cultural and

---

8   For more on this, read Nasser Abufarha's *The Making of the Human Bomb* (2009).
9   I understand Islam more broadly as a culture, so in this case even the understanding of most Christian Palestinians is somehow tied to an Islamic definition and popularization of the concept.

political dialects, consciously or unconsciously borrowed many of its acmes from Islamic culture.

Ṣumūd is not always a driving force in Palestinian refugee's lives. In Dbayeh, for instance, I found that although the idea of *ṣumūd* was still present, especially in the older generation's discourses, it was not particularly important for younger people and did not define either generation's social practices. Among the most important reasons for *ṣumūd*'s effacement from the discourse and practice of young people in Dbayeh was that most of these youths did not define themselves unambiguously as "Palestinian" due to the camp's specific historical context.

The fact that older people, who still tended to define themselves unambiguously as Palestinian, continued to assign great importance to the idea of *ṣumūd*, attests to the generalized indexation of Palestinianness through the subjects' commitment to being *ṣāmid*. Furthermore, in Dbayeh, the older generation's social practices did not reflect a *ṣāmid* posture as much as those of older generations in other Palestinian refugee camps in Lebanon. This relates to the difference between their identity discourses and their social practices and it can be explained by their lack of hope of returning to their now changed homeland, and the consequent tentative accommodation of their lives to a foreign environment, all the while maintaining a stereotyped discourse of Palestinianness. Thus, for this specific group in Dbayeh being Palestinian had more to do with how they lived their lives in the past than with how they lived in the present of my ethnographic fieldwork. In contrast, younger generations in the same camp tended to define their own identity through their present engagement with their Lebanese surroundings and the largely Lebanese composition of the camp itself.

The Palestinian time framing intimately interwoven with the concept of *al-ṣumūd* was historically generated and maintained within the context of the secular activism of a Muslim majority, but by the time of my fieldwork its vernacular language was becoming ever more Islamized. It was precisely in those cases where *ṣumūd* was an essential component of social practice and discourse that I found a broader tendency toward the hyper-expression of identity, leading to the ritualization of the quotidian. The ritualization process discussed throughout the book so far, and thus the ritual analysis I developed in the previous chapter, are based on the Palestinian social belonging process I witnessed while in the field, and which was firmly tied to variations of the abovementioned Palestinian framing of time.

e.   Resistance, Martyrdom and Ritualization

Al-Jalil had two sheiks, one affiliated with Fatah and the other with Hamas. They disputed authority and favor with political leaders, local Palestinians working for UNRWA, and local Palestinian associations at times partially funded by international NGOs. The camp's mosque played a central role in articulating public life in Al-Jalil. This was also a political role, as it tended to publicly meddle in politics on what could be considered common ground among the local political factions. The sheiks there tended to preach attachment to the Palestinian Cause, fomenting *ṣumūd*, martyrdom, and other forms of "resistance," and to mediate local disputes. They did this while promoting Islamic values and rooting their messages in an ideal of Palestinianness. The mosque's capillarity in daily life was very wide, as it organized public and private collective rituals such as funerals, weddings, daily prayers, as well as religious and even national ceremonies. As with authority and favor, however, the mosque shared many of these quotidian tasks with political leaders and social activists. UNRWA's influence was mainly felt publicly through the large school it ran in Al-Jalil, although many of its teachers were at odds with several UN positions regarding the Palestinian situation. In this way, both humanitarian and religious agents had to at once dispute and share influence with political leaders.

While the mosque played the call to prayer and sermons, political offices frequently played military marches as party hymns, whereas local foundations typically preferred Palestinian *dabke* or nationalist singers and poets such as Marcel Khalife[10] or Mahmud Darwish. In some cases, there could be a confluence of the two types of music, as when, for example, the headquarters of Fatah al-Intifada lent a large empty room in its office for local youth *dabke* rehearsals. As developed in *Chapter 3*, along with the sound density of the music, and the visual density of the posters and graffiti, the streets of the camp contained a multitude of people carrying their own personal charms. Necklaces, t-shirts, rings, wristbands, and other paraphernalia accompanied discourses with political, moral, and religious undertones, reproducing and disseminating Palestinianness throughout the public space of the camp in everyday life. What I witnessed in Al-Jalil was a hyper-expression of Palestinianness, which I understood to be highly associated with the imperative of national belonging

---

10   Marcel Khalife is a Lebanese singer and oud player, known for praising Palestine in some of his songs.

through the group's refugee condition, reinforced by the instigating environment of the camp. Even personal celebrations such as birthdays, marriages
and funerals were often flooded with nationalist expressions. At a marriage,
for example, it was common to hear speeches describing how committed a
Palestinian was the groom. At a funeral, a Palestinian flag, that of a political
party, or both would cover the deceased's coffin as a sign of moral rectitude.

In the celebration of an 'amaliyya istishhādiyya (martyrdom operation),
the istishhādy was different from the shahīd. Although any death could inspire
national feelings, the primary purpose of celebrating an istishhādy was to instill a shared sense of Palestinianness that tended to be experienced as sacred,
and to create a specific political effect, i.e., if not another istishhādy, then at
least ṣumūd (steadfastness) among the community. It is precisely in this entailment of generating and maintaining ṣumūd ritually – something akin to
Benedict Anderson's ideas on map, museum and census (1 9 8 3) – that I see
the basic general structural similarity between calendric and extraordinary
collective celebrations in Palestinian contexts, including the Al-Jalil refugee
camp and many others. As a result of the values instilled by these events and
the consequent establishment of an ideal Palestinian posture, it was common
to attribute moral value to a person's life depending on how "active" (nashaṭ)
they were in the Palestinian cause. The measure of one's commitment was in
terms of degrees of a ṣāmid posture – the istishhādy was generally considered
to have the highest level of commitment, while the collaborationist/traitor
invariably had the lowest.

As previously noted, the pace of daily life in Al-Jalil, as in most other Palestinian refugee camps in Lebanon[11] and the Occupied Territories, contained
the same ritual properties that were found in the circuits of celebrations described above. Like in Al-Jalil, the ritual tempo of other camps also tended to
instill Palestinianness and ṣumūd in the quotidian, mundane life. Perhaps the
most pervasive of this tempo's ritual properties was the instilment and dis-
semination of ṣumūd among the participants, and its frequent attribution as a
measure of Palestinianness. In fact, Al-Jalil's high level of ritualization in daily
life can be greatly attributed to the value of ṣumūd, which drove individuals
and groups to a hyper-expression of their personal and collective selves.

---

11   Urban, open, mixed, and often larger camps such as Shatila tended to be less cohesive
and thus less ritualized than other camps with a stronger sense of community and
tighter communal life.

f.   Sacralization and Ritualization of the Quotidian

Since the end of the 1980s, social movements and political parties explicitly characterized as "Islamic" have been gaining momentum in the Palestinian political and social landscape, as well as in other Middle Eastern countries. Islam has been increasingly incorporated into the nationalist, political, ethnic, and moral language in two different ways: first, as a rejection of discourses and practices seen as non-Islamic and their substitution with those seen as Islamic; and second, as the Islamization of discourses and practices that once were perceived as secular. Following this trend, the concept of *ṣumūd*, developed as a secular praxis although with inspiration from Islamic culture, has become increasingly inscribed into an Islamic praxis by Muslims, in the same way that political activism and Palestinian resistance have been increasingly conflated with Islamic resistance. While still mobilizing the discourse of *ṣumūd*, if not by mentioning the word, by supporting the existence=resistance formula, many Dbayeh Palestinian Christians expressed to me that this was one of the main reasons for their discontent with the Palestinian political scenario today, and why some no longer dream of returning to Palestine. Thus, niches exist whereby *ṣumūd* is not re-Islamized and the concept – as well as the "resistance" itself – continues to be expressed primarily in secular discourses, despite its religious undertones. In this way, *ṣumūd* continued to instill a moral sense of obligation to the Palestinian cause in the Christian camp Dbayeh, even among individual cases in which it was more a feature of rhetoric than a moral imperative.

As Olivier Roy explains structural radicalization in France, it is not the "radicalization of Islam," but the "Islamization of radicalism" (Roy January 7, 2016). Even though the contexts are vastly different, Roy's turn of phrase encapsulates the trend towards the moralization of Palestinian resistance in the refugee camps in Lebanon, and its deeper engagement with Islam as a vernacular for expression, more so than as a motivation for action in itself. While political resistance has become increasingly associated with Muslim resistance in many Palestinian contexts, what makes the concept of *ṣumūd* particularly susceptible to Islamization is that historically *ṣumūd* is one of the divine attributes, and *Ṣamad* His epithet. It is possible to find in the *Qur'an* and in the *Sunna* direct justification for the necessity of a *ṣāmid* posture and for the maintenance of its sacred meaning. In Lebanon, the term was frequently associated with divine attributes, such as "will" and "power." Given that most Palestinian political activists were Muslim and some at least somewhat pious, and given that Islam was also a cultural reference beyond religious praxis, the majority of Palestinian political activists ascribed Islamic connotations to the meaning of ṣumūd.

Even more pervasively, the concept of ṣumūd allows all Palestinians to feel and be recognized as *foci* of resistance. Thus, a considerable number of Palestinians, especially among refugees and inhabitants of the Occupied Territories, derive meaning in their lives, at least in part, from the idea of ṣumūd. This, in turn, confers to ṣumūd a variable measure of sacredness dependent on the subject in question. This sacredness may be Islamic or only a referent to the sacralization of the polyphonic idea of the Palestinian cause. Either way, as the mission is sacred, the subject invested in it can be compared to a missionary, and the propensity to advocate "the cause" as a form of proselytization is strong, even in cases where the cause is not directly infused with religious values.

In the case of the Palestinians living in most of the refugee camps in Lebanon, the social, territorial, and identity confinement to which they were subjected evoked and reinforced Palestinianness even in the most mundane of quotidian tasks. As with all things relating to the sacred, ṣumūd involved certain obligations while it gave meaning and legitimization to the subjects' actions and conceptions. Because the subjects invested with ṣumūd turned their own existence into something sacred, daily routines were by extension sacralized. Thus, enduring the hardships of the camp, the pain of dispossession, or the suffering of loss, separation, and prejudice became a moral imperative, a sacred mission in the name of Palestinianness. Sacralization was in turn an integral part of a process by which the quotidian became ritualized.

g.   Time and ṣumūd

I observed a general commitment among Palestinians to search for the possibility of living the plenitude of an ideal Palestinianness that could be found in a future that included a return to a pre-*Nakba* past. This commitment was then translated into a steadfast posture (ṣāmid), which was directed toward the Palestinian cause (or *al-niḍāl al-falastyny* – the Palestinian struggle) sacralizing the present, and thus the quotidian. The utopian objective of the cause was understood more generally – and almost independently of political orientation, and thus of the means in which it was employed – as *al-'awda* (the return). The return, however, was understood not as much as a practical aim (and many in fact did not want to "go back" to Palestine) as a collective ideal.

In this way, *al-ḥaqq al-'awda* (the right of return) was invested with exceptional meaning, inspiring social action and worldviews among groups of Palestinian refugees and individuals in Lebanon and elsewhere.

The present was thus understood twofold: first, as a temporary aberration to be abolished with "the return" (often through "the right of return"); and second, as an almost ineluctable but also unacceptable condition determining Palestinian fate – a "realistic" conception also motivating present agency, identity, and social organization. Only through *amal* (hope) and *imān* (faith), both directed toward the Palestinian cause and God, could the present predicament be escaped. Frequently, through the amalgamation of hope and faith, not believing in the Palestinian cause became synonymous with not believing in God, which gave the cause considerable impetus. The present was at the same time composed of repeated emulations of what Palestinians perceived as the Palestinian past, and a repudiated time to be suspended by advancing into a future idealized according to that ideal past. Performing Palestinianness unrestrictedly, that is, to be a Palestinian as one is supposed to have been in the times before the Nakba, or supposed to be to reach the subjunctive utopia, represented an important way of transcending the present. In this way, time folded within itself.

The refugee condition occupied much of the lives of Palestinians in Al-Jalil, Dbayeh, and camps elsewhere, as their refugee status locks the present within an idealized past and a future utopia mirrored in that past. This subjunctive and embodied framing of time constituted a force which compelled individuals to collectively articulate their existential condition through ritualized practices deployed in the quotidian. As we have seen, ritualization was more prevalent and overt in Al-Jalil than in Dbayeh. It tended to occur more frequently and to have more profound effects in camp environments that were closed off from their geographical and social surroundings, as Palestinian refugee camps in Lebanon tend to be for a variety of reasons. Dbayeh camp residents lacked the social practice of *ṣumūd* and other ritualized activities common in Al-Jalil, mainly because Palestinianness was not as fervently celebrated as it was in Al-Jalil and other camps. Yet, even for these residents, calling upon the rhetoric o f *ṣumūd* in the public sphere was still important, especially when faced with other Palestinian refugees, UNRWA, or international NGOs. The basic idea that living as a refugee was a form of resistance was still pervasive in Dbayeh, although this resistance was not as often associated with ideas as broad as the Palestinian cause or the Palestinian struggle. Instead, it was often framed as pertaining to the Dbayeh community, or Palestinian Christians at large. This praxis observed in Dbayeh, however, did not necessarily break the general linkages between a Palestinian ideal of ṣumūd and the ritualization of the present. Although different contexts generated certain internal differences in how Palestinianness was conceived of and lived, these differences did not completely interrupt the subjunctive Palestinian framing of time, but instead disputed iterations contributing to its dynamic. In the particular case of Dbayeh, it was not so much Palestinianness that changed, but the residents' own ambiguous attachment to it.

In contrast, the ritual tempo in Al-Jalil was firmly anchored in variations of this Palestinian framing of time, which was largely propelled by the embodiment and performance of ṣumūd. Overall, even when ritualization was weak or non-existent, as among Dbayeh residents, I still found iterations that characterized the present as a "time within time." While the performance of ṣumūd was not as prevalent in Dbayeh,[12] it fueled the sacralization and ritualization of daily life in most of the refugee camps in Lebanon.

h.   Point of No Return

Even among Palestinians who did not actually wish to "go back" to Palestine, in most cases one could still find this general way of conceiving of time, marked by the pre-*Nakba* past, the aberrant present, and the rightful return as defining features of Palestinianness. Among these individuals and groups, the professed unwillingness to return to Palestine tended to appear as though it had caused them to split from the group in terms of their life choices and trajectories, but not in terms of their Palestinianness or the commitment to the general right of choosing the Return or not. This held true in Dbayeh.

Every camp had its own specificities, as Al-Jalil was different from 'Ayn al-Helweh, Beddawy, al-Buss, Shatila, Mar Elias, and others. However, as demonstrated in *Chapter 4*, Dbayeh was different in an exceptional way. It was perceived as unique to the extent that most Palestinian refugees who actually knew of its existence would state that Dbayeh was not a Palestinian refugee camp. The most important differences included: the complete absence of Palestinian political parties, social movements, and charitable organizations; the absence of Palestinian clergy in the two local churches despite a long-standing demand for a Palestinian priest; the perceived lack of commitment to the Palestinian cause and thus the lack of ṣumūd; the isolation of the camp

---

12   Or in Shatila.

from others; the supposed higher standard of living of Dbayeh inhabitants; and, last but not least, the fact that virtually the entire camp was Christian. All these elements were mutually reinforcing and understood in conjunction with each other. Thus, other Palestinian groups frequently resorted to stripping Dbayeh's social space and its inhabitants of their Palestinianness.

Despite the apparent lack of *ṣumūd* in Dbayeh when compared to other camps in Lebanon, it is not religion alone (or even mainly) that explains its historical difference. Instead, the lack of *ṣumūd* corresponded more to the absence of Palestinian *tanẓimāt* (political organizations), since Dbayeh was located in an area that since the 1970s had been controlled by Lebanese Christian political parties overtly hostile to Palestinian refugee presence in Lebanon. As a consequence, the camp was completely devoid of Palestinian institutions and developed a very specific socialization process, especially concerning younger generations. The fact that local religious leaders were Lebanese reinforced the symbolic linkage between Christianity and Lebanon at the same time that it weakened local feelings and expressions of Palestinianness. This situation was further exacerbated because a Lebanese Christian organization, Caritas Migration Center, was *de facto* in charge of most social services in the camp, while the UNRWA office there remained closed most of the time during the period of my field research.

Without the support of Palestinian institutions, and given their tendency to accuse the PLO and other Palestinian political institutions of neglect, Dbayeh inhabitants were not socialized to emphasize their Palestinianness over other identity traits. Consequently, most of the camp's inhabitants expressed no identification with Palestinian politics and claimed that they did not wish to return to Palestine. Given this historical context and the general ethos it shaped, Dbayeh inhabitants were not committed to the idealization of a future return (*al-'awda*) as a possibility to live the plenitude of their Palestinianness. This, in turn, influenced the general Palestinian framing of time in ways that were different than in Al-Jalil. Personal idealization of the future tended to be open-ended and dependent on individual and group will. While many simply wished to become Lebanese t h r o u g h *tawṭīn* (taking up a local citizenship) and refrained from a more collective Palestinian discourse, others still invoked the importance of the return as a collective solution while choosing another path for themselves and their families. As *tawṭīn* was seen as precisely the opposite of *ṣumūd*, others perceived the camp as less Palestinian, or not Palestinian at all. The most common explanation for this perception was that the camp residents were Christian, and not

Muslim. Hence the strength of the association between Islam and a ṣāmid posture, and between the Palestinian Cause as protected by Muslims, while not an Islamic cause in itself.

Although Dbayeh residents' Palestinianness was (rarely) publicly performed, their most pressing demands were localized, having to do with the future of the group and not necessarily with all Palestinians. Therefore, there was ṣumūd involved in this resistance, but although the Palestinian Cause was frequently part of the discourse, it was not exactly Palestinianness that was at stake. While they may have attributed the cause of their dispossession to being Palestinian, instead of demanding a solution to the Palestine question, they tended to demand a solution for their own, immediate problems. From the perspective of many Dbayeh's residents, tawṭīn was not necessarily the opposite of ṣumūd precisely because of this relegation of the Palestinian cause to much more circumscribed local civic goals. Y e t , Dbayeh residents were an outright target for the assumption that its members' lack of ṣumūd was associated with their religion.

Thus, there was a difference between the ṣumūd called upon in Al-Jalil and Dbayeh. Underlying this was the fact that Palestinian social institutions did not socialize the refugees in Dbayeh, and this group did not develop the same hyper-expression of Palestinianness as Al-Jalil inhabitants. Given the lack of a vibrant Palestinian public sphere through and against which to live their quotidian lives, identity maintenance was not as much marked by Palestinianness, and these refugees seemed to have slowed down their resistance in the name of their Palestinianness, albeit without disputing much how other refugees imagined, felt, and performed it.

i.   Religion and Popular Culture

Hyper-expression of Palestinianness, along with the sacralization and ritualization of the quotidian, are features characteristic of certain contexts marked by physical and social isolation and the stigmatization of a given group. These social traits only came about in the refugee camps of Lebanon through a socialization process very much influenced by Palestinian institutions, especially those of the PLO during the Lebanese Civil War, which made possible shared social characterization and social action. Among the most consequential elements in this socialization was a Palestinian time-framing tendency that tended to push Palestinians toward understanding their present condition as an aberration to be amended by a posture defined by ṣumūd and geared toward what was understood as the Palestinian cause. But even when Palestinians were disenfranchised, and socialization lacked the Palestinian apparatus, a general notion of Palestinianness still tended to involve certain key elements, such as the notion of the disaster as characterized by the *Nakba*, the abomination of the present Palestinian condition, and the utopian *'awda* (return), at least as a collective possibility independent of personal choice. Furthermore, present life as a refugee tended to be lived, at least to some measure, as resistance against an existence of suffering associated with the refugee condition, which, in turn, was associated with Palestinianness. While refugeeness is not circumscribed to Palestinianness, nationhood, often infused with religious undertones, made the experience of the present unique in the Palestinian contexts I analyze in this book.

To conclude, the complex intricacies of the concept of *ṣumūd* and its local social expressions tend to be conceived in relation to the Palestinian cause as a sacred mission, a duty to all Palestinians, and a binding trait of Palestinianness (Schiocchet, 2015b). I have shown here that labeling certain phenomena simply as "religious" to isolate and study them mainly in relation to other such phenomena, is not, at least in this case, as constructive as analyzing the religious components of social belonging processes and expressions in light of the broader context of Palestinian refugeeness. This conclusion corroborates that of Stanley Tambiah (1979; 1996), who proposed approaching the study of ritual and religion in a way that resembles that of "popular culture." The conceptualization and expression of *ṣumūd* in Al-Jalil and Dbayeh was not bound to the religious realm, but was instead inextricably tied to the broader social conditions, which in this case is especially the condition of refugeeness and the utopia Palestinians have devised around making it surmountable. Thus, similarly to what Tambiah observed in the context of ethnoreligious clashes in the Indian subcontinent (1996), among Palestinian refugees in Lebanon religion is ineluctably tied to identity politics, while suffering and coping strategies are experienced through a religiosity not detached from the quotidian, but embedded in the present.

Chapter 7: Economies of Trust

Economic entrustment is not neatly distinguishable from ritual, symbolic, or spiritual entrustment. (Shipton 2007: 215) Some of these forms of entrustment make up part of reproductive, ritual, and symbolic life, and people feel strongly about them (...) These are dealings and sentiments. (Shipton 2007: xi)

The Marxist thesis is that the activities of the secular market – where all values are supposed to be measured by the strictest cannon of rationality – judgments are in fact influenced by mystical non-rational criteria. A full generation later, Mauss (in The Gift), developing his theory of gift exchange from an entirely differently viewpoint, reached an identical conclusion. Exchanges that appear to be grounded in secular, rational, utilitarian needs, turn out to be compulsory acts of a ritual kind in which the objects exchanged are the vehicles of mystical power. (Leach in Hugh-Jones & Laidlaw 2000: 167-68)

Chapter 1 described a generalized disposition toward suspicion as an imperative for social belonging and organization in Al-Jalil and Dbayeh. It also hinted at ritualized economies of trust embedded in interpersonal interactions, constituting a strong force shaping the way the refugees interacted among themselves and with outsiders. This chapter argues that each camp developed unique and distinct economies of trust, as they reflected the broader contexts informing each camp's ritual tempo. Trust and suspicion were rarely absolute, and this absence of certitude made subjects at once trust yet suspect contextually, and entrustments were bound to morality as much as to conscious negotiation. Thus, such economies of trust were disciplinary practices – and, as such, largely ritualized - shaping the boundaries of different categories of subjects, influencing in turn the making, maintenance, and transformation of groups' constituencies and alliances. While all contexts have their own economies of trust, cultural elements and local contexts marked some of the specific ways in which trust was negotiated in each of the refugee camps.

Moreover, this chapter aims to demonstrate, through the language of interpersonal relations, how religion, among other variables such as nationalism and ethnicity, influenced refugees' social belonging processes, notably through daily expressions of belonging and social organization. In this way, the chapter supports my argument that religion in itself cannot be simplistically held accountable for the camps' different social dynamics, while making a more general case for how suspicion and trust tend to define the lives of refugees and other liminal subjects.

Largely consisting of disciplinary practices, economies of trust were yet another form of ritualized expression contributing to the rhythms of daily life in both camps, alongside other expressions presented throughout the book. The distinctive property of trust as currency in many ritualized practices made economies of trust pervasive features of Al-Jalil and Dbayeh's ritual tempi, and were recurrently found to underpin interpersonal interactions. For example, while political rallies were demarcated in time and space, economies of trust were embedded in almost all aspects of daily life, being thus a form of ritualization of social interactions, following relatively loose and malleable scripts, and characterized by a relatively lower level of formalization and normativity than the public celebrations described in the previous chapters. Yet, it is precisely the embeddedness of these elements in a broader context – as indicated by Tambiah's example of rioting crowds' and other authors' interpersonal relational understandings of rituals (1996) – that gives meaning to life, creating a sense of belonging, evoking salient identities and inspiring collective commitment to patterns of social organization. Like music, ritual exists only in the performance, and so both are social in Rappaport's sense that "they are not entirely encoded by the performers themselves" (Rappaport *apud* Seligman et al. 2008: 165). Al-Jalil and Dbayeh's entrustment processes illustrate this point very clearly, as they represent both encoded features of a subjunctive tense of ideals and dispositions, and particular inflections (practical and/or not) of the subjects involved.

Furthermore, economies of trust in both Al-Jalil and Dbayeh were at once political and moral. They were political because, in both settings, trust was in part exchanged consciously according to strategy and aimed at individual and group goal maximization. Yet, economies of trust in both camps were also moral, because trust was not experienced as something utterly contingent upon entrepreneurial transaction, but entrustments also depended on imperatives, embodied dispositions, sensibilities, and affects translated into affinity, and commonly expressed through the idiom of honor. In other words, both camps' economies of trust did not rely completely on conscious, strategic, and unbound transactions; they were also bound to subjects' character, social standing, and reputation, with honor tending to embody all these features. That is, despite the risk, entrustments were often performed to forge or strengthen a bond. However, subjects did not choose freely who would be entrusted, instead they first classified who *could* be trusted. In this sense, familial, national, religious, ethnic, and political ties were the main repositories of trust for Palestinian refugees both in Al-Jalil and in Dbayeh. Moreover, although every individual would rank these belongings differently according to personal preference and context, there was a general predilection for national and kinship ties. Kinship ties were especially preferred above all, as not only were they the closest, but they also tended to overlap with national, ethnic, and most of the time also religious belongings. As I will elaborate in what follows, Dbayeh once more exhibited certain unique features when compared to other camps, which tended to be more similar to Al-Jalil in this respect.

a.   Symbolic Entrustments

As Parker Shipton states, "fiduciary thought and practice connect time, space, and social distance in cultural ways not yet widely acknowledged" (2007: 39). If by *fiduciary*, we understand not only financial, but also any other sort of symbolic entrustment - as I think Shipton would agree – this proposition touches upon a crucial aspect of social belonging processes: symbolic entrustments shape all things social, such as friendship, loyalty, group membership, alliances, and even marriages (Schiocchet 2017; 2014a). Accordingly, this final chapter tackles the question of social belonging processes in the two camps from the perspective of different subjects (groups, individuals, and networks), and the interaction among them inside each camp.

Economies of trust are largely embedded in the broad ritualization dynamics of each setting, and take a distinctive shape in the context of the refugee condition. They are affected by broad Palestinian symbology, as much as by the specific context of each of the refugee camps in Lebanon. In other words, entrustment processes, bound to contexts and thus constituting part of the socio-cultural language of interaction in the shape of economies of trust, are manifested as broad local tendencies in different camps in Lebanon synthesizing complex refugee, Palestinian, religious and other local undertones. They set the boundaries between, on the one hand, "us" – Palestinian, refugees, Muslims, Christians, and more specifically Dbayeh and Al-Jalil camp dwellers – and on the other hand, "them" – the Lebanese, the Westerners, the non-refugees, the foreigners, and whoever the "other" may be. Economies of trust are at the level of what Barth would call "boundary maintenance mechanisms," but subjects involved in them are not always conscious and strategic, as the Barthian model may assume (1958; 1966; 1987; 1993; 1998), being in this sense more similar to what Asad (1993), following Foucault, describes as "disciplinary practices" – which in turn I highlight in this book as an expression of the ritualization of quotidian life. Thus, despite a common ground, and beyond religious determinism, what make the economies of trust in Al-Jalil and Dbayeh singular are the diverging contexts in which they are embedded, as presented throughout this book.

Ritual life in the two camps was very different, especially because Dbayeh inhabitants did not usually aim to express their Palestinianness in quotidian life in the same way, or with the same intensity, as did Al-Jalil inhabitants. However, if on the level of highly formalized ceremonial rituals Dbayeh's ritual life was less active – save for rare exceptions such as Suleyman's funeral – this was not necessarily true at the level of less formalized daily social interactions. Local economies of trust were an important example of pervasive but less formalized and normative ritualization of daily life in Dbayeh as well.

In *The Nature of Entrustment*, Parker Shipton states that entrustments "Appear as part of 'multiplex' social bonds - they accompany kinship, friendship, church membership, commercial custom, and so on, which may coincide – and some local lenders depend precisely on these overlapping ties for their repayment" (2007: 208). As Shipton suggests, there is something universal about people's trust dynamics that lies at the basis of social exchanges and social bonding. At the very least, all social groups have socially accepted or contested ways to navigate entrustment. Beyond this potential universality, others have suggested that trust as a basic element for social bonding tends to be emphasized by the condition of being a refugee (Daniel & Knudsen 1996). Moreover, beyond socio-historical conditions, there are also cultural proclivities that make one people's suspicion and trust dynamics unique in relation to others.

In what follows, I explore *conditional* and *cultural* dimensions to what I call economies of trust in Al-Jalil and Dbayeh, where conditional relates to the condition of refugeeness and cultural relates to being Palestinian. While these dimensions can be seen as particular developments of a more prescriptive general human principle – trust is at the base of most social relations, from kinship to the market – here I am interested in how trust is constitutive of the specificities of social life in Al-Jalil and Dbayeh. Thus, while a case for a universal dimension could be made, here I will only make a case for conditional and cultural dimensions of local economies of trust found in the two camps.

In both Al-Jalil and Dbayeh, individuals and groups engaged in entrustment practices by mobilizing social referents, moral imperatives, and embodied dispositions, affects and sensibilities to determine affinity according to each ritual tempo's own properties, which in turn accounted for much of the dynamic process of identification and social organization in these camps. Even when trust was invested in a social relation due primarily to its formal and contractual basis, the supposed contract only existed based on a certain moral framing, at the same time that the contract itself often inspired moral principles. Morality was thus at the core of Al-Jalil and Dbayeh's economies of trust, which nonetheless still allowed space for negotiation.

The shared refugee experience coupled with a generalized mistrust toward official civic institutions led Al-Jalil and Dbayeh residents to depend solely on other social bonds as shared and legitimized references for identification, social organization, and trust. Like for Palestinian refugees in Lebanon in general, inner groups and institutions that were traditionally already the repository of trust, such as the family, the village neighbors, and the *ḥamūla* (a "clan," formed by groups of extended families, the *'a'ilāt*) (Peteet 1996; Giacaman 1998; Muslih 2005), allied to the party, the social movement, and the community association, tended to prevail. Honor, in turn, implied confidence, as an honorable subject would never lie, deviate from social norms, or dishonor an obligation or deal. Thus, honor was a main resource for building trust, and consequently for social bonding. All kinds of transactions tended to be taken as statements of the subjects' honor, especially those with more social goals such as friendship or marriage. However, if in both camps the main repositories of trust were the inner groups that assured continuity with the past, each camp's context differed in how they related to Palestinianness. In Al-Jalil, such inner groups were thus perceived as a continuity with the "national order of things" (Malkki 1995), giving the Palestinian nation priority in providing a sense of belonging, and institutions representing nationhood equal footing (Sayigh 1977, 1994, 2000; Lybarger 2007; Swedenburg 1990, 1992, 2003). Dbayeh's singular history and social context led to a different situation. Institutions representing "the national order of things" tended to be underrepresented, if not completely absent, in relation to the tradition-oriented inner groups. This reinforced other orders of belonging such as religion and ethnicity that, in the Al-Jalil case, tended to be more closely tied to nationhood.

b.   Trust and the Palestinians

The suspicion I found both in Al-Jalil and Dbayeh was heightened by the formative event of the community, that is, the coming to Lebanon as Palestinian refugees, as described in the first part of this book. Yet, much before 1948, like all other societies, Palestinians already had their own established procedures for navigating issues of trust. Many of the institutions that were the traditional carriers of trust – the family, the ḥamūla, the mosque, and the church – survived the original Nakba "critical event" (Das 1997). Apart from the family, neighborhood clusters were another traditional repository of trust. Julie Peteet describes the making of the refugee camps in Lebanon as "structurally arranged to mirror rural Palestine in a desire to re-form a physical and social geography of trust" (Peteet 1996: 173-74). Identifying and communicating one's Palestinian identity was to identify one's place of origin. The village of origin is thus where trust was, and still very much is, "sought and initially located" (Peteet 1996: 183).

Life in Lebanon shaped much of al-Jalil and Dbayeh's inhabitants' social imaginary of what Palestine was before 1948, and thus shaped what it meant to be Palestinian. Due to their distinctive cultural traits and historical development, Al-Jalil and Dbayeh inhabitants had to engage and make sense of different social actors, institutions, and contexts. Well-established institutions and values interacted with new ones, transforming relations between different groups and helping shape local perceptions of their own identity. In this process, local economies of trust were dialectically transforming and transformed by the new social situation. Authority was just one of the elements negotiated through this economy of trust, and others were as basic as friendship and love. As individuals and groups competed for allegiance in different sectors of daily life, from politics and religion to the market and interpersonal relations, the values governing these allegiances were interwoven in intricate patterns both at the level of groups and individuals.

In what follows, I will briefly present aspects specific to the Palestinian trust dynamic, most of which come from the broad academic debate on Palestinian civil society. This literature thrives on the idea that the PLO is a "surrogate state," a "proto-state," or supposes the Palestinian National Authority's (PNA) sovereignty or its possibility. In addition, for Muhammad Muslih (2005), at the center of this debate is the question if Palestinians were able to go beyond their historic forms of social organization to create other bonds surpassing the (extended) family and neighborly logic of trust.

There is a well-established Islamic argument to the contrary, which states that Islam replaced *'aṣabiyya*[1] with the idea of *maṣlaḥa al-'āmma*.[2] However, most research on Palestinian civil society tends to agree that today some measure of both principles are to be found in Palestinian society, and kinship still plays a central role. For Muslih, "the essence of [Palestinian] social organization is a network of hamulas and smaller families, as well as village, neighborhood and religious solidarities" (2005: 245). For Julie Peteet, trust is not axiomatic among Palestinians, but "closely tied to notions of family, where trust is assumed." The family "is a bulwark of sorts against precisely the domain of the extra familial relations that trust must be nurtured" (1996: 169).

Muslih analyzes associational life in Palestine in relation to three periods of Palestinian history. The first extends from 1917 to 1948 and can be characterized by the prevalence of a wide array of associations that emerged outside of the framework of British Colonial Rule, among village guesthouses, town cafes, charitable societies, and religious bodies. With the national struggle many of these were drawn into the orbit of the political apparatus of the Palestinian National Movement, or more directly under the control of Haj Amin Al-Husayni, then Grand Mufti of Jerusalem, who presided over a para-state formation (Muslih 2005: 246). Giacaman adds to Muslih's more urban forms of association, "ethnic, tribal, or kinship-based" forms that existed in relative autonomy from the state, forming the pre-modern forms of association in Palestine. As he states, "various communities organized aspects of their daily life with custom and tribal law as central elements contributing to their cohesion," due to the considerable autonomy Palestine had vis-à-vis Ottoman rule (Giacaman 1998: 5).

---

1   Partisanship. The concept became important in academia especially through Ibn Khaldun's *Maqaddimah* (2004), in which the Tunisian author underlines the early Islamic comparison between Islamic solidarity (more Universalist), and *'aṣabiyya* (clannishness).

2   Translated usually as "common" or "public" "good" or "interest," *maṣlaḥa al-'āmma* is an integral part of the Islamic *fiqh* (jurisprudence).

The second phase, from 1948 to 1967, was also rich in social formations. Upon the creation of Israel, Palestinian society was uprooted, and the Palestinian National Movement collapsed. As Jordan annexed the West Bank and Egypt the Gaza Strip, Palestinians found themselves unable to play an independent role. Nonetheless, Palestinians did create associations of students, professionals, workers, and women, all of which were in one form or another committed to the national cause. This second phase also witnessed the emergence of associational formations in the diaspora very much engaged in a "Palestinian political movement dedicated to a program of national reconstruction and liberation" that ended up co-opting many of these movements. The political movement in question was Fatah, which at the time was building an army, a bureaucracy, and a leadership role, from its base in Amman (Muslih 2005: 246-47). According to Peteet, in Lebanon the 1950s and early 1960s brought "ruptured identities" and "disorganization" in the refugee camps (Peteet 1996: 172). During the inter-war period, before the creation of the PLO, political parties tended to be led by noteworthy figures from land-owning or urban families, giving political life the taste of "traditional" family and clannish rivalry. Nonetheless, voluntary membership-based associations increased in twentieth century Palestine due also to the Zionist-Palestinian conflict, according to Giacaman. In addition, associations such as "unions, charitable societies, clubs, professional associations" greatly increased (Giacaman 1998: 5). Yazid Sayigh also points out that Palestinian grassroots associations, such as the general unions of students, women, and teachers emerged after 1948, enhancing a distinctive "national consciousness" and thus providing guerrilla leaders for the conflicts that arose after 1967 (Sayigh 2000: 220).

The third and last phase of Palestinian history, according to Muslih, started in 1967 and continues until today, as associational life endured despite the Six-Day War and despite the Jordanian government's competing with the PLO for Palestinian loyalty. As opposed to "days of passivity" between the 1950s and the 1960s, to Peteet, the "days of euphoria" were characterized by "the emergence of an inner-directed trust closely bound up with the rise of the resistance movement in the late 1960s" (Peteet 1996: 172). The "resistance movement deepened sentiments of solidarity and trust, turning them inward" (Peteet 1996: 182). According to Muslih, four types of organizations, which I describe below, characterized associational life during this period: "political shops, voluntary cooperatives, voluntary mass organizations, and Islamist groups." (Muslih 2005: 249). As Muslih points out, concerning Islamic inspired groups, people were not only drawn into these new formations by "a kind of *'aṣabiyya* or solidarity oriented solely toward furthering interest of the formation itself," but by more humanistic purposes as well, aiming at the common good. In addition, as Siddiq (1996: 90) suggests, border crossings are generally perceived as involving breaches of trust, as I will illustrate in what follows. Thus, despite the diversity of forms, the solidarity of these groups transcended their boundaries as it was rooted in the common goal of resistance (Muslih 2005: 265). The fact that the history and exegesis of Islamic expansion recounts how the prophet Muhammad had to break down *'aṣabiyya* ties to create a united Islam which was above all particularities only reinforces the quotidian moral and practical allure of Islamic inspired idiom to the Palestinian cause and forms of resistance associated with it. However, it is vital to note that, in practice, more traditional kinship-based principles of social organization not only live side by side with new ones, but also within them, as a few of the stories presented in this book demonstrate.

As soon as the PLO came to Lebanon in 1969, and more significantly in 1970 following Black September in Jordan, Arafat proceeded to build a social infrastructure, such as political offices, schools, militia, and civil associations, and to finance and maintain other institutions and groups inside the Palestinian refugee camps. Since most Palestinians had little or no work opportunities, many were on the PLO's payroll, and many others joined voluntary associations created or supported by it. Because of the new leadership, the role of UNRWA as ultimate manager of the camps, and the role of the so-called "traditional elite" in organizing the camps' social life, was soon radically diminished. However, as the case of Dbayeh demonstrates, the PLO infrastructure was not always evenly deployed in every one of the Palestinian refugee camps in Lebanon, nor did the locals naturalize its process of implantation. Also, after the PLO left Lebanon in 1982, the institutions in each of the camps were left to the locals to negotiate within their own local contexts, as the episode of the War of the Camps in Al-Jalil demonstrates. According to Yazid Sayigh, two processes are central for understanding the impact of the PLO in the refugee camps in Lebanon: *tajaīsh* (making-into-an-army) and *tafrīgh* (making-into-full-timers). *Tajaīsh*, refers to the transformation of guerrilla groups into "semi-conventional army units" in the early 1970s, first by Fatah and then by other groups, and *tafrīgh* was a process by which civilian members of the guerilla groups were added to the PLO payroll, and therefore established a relation based on "rent" (Sayigh 2000: 215). Controlling the allocation of posts and funds, and further weakening civilian organizations and traditional forms of leadership, this process led to the creation of networks of clientelism in the Palestinian refugee camps in Lebanon. This helps to explain why many perceived Hamas' coming into al-Jalil as a presage to new opportunities, as I will soon demonstrate. This also relates to how nationhood in Dbayeh was a wildcard, since, against the general tendency in other camps, Dbayeh was the only such site where the PLO and any other Palestinian institution could never really establish a foothold due to its location and close monitoring by the Lebanese.

In Al-Jalil, strong support for the rejectionist front parties can be partially understood as a consequence of the camp's political context. Being located in front of Baalbek, surrounded by the Shi'a population, and close to the border with Syria, helped shape Al-Jalil's sense of belonging in terms of identity and social organization. First, during the civil war, Al-Jalil Fedayeen struck a deal with Amal to give up their weapons in order to avoid being utterly crushed by the Shi'a militia. Second, after the entire area came under Syrian control, some of the Syrian-funded Palestinian parties and social organizations found refuge in Al-Jalil. In addition, political support for Hezbollah (and thus Islamic Jihad and Hamas) at the time of my fieldwork was more widespread in Al-Jalil than in most other camps. Finally, what varies from camp to camp is not only the character of the entrusted groups, but also the principles defining the local economies of trust per se, as demonstrated by the stories that follow in this chapter.

In Dbayeh, by contrast, isolation in Maronite dominated Mount Lebanon prevented inhabitants from being socialized in the same PLO institutions, as was the case in other camps such as Al-Jalil. Therefore, they took a different route in their process of identity construction and social organization. On account of full Lebanese control over the camp until 1991, and given their ongoing isolation from other camps, for decades Palestinians living in Dbayeh had to deny their Palestinianness or make it coincide as much as possible with the identity of the Christian Lebanese who lived in the camp surroundings and even inside the camp itself. This quest for identification with the Lebanese around them was already at play to some extent before the war – as presented in *Chapters 2* and *4* – but a sense of distinctiveness and inferiority violently imposed onto them by their Lebanese neighbors also contributed to shaping it.

c.   On the Disposition toward Suspicion and the Situational Character of Trust

Parker Shipton notes in *The Nature of Entrustment* that Keith Hart, referring to Henry Maine's *Ancient Law*, situates trust "in the no man's land between status and contract." For Shipton, to trust is to risk betrayal. "What gives trust its value is the uncertainty about how someone or something will respond to an action or situation, together with the possibility that the response will disappoint" (Shipton 2007: 34). I agree with this perspective in that trust would be especially highlighted in a context very much marked by what I defined as a disposition toward suspicion in the previous chapter.[3]

The edited volumes *Engaged Observer* (Sanford and Angel-Ajani 2006), *Ethnography in Unstable Places* (Greenhouse et al. 2002), and *Fieldwork Under Fire* (Nordstrom and Robben 1995) are all part of an emergent field in anthropology primarily focused on reflexivity. In one way or another, almost all the forty authors of these three collections present suspicion by and toward the anthropologist as a key element defining their fieldwork experiences. Their main merit is to show that, although suspicion and trust are to be found in any context, their intensity is a significant variable in certain situations. Doing fieldwork in a refugee camp or in a war-torn country brings special attention to matters of suspicion and trust in relation to the populations studied, the host country authorities, or the anthropologist's own academic peers. While *Ethnography of Unstable Places* and *Fieldwork Under Fire* generally revolve around suspicion and trust between anthropologists and the groups with whom they interact during fieldwork, *Engaged Observer* is focused on how anthropologists' political positioning affects not only their field research, but also their relationships with peers and with the discipline itself.

Based on the variety of fieldwork situations presented in these books and my own fieldwork experiences, especially those detailed in the previous chapter, I argue that on a continuum ranging from an ideal typical state of generalized suspicion to another of generalized trust, camp refugees tended towards the radically suspicious pole. Other populations, like those of war-torn countries, sectarian or deeply divided societies (as we have seen, the Lebanese being all of these), tend to also be marked by suspicion. In contrast, places with

---

3   For more on the relationship between refugee status and suspicion, see Valentine Daniel's *Mistrusting Refugees* (Daniel & Knudsen 1996). See also (Malkki 1995; Greenhouse et al 2002; Nordstrom and Robben 1995; Sanford and Angel-Ajani 2006).

more of what neo-Tocquevilians call "civil society" would be closer to the other ideal pole of this continuum.

Liisa Malkki's *Purity and Exile* (Malkki 1995) is not about trust, nor does it elaborate on the theme of suspicion. In fact, she advises caution to those who seek to define a standard refugee experience. The focus of her criticism is directed at caseworkers who strip refugees of their culture and history, thereby (re)producing a stereotype that defines the refugees' condition and needs. Far from disagreeing with Malkki, my own fieldwork experience only reiterated the unfortunate existence of such stereotypes. However, in spite of never developing the themes of suspicion and trust, there are many passages in Malkki's book where she addresses the mutual sense of suspicion between the Hutu refugees and the Tutsi. Among the Hutu, for example, there was a sense of suspicion about everything that was not Hutu as idealized by the refugee camp and represented by its inhabitants. For instance, she mentions that for the Hutu "the Tutsi are 'weak of body.' They govern through 'malignity,' 'trickery,' and 'secrecy'" (Malkki 1995: 81). That is, there is a sense that the Hutu cannot anticipate Tutsi actions because they are either deceptive or protected by the Tutsi in-group from the Hutu knowledge.

We can find in this example similar kinds of segmentation to those found in Al-Jalil and Dbayeh. According to Malkki, "mythico-historical" themes "reinforced the importance of maintaining this difference and laid out the danger embedded in trying to blur categorical boundaries" (Malkki 1995: 82). The "national order of things" is for Malkki what generally defines the in-group borders, because that is what defines the refugee condition per se. Besides, as I have been doing so far, Malkki also tends to talk about partisanship and belonging as a local moral issue. For example, "the Tutsi were cast 'the impostors from the north,' 'the foreigners,' and further, as morally unworthy of membership in the nation because of their parasitism, thievery, and trickery" (Malkki 1995: 93). And again:

> Living in the camps signaled undesirable forms of social and economic control. Notably, it was not only the discipline exercised by the camp authorities that was at issue. For the refugees, inhabitants of the camps themselves were seen by many as the agents of unwelcomed forms of control. It was specifically moral prescriptions and proscriptions that were foreseen by those in town. (Malkki 1995: 201)

The linkage of the Kigoma refugees [refugee town dwellers, as opposed to the camp ones] to impurity in the mythico-history was also evident in the specific accusations of what may be called moral pollution (...) and finally – most dangerously of all, acting as paid informers to the Tutsi-led government in Burundi. (Malkki 1995: 216)

Malkki's *Purity and Exile* (1995a) therefore supports my argument that life in refugee camps tends to be marked by generalized suspicion, and refugees treat trust largely as a moral issue, although in the Palestinian case this was often played out through the idiom of honor. As I found through my own research, as moral issues, these themes require radical displays of character to be maintained. This is so because, as Julie Peteet states, trust is "a fragile and situational concept, easily broken but difficult to restore" (Peteet 1996: 169). Such radical displays and statements of morality underpinning al-Jalil and Dbayeh's economies of trust, as developed by the examples in this chapter, are what primarily constitute honor dynamics. In addition, following Mauss' gift economy model, honor is at least tacitly being exchanged, shaping identity and social organization in al-Jalil and Dbayeh, as in most social relations and even in local, modern market transactions (Mauss 2000).

Like Malkki, Mohamed Kamel Doraï also points toward the diversity lumped within the analytical category "refugee," underscoring the fact that the category "Palestinian refugee" encompasses a diverse range of statuses: "social," "legal," "economic," and "of personal trajectories" (Doraï 2006: 212). Nonetheless, in practice, Doraï also uses the term "refugee" in a general way. The legal definition, for example, ascribes similarity to widely diverse experiences and needed to be stripped of more substantive qualities regarding subjects' experiences to be useful. Malkki and Doraï's point is an important one. Yet, in what touches refugee subjects' experiences of refugeeness, Valentine Daniel and Chuck Knudsen are also right to assert a certain widespread substantive tendency, thereby opening the possibility for a more experiential definition of refugeeness, and filling the vacuum left by Malkki's exclusively legal definition. With Daniel and Knudsen, I recognize that "from its inception the experience of a refugee puts trust on trial. The refugee mistrusts and is mistrusted." Building on this statement, I understand that the experience of suspicion (more than just mistrust) is at the core of different groups of refugees' politico-moral economies of trust. Daniel and Knudsen also recognize that "The process of breaking down of trust may range" (Daniel & Knudsen 1996: 1), as it did from Al-Jalil to Dbayeh. In this sense, Malkki's own description of the refugee experiences she studied resonates with Daniel and Knudsen's more experiential definition. Broadly defining trust as something akin to Pierre Bourdieu's *habitus*, as opposed to "a largely conscious state of awareness," Daniel and Knudsen state that if the refugees were to be reincorporated into a new culture, which they understand as a rare instance, trust would be "reconstituted, if not restored." However, "in the life of a refugee, trust is overwhelmed by mistrust, besieged by suspicion, and relentlessly undermined by caprice" (Daniel & Knudsen 1996: 2).

Trust, as any other universal or conditional social element, has to be made sense of culturally and historically. On the universal-conditional dimension, Daniel and Knudsen's definition of trust as lived through habitus does not preclude them from understanding that trust becomes highlighted by a refugee condition. On the conditional-cultural dimension, this disposition toward suspicion, as part of the ontology of the refugee, has also to be made sense of sociologically, through culture. As the editors of *Mistrusting Refugees* state:

> Mistrust is a cultural value in many societies. But there is a difference. The distinction lies, we believe, in the measure of mistrust's magnitude in the experience of a refugee: not only does mistrust push itself onto a surface of a quickened consciousness but the agitated state of awareness that it creates bars it from settling back into a state of comfortable and largely unconscious comportment with the surroundings of its world. By contrast, where mistrust is a cultural value, available for invocation into conscious ideology or normative recitation, such a comportment is commonplace. (Daniel & Knudsen 1996: 2)

Yet, this difference in the experience of mistrust (by refugees and non-refugees) does not hinder Daniel and Knudsen in recognizing that mistrust becomes "profoundly cultural" once refugeeness conditions the state of affairs, due to what Max Weber calls "the need to affirm 'the ultimate explicableness of experience'" (ibid: 2). In Julie Peteet's chapter in the collection, trust is said to underlie "a certain predictability and therefore cultural practice and communication," pointing to a "feeling of safety and well-being." While "basic to social life, [trust] is a multilayered sentiment and relationship" (Peteet 1996: 169). The refugee condition thus spawns what she calls "a culture of suspicion and mistrust" (ibid: 170).

For Daniel & Knudsen, being a refugee conditions the experience of suspicion through the two diametrically opposed but interrelated processes of "hyperinformation" and "hyperredundancy."[4] Due to extreme uncertainty and unpredictability, the refugee experience is difficult to comprehend. This is what Daniel and Knudsen call hyperinformation, that is, experience devoid of redundancy. However, as presented by Malkki, "well-meaning casework-ers" such as UN and NGO representatives generally develop "blueprints for behavior" for refugees. As refugees are asked to make sense of their extreme experience as a group, all are to be radically treated as equals among them-selves. Supporting this thesis, for Muhammad Siddiq, "to be a refugee is to be deprived not only of home and country, but also of individuality and all at-tributes of personal identity" (Siddiq 1996: 90). Besides this, Julie Peteet states that as Palestinians became refugees, there was a "leveling of statuses and identities in the refugee camps" (Peteet 1996: 168). Due to a refugee condition like this, "Individual identities and continuities" tend to be "systematically neutralized," generating a condition of hyperredundancy, "once again mak-ing for meaningless existence" (Daniel & Knudsen 1996: 3).

Due to the competing national and local narratives and social practices relating principally to the refugee condition, in Al-Jalil and Dbayeh, hyperre-dundancy and hyperinformation, as expressions of the local necessity of mak-ing sense of the refugees' ontological reality, were major motivations trigger-ing the disposition toward suspicion. This disposition intensified the experi-ence of suspicion, highlighting the importance of entrustment and enhancing its selectivity, being thus a major component motivating and shaping local economies of trust.

On the one hand, we cannot lump all the world's refugees in a single le-gal, social, and political category if we wish to understand who they are. On the other hand, it is vital to note and discuss general processes related to refugeeness. The idea that a disposition toward suspicion might indeed be a widespread tendency among refugees in general is one such discussion. Dis-position toward suspicion must then be understood as a social imperative to be dealt with, which in turn entails a necessity to highlight socio-cultural and context related rules for entrustment that thus become integral to unique so-cial belonging processes. Descending to the level of interpersonal interaction

---

4   In dealing with the relation between camp refugees and their hosts, Malkki, inspired by Michel Foucault, defined the space of the refugee camp as both a "dungeon" (where the prisoners are invisible to the guards) and a "panopticon" (where they are always accessible to the guard's gaze) (Malkki 1995). I understand that Malkki's observations and those of Daniel & Knudsen are possibly interconnected.

to illustrate Al-Jalil and Dbayeh's peculiarities will help to support this argument.

d.   Suspicion, Trust, and Honor

I was midway into my fieldwork when I witnessed an historical event in Al-Jalil. It began in the late afternoon as I was resting in my apartment in the camp and I heard people knocking on my door. This was not unusual. Often, refugees came to tell me that it was time to go back to the *Markaz*, where we worked or volunteered for the most part of our days. At night, however, we would not go there to work, although the general manager of the Center, Amid, always had something to do while he chatted on the computer with random people. A different crowd gathered at the center at night. During the day, there was a (not well respected) no loitering policy, but at night, when the Center was closed, it served as a meeting place for local workers and activists. These were all friends, and I was among them. We would smoke *argile*, drink tea or coke, and chat, sometimes until almost everyone else in the camp was asleep. I was once told that we were not supposed to circulate in the camp late at night, especially after midnight, but these people who gathered at the Center seemed to care less about this than I did. However, this time the people knocking on my door were not the usual faces, and they were not there to take me to the Center. I knew one of them who was smiling. He was a son of a local politician and as usual, also involved in politics himself. His name was Hassan, and he was the same young man who was involved in an argument with Abu Nizam at a café in Al-Jalil, days after the death of George Habash.[5] He was asking me to come and take my camera with me. It would not take an anthropologist to sense that something important was about to happen.

People were gathering in the streets of the camp. There were different groups whispering, giggling, and smiling. Some others, generally men, were agitatedly walking and directing other people. The women were gathered in groups. I thought to myself that this would be another political demonstration or celebration of some kind, like the many I had seen during my stay in Al-Jalil. My assumption was correct, but this time the celebration was unique.

Posters of Khaled Mashal, the leader of Hamas during my fieldtrip in Lebanon, and Shaykh Ahmed Yasin, one of Hamas' founders who was assassinated by Israel, were displayed, and rumors started circulating that what

---

5   I described their dispute in the introduction to this book.

we were witnessing was a Hamas event. I had always perceived the political arena there to be disputed mainly among PLO factions and their pro-Syria dissidents. I had attributed this dynamic to the fact that the PLO was once headquartered in Lebanon, and after its withdrawal the militants left behind were almost all PLO members. Historically, this tended to be the case in most other refugee camps in Lebanon. The PLO in Lebanon was financially better situated than most other groups and could therefore afford to maintain a larger number of members on its payroll. Fatah had the largest membership in Al-Jalil because of money, and not will, at least according to a PFLP local chapter leader. Islamic Jihad was the important exception to that rule, as it seemed to enjoy great support among the locals, and to have developed a decent infrastructure in Al-Jalil. I never learned much about its financial situation, but together with other so-called "pro-Syrian" groups, it had stronger financial support in Lebanon, especially in Al-Jalil, than in the Occupied Territories.

Soon, the procession started, and people gathered inside the main entrance of the camp. There were boy scouts, political-military marchers, and a truck with six people, one of whom was delivering a speech. Local camp residents were holding Hamas flags and calling out a variety of political and religious slogans, including praise for Hamas, the Prophet Muhammad, and the Islamic dictum *Allah akbar (God is the Greatest)*. Local social, religious, and especially political leadership figures came from the back of the camp near where I lived; they walked arm in arm in a tight clasp forming a human chain, just like they did during the pro-Gaza demonstration described in *Chapter 3*. Bodyguards and supporters followed them to the entrance of the camp, where they joined the rest of the crowd.

Following the local leaders, a crowd of a few hundred people advanced into the main street. Fatah men, some in military uniform, held their weapons as they gathered around their checkpoint at the main entrance of the camp, talking and whispering among themselves. Although most were smiling, they seemed to be surprised by the event. One of them told me that until recently most of these event participants had been saying they were with Fatah. "Look at them now," he exclaimed. He knew each and every one of them, their families, their villages of origin, their neighbors, and more.

The parade ended with some supporters following the leaders who were to deliver a speech, which to my surprise was held at the headquarters of Fatah al-Intifada, a split from Fatah that was then allied with Hamas through the so-called "Rejectionist Front." Many of those participating in the parade dispersed before the speech. Some were not interested in the content of the talk, while others thought it was not of their concern. The important message was that Hamas was now formally opening an office in the camp. Until then, I had identified many offices of Palestinian political parties in Al-Jalil, but I had never seen a Hamas party office. This new development indicated that Hamas would be sponsoring the Palestinian resistance in Al-Jalil more directly, and that practical and ideological opportunities for the locals were now newly available.

Puzzled that Hamas' formal entrance into the camp was being celebrated at the local office of Fatah Al-Intifada, I asked one of the local workers at the entrance of the Center for an explanation. She seemed hesitant about providing an answer, maybe because I was an outsider, maybe just because she did not know for sure herself, and most likely a combination of both. I asked if they would not have their own office. She looked at me smiling and told me that they would have one, but since it was not ready yet, they were using that of Fatah al-Intifada for the moment. Pushing too far without realizing it at first, I asked where their office would be, as I was interested to know whether physical political territoriality existed in the camp as it did in others.

Gazing at me from the Center's door was Marwan, my Palestinian friend from Shatila with whom I shared many of my days during the 2006 war. After hearing my question, he immediately came toward us displaying a half smile and one eye closed. He abruptly questioned why I wanted to know such information. I explained that I was curious about this just as I was curious about many other things in the camp, and redirected the question by asking him why he was asking me that. Was the office location to be secret? Why would it be secret? Did I not know of Hamas' involvement in the Palestinian resistance, and, especially after that parade, was I not supposed to know about its presence in the camp? Why would the location of their office be a secret while the locations of all other offices were not, and conversely, why should Hamas not proudly display its presence everywhere it went? He told me he was "joking," but he did not answer my questions. My guess was that he did not know the answers either and that he was not simply joking. Teasing and taunting with potentially hazardous subjects constituted a very common local way to obtain information and avoid making compromising statements.

Similarly, I remember once when Bakri, one of those who frequented the Center at night, appeared for the first time with a yellow Hezbollah scarf. Everyone in the Center that night teased him at some point, including me. Like the others, I wanted to know why he was wearing such a scarf, as until then I had rarely seen anyone in the camp wearing that or any other Lebanese symbol. My question was even more pertinent, as I saw it then, since Bakri was among those who used to boast about his Palestinianness. I reminded him that he had once even asserted that all that Hezbollah knew, it had learned from Fatah Fedayeen during the Civil War. He told me that this was precisely the case; he admired Hezbollah for continuing the resistance and keeping Fatah's military legacy alive. Others started to joke that he was working for Hezbollah, that he was taking Hezbollah's money, and that, if that were the case, he may be a Hamas supporter. The discussion turned very serious then, and I retreated. People started to question his loyalties, upon which he became defensive and upset. At the core of his main argument was that after the Oslo Peace Process he had become "anti-Fatah Mahmoud 'Abbas,"[6] but that he would never support Hamas because of the coup they had just recently mounted in Gaza, among other reasons.

Discussions like these tended to be important public statements in Al-Jalil. Sometimes the only way to make a statement or question a position was to jokingly introduce otherwise taboo subjects. That day, Bakri looked straight at me and told me that he was using that scarf because "like all those in the al-muqāwama al-Lubnāniyya [Lebanese resistance], we [the Palestinians] are all shuhadā [martyrs]." After Hamas' celebration, however, Bakri had difficulties defending these statements publicly.

Back at the Center after the parade, I found myself surrounded by people discussing what was likely to change. Some were excited, some not. Nonetheless, they all seemed to take for granted that the camp's political composition was about to undergo a major shift. Smiling in great excitement, clapping his hands, and holding me in his arms, Bakri told me before telling anybody else, "ya 'Abbas![7] Now we are going to see it, ya 'Abbas! Now everything will change!" I read Bakri's choice of delivering first to me, the foreign researcher, his awaited public statement about the situation as a way to ensure that his position be placed on record. While still trying not to contradict his earlier statement, he then told us all that Hamas' presence in the camp was good, as the other groups would now need to be concerned with it and therefore "do

---

6   Palestinians tend to refer to the many branches of Fatah by adding the name of the faction leader as a suffix to the party's name.

7   Most in Al-Jalil would call me by this name, which was given to me both as an endearing joke and to simplify my own which many had difficulties pronouncing.

something for the resistance." Days later, he was openly supporting Hamas like many others in Al-Jalil. I did not know exactly when he officially changed his position, if indeed there was such a moment. Bakri was not more religious than any of the other refugees supporting Fatah in the camp. The reasons he later gave me for supporting the Islamist group could not be construed as mainly religious, but rather as moral. Hamas, being an Islamist movement, lent the group a strong aura of morality, especially while the memory of Shaykh Ahmad Yasin's martyrdom was still fresh for the Palestinians. This aura was reinforced by the contrasting and at the time very much present charges of corruption that Fatah, the PLO, and the Palestinian National Authority faced. These charges resounded strongly among the Palestinian population, especially among refugees after the Oslo Peace Process, and particularly after the death of Arafat.

Bakri's sister, who like him worked at the Center, was admittedly a Hamas supporter even before the welcoming parade, as was most of his family. That politics is at least as much a family matter as it is an individual choice is a commonly known fact among Palestinians and Lebanese alike. Bakri once mocked an Al-Jalil camp resident who told us that, as a Sunni, he supported Hariri. At the time, Bakri's asserted that he himself was not a supporter because "politics is not a matter of religion." As I would learn throughout my research, while many Al-Jalil and Dbayeh inhabitants alike agreed with this position, many others tended to believe that politics was indeed a "matter of religion," as the story that introduced this book highlights. Furthermore, as we have seen, while some did not admit or frame their views in this way, religion did influence much of political belonging among Palestinian refugees in Lebanon, especially through the Lebanese confessional system with all the possibilities and limitations it provided. However, given the plurality of variables, it was usually impossible to single out one sole motivation behind a person's identification with (and belonging to) a certain group. As previously indicated, social referents motivating identification and action usually evoked more than one overlapping mode of belonging at a time, particularly nationhood, religion, and ethnicity. Similarly, practical reason and morality were intertwined, motivating action and processes of belonging.

Returning to Hamas' arrival story, perhaps those perplexed Fatah members were not as surprised as I first thought, but were rather feeling helpless as they grappled with the new turn of events. Some did not see Hamas' arrival as indicative of a major structural political shift, like the local leader of the PFLP, who told me the following: "It is always like this. Whoever brings money has bigger offices and more supporters. Yesterday it was Fatah; today it is Hamas; tomorrow who knows?"[8] It is important to understand that his rather profane assessment of the situation was based on his own disenchantment with the present historical and political moment. There was some truth to the PFLP leader's statement, although I realized that his answer might have been influenced by the disappointment of his own office shrinking over the years. However, most Palestinians in Al-Jalil were not simply "with"[9] or "from" one or another party due to economic reasons and despite ideological concerns. Given the difficult situation characteristic of a refugee camp, some Palestinians did join a political party (or any other group) for purely pragmatic and economic reasons, despite their ideological positions or familial loyalties. Yet, not all or even most Al-Jalil inhabitants acted in this way. Even among those who did, such as Bakri, it was unclear how much of what they thought and did was concealed and how much sincere.

As the story illustrates, Bakri had not "changed sides" at once. The transition from one to the other was gradual. It can be argued that he strategically prepared the transition, but it can also be argued that he was simply carried away by the excitement of a new context. Either way seems too simplistic. While he appeared to act deliberately in realigning his allegiances, the move was not simply (and as I understood it then, not even primarily) driven by any hope for personal gain. He sincerely seemed to believe that Hamas' leadership was the "right" path (ṣaḥīḥ; or ḥaqq, the former meaning true). As earlier indicated, given the frequent allegations of corruption directed at Fatah, issues of morality were a common motivation for supporting Hamas. Furthermore, Hamas was also commonly said to be "right" as opposed to its main rival because it was still engaged in the "resistance." Finally, the idea that Hamas was "right" because it was Islamic – as opposed to Fatah, which was secular – was also among the most common justifications I heard in Al-Jalil for growing Hamas support. However, in practice, most who supported Hamas only did

---

8   Most of this dialogue happened in English.

9   Most Palestinian refugees in Lebanon expressed interchangeably "to be with" (ma') or "to be from" (min) in the sense either that someone was a supporter of a given group, or that someone was part of that group. Even though the second at times placed the subject more definitely within a group, the first could also be used in the same way. Thus, the boundaries between favoring, supporting, and belonging were often blurred. Depending on the context, they could be blurred reinforcing belongings and alliances or effacing them.

so because of what Al-Jalil refugees in general perceived as an excellent performance of resistance. Many actually put the matter to me in terms such as "it is not what they say, it is what they do." Yet, once more it would be too simplistic to separate the religious appeal of Hamas rhetoric from the practical reason behind the resistance performance. Both often went hand-in-hand, albeit not always. Whenever they met, they reinforced each other, recalling the teleology of fate and hope previously described. That is, whatever follows the religious path, the right path, must succeed, while every perceived success is God's will.

The idea that something is "right" can be beyond self-interest, for it is a matter of morality. Some rights and wrongs exist as truly moral imperatives, and some are very much similar to what Charles Taylor describes as a moral ontology (1992). Being part of such moral ontology or not, some sets of moral imperatives are strong enough to be at best difficult to manipulate. Nevertheless, while what constitutes certain rights and wrongs may sometimes be principles which precede given situations, people do articulate rights and wrongs as reflections of particular circumstances. Often, they do this to achieve their own goals, but perhaps just as often they find that there are certain things they cannot justify. The arbiters of such successful and failed attempts to give meanings that coincide with one's own goals are not only expressed in public, but also within the confines of one's own personal moral judgments. As I understand it, the impossibility of a purely entrepreneurial manipulation of moral values at all times is easily seen through examples of the constraints imposed by religious practices and beliefs. However, what Bakri's example displays is the dialectical role played by the complementary opposition between morality and self-interest, and between the resulting complex motivations and social performance.

In Al-Jalil, as in Dbayeh, doing or not doing what is right was considered a matter of honor. Being a matter of morality, honor binds people to their respective families, ḥamā'il (plural of ḥamūla), political parties, religious, ethnic, and political communities. Although sometimes contradictory in its implications, thereby creating space for articulation and manipulation, honor was something that one possessed beyond social display. Many in Al-Jalil, including Bakri, perceived their identity as closely connected to issues of honor; for example, one can be a good Muslim, a bad brother, a Palestinian martyr, and so on. Bakri's shift in allegiances involved mobilizing his own rights and wrongs, but at the same time did not allow for deliberate unrestrained manipulation out sheer self-interest. It involved his honor, although words expressing honor (*sharaf*, *karam*, and others) were not clearly articulated.[10] He could not have switched allegiances without a clear justification to himself, a necessity that was only deepened by the need to be trusted by the community. Honor indexed Bakri's social performance with personal moral imperatives, but it also indexed trust.

I did not doubt that Bakri had mixed feelings about Hamas and Fatah, and I had not fully trusted his earlier claims that he would never support Hamas. There were family, political, religious, ideological, and probably other matters involved. Some had more or less weight depending on his own accessing and processing of the situation and on specific occasions and opportunities as well. Perhaps tipping the balance at that moment was Hamas' successful attempt at establishing itself in the camp. I realized that Bakri's excitement was not only due to Hamas' arrival, but was also partially caused by the organization's remarkable public defiance of Israel and the effervescence generated by its ritual of arrival, which raised hopes and stirred up enthusiasm for their own campaign.

In Al-Jalil, the backbone of the local social economy of trust was that every subject (individual or group) had to display clearly defined allegiances as much as possible, despite the fact that identity and belonging for most were indeed complex and multi-faceted matters. It was socially required that these allegiances be shown without reserve, so that the individual could be seen as committed beyond suspicion. Bakri too had to make his public statement as clear as possible, and to be clear meant to choose one or another party only. Thus, the local economy of trust in Al-Jalil, as I knew it, tended to pull apart the local complex network of belonging, and polarize one group and individual against the other. In the Lebanese political landscape, being defined as "pro-Syria" or "anti-Syria," regardless of what one actually believed and supported, was a polarizing designation that almost dragged the country into another civil war. Similarly, being "pro-Palestinian Authority" or "pro-Rejectionist Front"

---

10   Beyond *sharaf*, the Arabic language is rich in expressions accounting for the importance of honor, as, for instance, *karamak*, meaning "your honor" (for a man). *Karam* means to be noble, generous, polite, kind, and hospitable. Hence, there is an immediate connection between ritual and honor. Another common way to express honor is *ḥasab wa nasab*, meaning roughly, the status individuals loose or gain during their lifetime and inherited social status [generally through family]. This last expression is thus also connected to nobility and virtuosity.

defined much of what a person was in Palestinian politics. Incontestable belonging in Al-Jalil was a matter of honor, worth even dying for. In Dbayeh, however, the local social economy of trust functioned according to different principles.

*

Performances negotiating trust were also common in Dbayeh. To start, Palestinian scholars and activists tended to discuss what they called the Palestinian cause in national terms, which was much harder to grasp from most Dbayeh refugees' point of view as they did not tend to parse out such matters in their quotidian lives, as modernists would have liked. Dbayeh inhabitants were Christians and had already been "left" by the Palestinian resistance to fend for themselves when they were most in need, or so was the dominant perception in the camp. Thus, many were also suspicious of what they called "the Muslims," fearing that "the Palestinian cause" was not theirs any longer. Nationhood tended to be less relevant in Dbayeh for the formation and maintenance of the inner groups than it was in Al-Jalil. In Al-Jalil, at least in discourse, the moral commitment to what was called the "Palestinian cause" was at the center of the formation of such groups. Furthermore, however framed, Islam was generally a language of resistance interwoven with "the Palestinian cause" and daily suffering, as *Chapter 6* illustrated.

The Al-Jalil case shows that individuals and groups generally strove to create unambiguous profiles. By contrast, in Dbayeh ambiguity was an asset allowing the population to go about constructing its own economy of trust. While the disposition toward suspicion, in the absence of national institutions, led Al-Jalil to political polarization, this same disposition led Dbayeh to social fragmentation. Al-Jalil represents an instance in which local economies of trust were put into play. In both camps, economies of trust were at least partially produced by what I have been calling a *disposition toward suspicion* that made subjects turn toward their own inner groups due primarily to their refugee condition. This inwardness, coupled with generalized suspicion toward outsiders, tended to lead to political polarization and/or social fragmentation, depending on the case.

Philosophers and social scientists have debated for a long time the importance of trust as indispensable for social organization, and there is evidence to suggest that the organization of trust is a general feature of all societies. However, in the previous chapter I presented evidence supporting the notion that a generalized disposition toward suspicion engendered by the condition of refugeeness heightens the importance of economies of trust. Such economies of trust can take different shapes, depending on the context.

e.   Honor, Trust, and the Orders of People

Following Mauss and Shipton, I understand that honoring a debt, or the desired possibility of doing so, holds together some of the most important social bonds. However, to "have" honor goes beyond honoring a debt, as Shipton claims. My experience in Middle Eastern societies corroborates his findings, and many authors have stressed the centrality of honor for interpersonal interaction and the ordering of things in the region. To name two, Andrew Shryock (1997) wrote about this matter in the context of tribal Jordan, while Michael Gilsenan (1996) wrote about it in rural north Lebanon. Both authors approached honor as an index of the orders of people in the world, through narrative modes in which subjects engage to manipulate their own standing in society. The fact that Shryock and Gilsenan wrote, respectively, about tribal Jordan and agrarian Lebanon in this way suggests that the centrality of honor is culturally more prevalent than just what is limited to Palestinian refugee camps in Lebanon. The way people deal with honor might be different, but I encountered similar forms of narrative disputes among the Palestinian refugees. Honor in Al-Jalil and Dbayeh was at the core of identification and self-identification processes, indexing subjects to disputed orders of peoples and things.

For Gilsenan, in rural north Lebanon narratives about events, happenings, and of their own selves and the others tended to present subjects with accounts of "how they are" (Gilsenan 1996: 116):

> The account of 'what happened', whether or not an 'event' had occurred and, if so, what was its nature, always had a rhetorical purpose, however veiled: each account sought to persuade or impose upon others, 'the truth' of a situation and a social order. And every narrative of a present event tacitly or explicitly drew on claims and assumptions about the value of different genealogies, past, and biographies. That the reproduction of social honor and the avoidance of social dishonor were problematic was a given of local discourse. (Gilsenan 1996: 59)

Gilsenan's point is valid for the cases presented in this book. However, here "honor" was not divided between "social honor" and "individual honor," since honor in Al-Jalil and Dbayeh was not just a conscious strategy for public display. Rather, it was also something one felt for/about oneself, a matter of self-identification that had a moral basis and was thus sometimes beyond complete manipulation. "Collective honor" (Gilsenan 1996: 196), or what I would call the collective dimension of honor, is present in Gilsenan's examples through party decisions, and the moral imperative that the dishonored (even the dead) must be avenged. The very relationship between collective interest and moral imperatives is a central point limiting the possibilities of individual entrepreneurship, for identification with a group does not always go hand in hand with personal interests, as Bakri's story above suggests. Nevertheless, Gilsenan's analysis is rather limited as regards the relation between morality and self-interest, between material and immaterial social capital, and at times between individual and social honor. For instance, in one case he noticed that the narrator sees himself as a "prisoner of its own language of honor confrontation, trapped in narratives of autonomous, individual action that paid no attention to material constrains" (Gilsenan 1996: 116). In opposition, the thrust in this book has been to not separate "collective honor" and "personal honor," as Gilsenan did.

What I take from both Gilsenan and Shryock is the centrality of dispute to the moral order of subjects and things. As Gilsenan states, "Honor does not guarantee its own eternal values, as in the heroic tales it should" (Gilsenan 1996: 117). That is, honor is a matter of dispute, and yet "above the law" (ibid: 260). This holds true especially in the Palestinian case because of the refugees' stateless condition, and even more so in the refugee camps in Lebanon where they benefited from partial social autonomy. Especially in the refugee camps outside of Palestinian territory, law tends to be defined much more as a deeply felt interpersonal convention than as a rational order emanating from an over-arching and impersonal social institution. Either that or law and authority in general were much more disputed in larger and more polarized camps such as 'Ain el-Helwe and Nahr al-Bared. In the cases of Al-Jalil and Dbayeh specifically, honor was a major element indexing entrustment processes, very often serving as a local legal framework for social disputes.

As we have seen in in this chapter and throughout this book, entrustments were achieved when obligations to honor debt were not yet in place. These entrustments created or strengthened social bonds due to the necessity of reciprocity – as Mauss and Shipton recognized – but even if mainly social in character, honor did not exist purely for display. Honor was an index of social belonging and identity also in the sense of the moral imperatives that subjects felt constrained or pulled toward when acting beyond social display. In other words, subjects defended their honor and the honor of the groups to which they belonged at the same time. In addition, while in Al-Jalil and Dbayeh the personal and the collective usually went hand in hand, there were also exceptions. Admitting that one is not a good Muslim or Christian, a good father, a good militant, and so on, is to place the honor of the group before personal honor, and vice versa. Navigating and negotiating these constraints was a part of daily life, and subjects frequently had to make difficult decisions that went beyond pure strategy to maximize their goals. The contrary also held true. Personal strategies were sometimes perceived, even by the entrepreneur, as going against the subject's honor. In all cases honor was still at stake, and placed individuals and groups closer or further away from other subjects' moral ideals and thus closer or further away from the subjects' core of belonging and identity.

For instance, Bakri's political alignment was an issue of honor. Not only did he have to display unambiguous allegiance to defend his honor and the honor of those around him when confronted by others, but he also dealt with the process as a matter of personal honor and identity in a way that would appease his own self. Furthermore, he had to defend his own honor and loyalty, while adhering to his family, which already openly supported Hamas. Doing this could mean a compromise in terms of arguments and justifications, but not in terms of breaching honor and trust.

As Shipton states, entrustment exercises and shifts power not only in one way and not always by force. Because of the local emphasis on trust and entrustment following a complex of moral imperatives and personal interests, in Al-Jalil and Dbayeh friendship and social membership were not merely "the elusive, interpersonal chemistry of optative bonding that seldom seems to follow rules" (Shipton 2007: 27). Among the Palestinian refugees in Lebanon – as it was the case among the Luo studied by Shipton – making friends and belonging to a social group is also "the crucial thing on which so much else depends" (ibid: 6). Thus, I follow Shipton's lead in positing that entrustment is not just a matter of practical considerations, "but moral and sometimes aesthetic ones as well," and that, "reason and rationality pertain not just to individuals but also to groups, networks, and categories; and they do not always involve measurable gains. Nor are reason and rationality the only human aspirations. Too often they leave out the intuition, the experience, the feel" (ibid: 12).

In line with social contract theorists, I understand trust to be universally constitutive of social bonding. However, along with neo-Tocquevillian civil society theorists, and by way of Mauss and Shipton, I understand that trust is not generalized throughout a given society, but it is a matter of investment. While perhaps not all human bonds must entail trust, in all societies there are social relations based on trust. Finally, economies of trust will vary situationally and culturally. Variation can occur even between two different populations of Palestinian refugee camps in Lebanon. While in Al-Jalil ambiguity was likely to cause problems or have adverse consequences, in Dbayeh it was generally an asset that allowed the population to live among the Lebanese. While in the first case the local economy of trust led to political polarization, in the second case it was the main force contributing to social fragmentation. In addition, while in Al-Jalil religious referents were associated with the inner groups, the national cause, and with morality, in Dbayeh religious referents were mainly associated with bridging national differences, and thus not infrequently with private interests.

As suggested in *Chapter 1*, refugeeness in combination with the political circumstances of life in Lebanon generated a disposition toward suspicion in Al-Jalil and Dbayeh. This disposition became part of the reality that had to be dealt with throughout social life. As suspicion is marked by the lack of trust, the disposition toward suspicion had a great impact on the local dynamics of entrustment in Al-Jalil and Dbayeh. Furthermore, this chapter demonstrates that these dynamics of trust were equally affected by the necessity to manage trust as a resource. Entrustment thus worked as boundary maintenance dynamics, but without the Barthian assumption that entrustments were always conscious and strategic. Such dynamics were instead often moral and embodied disciplinary practices. While the situational aspect of refugeeness entailed a more immediate need and expediency for entrustment processes, such need and expediency were further shaped by cultural aspects, some of which were common to Palestinians and some unique to each of these camps. Religion was certainly an important element in both economies of entrustment, both politically as an institutional repository of trust for some, and, more often, morally as an index of honor.

In Al-Jalil, entrustments pointed to how Islam and other traditions motivated social belonging. Bakri's story illustrates the extent to which membership in a political party was entangled with financial opportunities, ideology, and the motivations behind joining Islamist parties. In Dbayeh, by contrast, religion tended to be socially more important in interactions with the Lebanese population then when indexing trust among the Palestinian refugees themselves. In other words, in Dbayeh, religion was not significantly tied to Palestinianness but was one of the main elements enabling the blurring of nationhood.

f.   Clash of Civilizations versus Fusion of Horizons

The stories recounted in this chapter demonstrate that in Al-Jalil ambiguity was generally dangerous while in Dbayeh it was generally an asset allowing residents to live among the Lebanese. While elsewhere among Palestinians in Lebanon religious referents generally indexed and reinforced the refugees' sense of national belonging, in Dbayeh they generally entailed bridging the gap between refugees and the Lebanese local population.

To reiterate, while not all human bonds must entail trust, in all societies there are social relations based on trust. However, the value ascribed to trust and the dynamics of the economy of trust in its more objective sense is also situational and always has a cultural dimension. Furthermore, the refugee condition in Al-Jalil and Dbayeh generated a disposition toward suspicion characterized by generalized suspicion as an existential condition that can only be surpassed by social bonding. The experience of suspicion is thus of great importance for the constitution of social organization and identity in both camps. This chapter argued that the historically and culturally constructed experience of suspicion has a dramatic impact on local economies of trust, which are in turn knowledge- and context-bound and thus render unique tendencies in each of the two camps, rather than being a direct consequence of culture, theologies, or ideologies of any kind.

I argue that within an environment fostering suspicion, and the consequent increase in the value of trust as a necessary element of social dynamics, in both camps social networking became fundamentally bound to the act of entrusting subjects, although this often occurred subtly. Even though the universes of those entrusted were similar in both camps, the public display of trust varied greatly. In Al-Jalil, individuals and groups generally strove to create unambiguous profiles, and the local economy of trust led to a tendency toward ideological polarization. In Dbayeh, by contrast, it was precisely ambiguity that allowed part of the population to achieve a generally desired intermingling with the Lebanese population surrounding the camp. Thus, entrustments involved more private and less overt displays. In both camps, however, rather than a sign of an unbounded entrepreneurial agency, entrustments were also largely moral. Thus, due to both culture and context in the two cases presented, honor was a key element indexing trust.

Religion was often among the most important criteria for entrustment, and especially in Al-Jalil, an anti-Western posture was very much a consequence of the Palestinian refuge associated with the postcolonial context of the region. However, as I have argued throughout, differences between Al-Jalil and Dbayeh cannot be read in light of an intrinsic polarization between Christianity and Islam. Rather, a variety of processes led to social fragmentation in Dbayeh and political polarization in Al-Jalil. The type of distinction presented here is not to be taken as the same as Samuel Huntington's *clash of civilizations*[11] (Huntington 1993; 1996). Different from what Huntington describes the Palestinian polarization I witnessed was not ontologically religious, cultural, and anti-Western. On the contrary, even though not always locally perceived as such, culture shaped but did not determine each camp's local economy of trust.

In this way, my own approach to knowledge, very much influenced Barth's and Asad's, but also by Hans-Georg Gadamer's (2005), is fundamentally different from Samuel Huntington's (1993; 1996). Huntington does not foresee the possibility of dialogue and understanding as a possible productive consequence of the intercultural meeting – a *fusion of horizons* in Gadamer's terms – but only the impossibility of communication – a *clash of civilizations* in Huntington's terms. In addition, a fusion of horizons is a precondition to the production of any anthropological knowledge, allowing, for instance, for the possibility of writing this very book and for the readers' own understandings of the material.

Although I found a strong disposition toward suspicion in all Palestinian refugee camps in Lebanon, the local economies of trust delineated above represented unique mechanisms of social and individual junction and disjunction. These mechanisms only made sense embedded in their respective contexts, and in varying from group to group and individual to individual. Furthermore, like other communicational elements, they produced meaning, gained strength, and became disciplinary practices acting as partially embodied boundary maintenance dynamics through the ritualization of the quotidian, as argued throughout this book.

---

11   The term was first used by Bernard Lewis but entered into a major international debate with Huntington's 1993 Foreign Affairs' publication. (1993; 1996). See also (Schiocchet: 2011).

8. Conclusion

There is no simple formula for understanding how Palestinian refugees in Lebanon relate to religion, ethnicity, politics, and their current condition of refugeeness – or any other category of belonging. Nonetheless, I hope that the reader will be more informed about the interplay of the plural processes of identification and motivation at play. External domination, although present, was never completely achieved in the cases presented, and military resistance is not the only way in which domination is denied its powers. Rather, the refugees I encountered found much more nuanced ways to go about alleviating or obscuring their conditions of repression and marginalization. These ways did not depend simply on conscious strategy, or even totally on choice – since the word choice suggests consciousness.

Of course, Palestinians did try to take control over their lives as much as they could but making sense of themselves and others was a far more complex and internalized process. Existing alongside practical reason, this process was embedded in a broader apparatus wherein moral imperatives, conscious choices, adaptive survival, preferences and sympathies, feelings, thoughts, resistance, acceptance, and other possible influences, known or unconscious, spoken or mute were synthesized, motivating individual and collective action and reflection. Religion was certainly an important element engendering the two camps' very distinct characters, but never on its own, and not so much by way of orthodox dogma as through religiosity embedded in everyday life.

What ultimately constitutes Palestinianness to refugees and non-refugees does not reside necessarily in objective concepts such as *dīn* (religion), *jensiyya* (nationality), *qawmiyya* (national identity, widely understood in ethnic terms; nationalism) or even *aṣl* (genealogical descent), but rather resides in the concrete collective experiences of individuals. Due to their stateless status, in the case of Palestinians *jensiyya* may equate even more than usual to *qawmiyya*.

Besides, from all such categories, *qawmiyya* is perhaps the most dangerous one for reasons well expressed by Charles Lindholm:

> In polar contrast to the effort to disintegrate restrictive racial categories is the assertion that ethnic and national identities are natural, oppositional, and hierarchical. As a result, what is in principle an open category turns into a closed one. The danger of naturalizing ethnicity (and viewing the nation as an ethnic entity) is horribly evident in events such as the destructive internal wars ethnic cleansing in Yugoslavia and the genocidal slaughter of Tutsis in Rwanda. (Lindholm 2007: 225)

When discussing the "politization of ethnicity in South Asia," Stanley Tambiah also enlightens by showing how the new polities generated

> have become, or made to become, conscious of ethnic identity, and how in turn they have energized as collectivities to engage in political action (...) This instrumental efficacy of ethnicity in making claims on the resources of the modern state inevitably in turn reinforces and maintains ethnic political machinery – patron/client networks, bossism, and patronage structures – through which affirmative action and pork-barrel distributions are dispensed. (Tambiah 1996: 335)

To these authors' insights, I would add that such a situation can be even exacerbated by an already national context marked by sectarianism, especially as it regards its relation to a refugee population that does not fit the system in any way. As Peteet states, "Palestinian Otherness" is juxtaposed not with a homogenous, singular category of Lebanese, but with a shifting set of sectarian groups and alliances. Palestinians, perceived as a threat, serve as a "common denominator" to unify disparate elements of polity (Peteet 1996). The consequence is again well expressed by Tambiah: "The quests for group worth, group honor, group equivalence, and so on are central foci in the politics of ethnicity and critical ingredients in the spirals of intense sentiments and explosive violence that ensue" (Tambiah 1996: 337).

This book focused on the realm of social belonging and organization. In this sense, I argued that largely due to their refugee condition, the present was also lived in both camps as a suspended time in contrast to the normal time of non-refugees, when the idealized plenitude of their national identities was unreachable. Nationhood set a flexible framework for the experiencing of time in both camps. First, there was *al-Nakba* ("The Catastrophe"; evoking the original displacement caused by the creation of the state of Israel in 1948) marking the boundaries between an idyllic past and the present condition of refugeeness, followed by al-'Awda ("The Return") setting the boundaries between the present condition and a utopic future. Al-'Awda was often lived as a messianic religious and/or nationalistic return to a pre-*Nakba* past. In other words, a way out of the suspended time that would bring up the end of present suffering. Accordingly, al-Ḥaqq al-'Awda ("The Right of Return"), especially inspired by the UN General Assembly Resolution 194 from December 1948 – that foresees the right of return of Palestine refugees to the territory that is today within Israeli borders – was closely connected to al-Qaḍiyya al-Filastyniyya (The Palestinian Cause), motivating the refugees' present social belonging and dynamics. However, each one of the camps I described developed unique ways of collectively negotiating such themes, revealing different perspectives, moods, strategies, interests, and goals, but also affects, dispositions, and sensibilities. Within these themes, I also found rich individual variation. This book showed how the principles informing this suspended time, in conjunction with the postcolonial and settler colonial contexts of the Near East, refugee camp environments, and a drive to take back control of their own identities, often constituted a strong force pulling individuals to collectively articulate their existential condition, further ritualizing their quotidian routines.

Furthermore, concepts such as interests, goals, and moral imperatives are heuristic devices often used by social scientists to qualify social action as inherently determined, for example, by economic interests, ideology, or morality. This tactic often fails to account for the complexity of personal/social motivation and social action. This book challenged these heuristic divides altogether to more thoroughly appreciate people's actual and varied experiences of motivation and belonging. Motivations are not directly derived solely from either religion, ethnicity, nationalism, political ideology, economical strategy, or other social/cultural value systems. Rather, motivations generally compound at least some of these variables, mobilizing multi-faceted sets of referents. In turn, dispositions, affects, and sensibilities in the form of partially unconscious embodied drives, generated by subjects' mobilization of sets of referents, pushed them to respectively act and feel in certain ways. Ritualized expressions of embodied dispositions, affects, and sensibilities thus, along with conscious strategies, desires, and objectives, strongly motivated social action. Social referents associated with religion, nationhood, or the refuge only acquired meaning through their linkages with motivations and in context. Both referents and motivations varied according to context and according to the personal biographies of individuals and characters of social actors.

In other words, Al-Jalil and Dbayeh refugees were neither living in a world of instrumental entrepreneurship, nor in a world molded by inescapable moral demands. Sometimes they were divided between the two, and often tried to merge both. Yet, at least just as often, they did not recognize both as different realms, and thus were not split between one and the other. Such "merged" worlds gave rise to selves different from Erwin Goffman's (1963; 1967) mechanist competitive role-sets, and yet the tension between practical reason, desires, sympathies, moral imperatives, and social obligations created an environment where self-consciousness must be accepted with caution (Cohen 1993). That is, in Al-Jalil and Dbayeh, people made sense of themselves and the world around them also largely at the margins of the boundaries of such self-consciousness, by being part of something larger than themselves. These were collectives with which they were organically connected at least as much through daily routine that ritualized and sacralized the quotidian as through rituals that set the mundane world apart.

In both camps, the actions and reflections of individuals were embedded in the context of their respective ritual tempo. Ritualization can also produce autonomy, even extreme autonomy, as we have seen in *Chapter 7*. Thus, along with socializing members of a community into a set of values and practices and behaviors, helping demarcate its boundaries vis-à-vis others, organizing history, and providing frameworks for understanding the world, ritualization can also be engaged to transform that very reality. Like Charbel, many Palestinian refugees I met were deeply motivated by transforming the world around them, which they were pursuing also within the realm of the ritual tempi they were respectively immersed in.

Thus, I utilized a ritualization approach for understanding contrasting processes of belonging encompassing matters of social organization and belonging processes. To do so, in turn, I presented the social dynamics that occurred along two different axes among the Palestinian refugee population in Lebanon. The first axis aggregated processes of inclusion and exclusion that consisted of the relations between people's social organization and their complex and individual processes of identification to groups such as the party and the family. The second was composed of the dynamic interplay between ingroups and out-group that occurred at the levels of the camp and the nation. The resulting ethnography I presented avoided the essentialist trap of generalizing "the Palestinians," but still permitted an overall understanding of the camp's and individual's contexts that went beyond a mere statement of the uniqueness and subjectivity of groups or individual selves (including the self of the anthropologist).

In this regard, I hope to have shown that in many Palestinian communities, existence as a refugee is already widely understood as resistance (Schiocchet 2013), just as enduring suffering is seen as resistance (Schiocchet 2018). Collective suffering is by no means general among Palestinians, but as I also found among Palestinians in Brazil, Denmark, Austria, and the West Bank, it was exceedingly common to the Palestinian experience everywhere, or at least to the understanding of Palestinianness. However, not unqualified suffering that reminds us we are all human, but qualified suffering as an essence shared only among those who went through one of its particular iterations. In this sense, two of the main themes of Palestinian public expressions of suffering, in many ways re-appropriated through activism, are the ongoing character of the *Nakba*, and the drive against narratives of pure victimization towards narratives of resistance. Both are part of a same set of discourses, colored by the notion of the "Palestinian Cause," and thus inherently intertwined. While the first calls for witnessing Palestinian suffering, the second qualifies how that suffering must be apprehended. As I also developed elsewhere, among the refugees, and ironically largely through PLO nationalist jargon that has gone out of PLO's control, resistance needs not be experienced as bellicose or even apart from routine, but can be essentially embedded in the quotidian[1] (Schiocchet 2015, 2013). This is in line with Foucauldian thought. As Catherine Bell reminds us, to Foucault, power must be understood beyond pure coercion and violence: "At the heart of power relationships lies an insubordination or resistance (...) Hence, to explore power is to explore the necessary and simultaneous resistance to power that continues to provoke and legitimize its exercise" (Bell 2009: 201).

Overall, by way of the ritualization approach focused on Palestinianness and on to what extent religiosity informs different social belonging processes, this book explored boundary making and maintenance in both camps. It presented relations between individuals at multiple levels of sociality, and the layered relationships between individuals, social groups, and the polyphonically imagined Palestinian community. Dbayeh's lower level of ritualization,

---

1   It does not follow that all Palestinian agency is resistance - see, for instance (Mahmood 2005) - only that resistance is embedded in much of daily life, rather than only present when expressed overtly.

when compared to al-Jalil, can be partially attributed to its social fragmentation and hesitation to assert nationhood clearly and loudly, leading to different engagements with social belonging such as the local economies of trust
explored in *Chapter 7*. Al-Jalil's higher level of ritualization of daily life can be,
in turn, largely attributed to the value of ṣumūd (steadfastness), which drives
individuals and groups to a hyper-expression of their personal and collective
selves, especially when compared to Al-Jalil. Therefore, ritual tempo, or the
ritualization of the rhythm of daily life, is not simply a synonym for ritual as
a rupture with the quotidian, but rather a pervasive context in which actors
frame much of daily life. Although not everything inhabitants of al-Jalil did
was ritual, they ritualized the very quotidian largely because of the refugee
experience of the present time, which pulled them towards constantly reartic-
ulating their condition and a collective overcoming through ritualized modes
of behavior. That is, ritual tempo is the ritualized context, pace, and rhythm,
of daily life; it is not a clearly demarcated ritual with a structure, narrative,
and pre-existing symbolic system, but a broad context marked by ritualization. On the other hand, resistance in Dbayeh tended to take a different shape,
less marked by Palestinianness and collective ritualized engagement with different notions of resistance. A common form of resistance then was simply
to mobilize that which was common between Palestinian refugees and the
Lebanese surroundings, and Christianity was one such noteworthy common-
ality.

As to the different ways refugees from each camp understood their lives
and acted upon the world, some general tendencies were presented in Part
I and II, but these tendencies were by no means straitjackets. While context
was indeed evocative, different subjects within the same refugee camps understood and engaged ritual and religious life differently. Nonetheless, the
deep imprint of the different socio-historical conditions that each camp was
subjected to, as outlined in Parts I and II, should not be underestimated.

Each part of this book covered different aspects of the quotidian, but all
of them were concerned with the same tension between integration and par-
ticularity, and between religion and quotidian life. The dynamic interplay between groups and individuals (at any level, from national, religious, political
or ethnic belonging, to individual uniqueness) was presented according to
centripetal and centrifugal tendencies – to use Marshall Sahlins terms (1972)
– towards integration or dissolution. Dispute, management, conflict, and in-
ternalization of ideas and practices all acted in composing daily life largely
through ritualized processes of communication.

Finally, as to religion as an index for social belonging, due to the differences in the two camps, which include for instance the value of *ṣumūd* in Al-Jalil and the relative lack of this value in the Dbayeh, social investments tended to manifest differently. As we have seen, in Al-Jalil, there was the tendency to disclose one's allegiances within the community. These displays were performed both as ritualized rehearsals and as public expressions of one's identity. By contrast, Dbayeh's quotidian also contained ritualized routines, although such investments tended to be less public and more situational, and to detach religion from nationhood.

In both camps, subject's motivations were not directly derived solely from either religion, ethnicity, nationalism, political ideology, economic strategy, or other social/cultural value systems. Rather, motivations generally seemed to merge at least some of these referents. The intrinsic amalgamation of referents that generates social motivations is in turn essential to the understanding of the relative place of religion in each of the camps' social belonging dynamics. Context was central. For instance, although the Palestinian flag was often a symbol of belonging in Dbayeh as it was in Al-Jalil, it was displayed in different ways,[2] evoked different experiences and behaviors, and represented diverse ideas of Palestinianness.

If in Al-Jalil nationhood was sometimes superposed with ethnicity (Arabness), in Dbayeh some (usually younger generations) instead expressed their Christianity and displayed it as a mode of ethnic belonging in a bid for shared identification with the Lebanese population surrounding them. Perhaps if there had not been a heavy toll to be paid for being a Palestinian in Dbayeh, the situation might have been different. Yet, if there had been no deep, local identification with Christianity, such a bridge could not have been spanned either. The articulation of Palestinianness and Christianity I witnessed in Dbayeh was by no means the same as in other contexts, from Christian families living in Mar Elias' camp, to Palestinians with Lebanese citizenship living in large Lebanese urban enclaves. This strongly reiterates that both ritualization and religiosity are bound to context.

In the cases presented, religion was indeed a central referent to refugee's vernacular expressions of the self, as well as a currency to fundamental organizational principles such as local economies of trust, which were in turn heightened by a disposition toward suspicion strongly associated with

---

2   In Dbayeh I only saw it inside the houses, as opposed to Al-Jalil where they dominated the public space.

the refugee condition, and very much embedded in each camp's own ritual tempo. Yet, *religion*, as presented in this book, rather than doctrine alone, or cultural determinism, refers rather to religiosity. Thus, I approached religion in the same way that I approach rituals through ritualization: both are processes in-the-making and embedded in the much broader and more pervasive language of everyday life. My argument is not that religion was nowhere to be found in the cases I present in this book, but precisely the opposite: religion was everywhere, and therefore hardly ever being the sole defining factor of social experiences and forms of belonging. Even though not entirely new, this is an argument still worth making, both for scholars interested in Palestine studies and, more generally, for those who insist on portraying religion as a distinct domain of social life apart from others. However, more than simply making this case, this book aimed to describe ethnographically, through concrete instances, how religion is embedded in the quotidian of Palestinian refugee camp dwellers in Lebanon, which may inspire others to take this thought elsewhere.

References

Abu-Lughod, Lila, and Ahmad H. Sa'di, eds. 2007. *Nakba: Palestine, 1948, and the Claims of Memory*. New York, NY: Columbia University Press.

Abu-Lughod, Lila. 2007. "Return to Half-Ruins." Essay. In *Nakba: Palestine, 1948, and the Claims of Memory*, edited by Ahmad H. Sa'di and Lila Abu-Lughod, 1–24. New York, NY: Columbia University Press.

Abu-Lughod, Lila. 2008. *Writing Women's Worlds: Bedouin Stories*. Berkeley, CA: University of California Press.

Abufarha, Nasser. 2009. *The Making of a Human Bomb: An Ethnography of Palestinian Resistance*. Duke University Press.

Agamben, Giorgio. 2005. *State of Exception*. Chicago, IL: University of Chicago Press.

Agier, Michel. 2008. *On the Margins of the World: The Refugee Experience Today*. Cambridge, UK: Polity.

Agier, Michel. 2016. *Managing the Undesirables: Refugee Camps and Humanitarian Government*. Cambridge, UK: Polity.

AJIAL. 2001. "Palestinian Non-Government Organizations in Lebanon (Ajial Center)." Palestinian Refugee ResearchNet. McGill University. November 5, 2001. https://prrn.mcgill.ca/research/papers/ajial.htm.

Allan, Diana. 2014. *Refugees of the Revolution: Experiences of Palestinian Exile*. Stanford, CA: Stanford University Press.

Allen, Lori. 2013. *The Rise and Fall of Human Rights: Cynicism and Politics in Occupied Palestine*. Stanford, CA: Stanford University Press.

Anderson, Benedict. 2006. *Imagined Communities*. London, UK: Verso Books.

Anjum, Ovamir. 2007. "Islam as a Discursive Tradition: Talal Asad and His Interlocutors." *Comparative Studies of South Asia, Africa, and the Middle East* 27 (3): 656–72.

Asad, Talal. 1972. "Market Model, Class Structure and Consent: A Reconsideration of Swat Political Organization." *Man* 7 (1): 74–94.

Asad, Talal. 1973. *Anthropology and the Colonial Encounter*. London, UK: Ithaca.

Asad, Talal. 1983. "Anthropological Conceptions of Religion: Reflections on Geertz." *Man* 18 (2): 237–59.

Asad, Talal. 1986. *The Idea of an Anthropology of Islam*. Washington, DC: Center for Contemporary Arab Studies, Georgetown University.

Asad, Talal. 1993. *Genealogies of Religion: Discipline and Reasons of Power in Christianity and Islam*. Baltimore, MD: Johns Hopkins University Press.

Asad, Talal. 2003. *Formations of the Secular: Christianity, Islam, Modernity*. Stanford, CA: Stanford University Press.

Asad, Talal. 2015. "Thinking About Tradition, Religion, and Politics in Egypt Today." Critical Inquiry. University of Chicago. 2015. https://criticalinqui ry.uchicago.edu/thinking_about_tradition_religion_and_politics_in_egy pt_today/#_ftn1.

Atran, Scott. 1986. "Hamula Organization and Masha'a Tenure in Palestine." *Man* 21 (2): 271–95.

Austin, J. L. 1975. *How to Do Things with Words*. 2nd ed. Cambridge, MA: Harvard University Press.

Barbosa, Baptista Gustavo. 2013. "Non-Cockfights: On Doing/Undoing Gender in Shatila, Lebanon." Dissertation, London: London School of Economics. London School of Economics.

Barth, Fredrik. 1958. *Political Leadership among the Swat Pathans*. London, UK: Athlone Press.

Barth, Fredrik. 1971. *Models of Social Organization*. Occasional Papers No. 23. London, UK: Royal Anthropological Institute of Great Britain & Ireland.

Barth, Fredrik. 1987. *Cosmologies in the Making: A Generative Approach to Cultural Variation in Inner New Guinea*. Cambridge, MA: Cambridge University Press.

Barth, Fredrik. 1993. *Balinese Worlds*. Chicago, IL: University of Chicago Press.

Barth, Fredrik. 1998. *Ethnic Groups and Boundaries: The Social Organization of Culture Difference*. Long Grove, IL: Waveland Press.

Barth, Fredrik. 2002. "An Anthropology of Knowledge." *Current Anthropology* 43 (1): 1–18.

Bateson, Gregory. 2000. *Steps to an Ecology of Mind: Collected Essays in Anthropology, Psychiatry, Evolution, and Epistemology*. Chicago, IL: University of Chicago Press.

Bell, Catherine M. 1997. *Ritual: Perspectives and Dimensions*. New York, NY: Oxford University Press.

Bell, Catherine M. 2009. *Ritual Theory, Ritual Practice*. New York, NY: Oxford University Press.

Berger A, Cox H, Kelman HC et al. 2010. "Israel and Palestine-Two states for two peoples: If not now, when?" Policy Statement of the Boston Study Group on Middle East Peace. In: A. BERGER et al., *Israel and Palestine–Two states for two peoples: If not now, when?* Foreign Policy Association, pp. 1-14.

Bloch, Maurice. 1973. "Symbols, Song, Dance and Features of Articulation Is Religion an Extreme Form of Traditional Authority?" *European Journal of Sociology* 15 (1): 54–81.

Bowman, Glenn. 2011a. "'In Dubious Battle on the Plains of Heav'n': The Politics of Possession in Jerusalem's Holy Sepulchre." *History and Anthropology* 22 (3): 371–99.

Bowman, Glen. 2011b. "Identification and Identity Formations around Shared Shrines in West Bank Palestine and Western Macedonia." Essay. In *Sharing Sacred Spaces in the Mediterranean Christians, Muslims, and Jews at Shrines and Sanctuaries*, edited by D Albera and M Couroucli, 10–28. New Anthropologies of Europe. Bloomington, IN: Indiana University Press.

Bowman, Glenn. 2013. "Popular Palestinian Practices Around Holy Places and Those Who Oppose Them: An Historical Introduction." *Religion Compass* 7 (3): 69–78.

Chakrabarty, Dipesh. 2007. *Provincializing Europe: Postcolonial Thought and Historical Difference*. Princeton, NJ: Princeton University Press.

Chatterjee, Partha. 2007. *The Nation and Its Fragments: Colonial and Postcolonial Histories*. Princeton, NJ: Princeton University Press.

Chatty, Dawn. 2010. *Displacement and Dispossession in the Modern Middle East*. New York, NY: Cambridge University Press.

Cohen, Anthony Peter. 1993. *Self Consciousness: An Alternative Anthropology of Identity*. London, UK: Routledge.

Crenshaw, Kimberle. 1989. "Demarginalizing the Intersection of Race and Sex: A Black Feminist Critique of Antidiscrimination Doctrine, Feminist Theory, and Antiracist Politics." *The University of Chicago Legal Forum* 1 (8): 139–67.

Daniel, E. Valentine, and John Chr. Knudsen, eds. 1996. *Mistrusting Refugees*. Berkeley, CA: University of California Press.

Das, Veena. 1997. *Critical Events: An Anthropological Perspective on Contemporary India*. Delhi: Oxford University Press.

Davis, Rochelle. 2010. *Palestinian Village Histories: Geographies of the Displaced*. Stanford, CA: Stanford University Press.

Dias, Amanda. 2013. *Aux Marges De La Ville Et De L'état Camps Palestiniens Au Liban Et Favelas Cariocas*. Paris: Karthala.

Doraï, Mohamed Kamel. 2006. *Les Réfugiés Palestiniens Du Liban: Une Géographie De L'exil*. Paris: CNRS Éditions.

Doumani, Beshara. 1992. "Rediscovering Ottoman Palestine: Writing Palestinians into History." *Journal of Palestine Studies* 21 (2): 5–28.

Doumani, Beshara. 1995. *Rediscovering Palestine: Merchants and Peasants in Jabal Nablus, 1700-1900*. Los Angeles, CA: University of California Press.

Dumont, Louis. 1981. *Homo Hierarchicus: The Caste System and Its Implications*. Chicago, IL: University of Chicago Press.

Durkheim, Émile. 1998. *Selected Writings*. Edited by Anthony Giddens. Cambridge, MA: Cambridge University Press.

Durkheim, Émile. 2008. *The Elementary Forms of the Religious Life*. BN Publishing.

Farah, Randa. 1997. "Palestinian Refugees and UNRWA: Oral Histories and Popular Memories." Essay. In *A History within a History: Oral History and Popular Memory*, 289–99. Amman: CERMOC.

Farah, Randa. 1998. "UNRWA in Popular Memory Al-Baq'a Refugee Camp." Essay. In *A History within History: Humanitarian Aid and Development*. Amman: CERMOC.

Farah, Randa. 2003. "Palestinian Refugee Camps Reinscribing and Contesting Memory and Space." Essay. In *Isolation: Places and Practices of Exclusion*, edited by Carolyn Strange and Alison Bashford, 191–208. New York and London: Routledge.

Farah, Randa. 2009. "Refugee Camps in the Palestinian and Sahrawi National Liberation Movements: A Comparative Perspective." *Journal of Palestine Studies* 38 (2): 76–93.

Fassin, Didier. 2008. "The Humanitarian Politics of Testimony: Subjectification through Trauma in the Israeli-Palestinian Conflict." *Cultural Anthropology* 23 (3): 531–58.

Feldman, Ilana. 2008. *Governing Gaza: Bureaucracy, Authority, and the Work of Rule, 1917-1967*. Durham, NC: Duke University Press.

Foucault, Michel. 1975. *Discipline and Punish: The Birth of the Prison*. New York, NY: Random House.

Foucault, Michel. 1980. "Truth and Power." Essay. In *Power/Knowledge: Selected Interviews and Other Writings 1972-1977*, edited by Colin Gordon, 109–33. New York, NY: The Harvester Press.

Foucault, Michel. 1984. *The Foucault Reader*. London, UK: Penguin Books.

Foucault, Michel. 2000. "The Subject and Power." Essay. In *Readings in Contemporary Political Sociology*, edited by Kate Nash, 8–26. Malden, MA: Blackwell.

Foucault, Michel. 2007. *Security, Territory, Population: Lectures at the Collège De France, 1977-1978*. New York, NY: Palgrave Macmillan.

Furani, Khaled, and Dan Rabinowitz. 2011. "The Ethnographic Arriving of Palestine." *Annual Review of Anthropology* 40 (1): 475–91.

Gabiam, Nell. 2006. "Negotiating Rights: Palestinian Refugees and the Protection Gap." *Anthropological Quarterly* 79 (4): 717–30.

Gabiam, Nell. 2012. "When 'Humanitarianism' Becomes 'Development': The Politics of International Aid in Syria's Palestinian Refugee Camps." *American Anthropologist* 114 (1): 95–107.

Gadamer, Hans-Georg. 2005. *Truth and Method*. London, UK: Continuum.

Geertz, Clifford. 1973. "Religion as a Cultural System ." Essay. In *The Interpretation of Cultures: Selected Essays*, edited by Clifford Geertz, 87–125. New York, NY: Basic Books.

Gellner, Ernest. 1983. *Nations and Nationalism*. Ithaca, NY: Cornell.

Giacaman, George. 1998. "In the Throes of Oslo: Palestinian Society, Civil Society and the Future ." Essay. In *After Oslo: New Realities, Old Problems*, edited by George Giacaman and Dag Jørund Lønning. London, UK: Pluto Press.

Gilsenan, Michael. 1996. *Lords of the Lebanese Marches: Violence and Narrative in an Arab Society*. New York, NY: I.B. Tauris.

Gluckman, Max. 1944. "'The Bridge': Analysis of a Social Situation in Zululand." Essay. In *The Anthropology of Politics: A Reader in Ethnography, Theory, and Critique*, 53–59. Malden, MA: Blackwell Publishing.

Gluckman, Max, ed. 1966. *Essays on the Ritual of Social Relations*. Manchester: Manchester University Press.

Goffman, Erving. 1959. *The Presentation of Self in Everyday Life*. New York, NY: Doubleday Books.

Goffman, Erving. 1963. *Stigma: Notes on the Management of Spoiled Identity*. New York, NY: Simon & Schuster.

Goffman, Erving. 1967. *Interaction Ritual: Essays on Face-to-Face Behavior*. New York, NY: Pantheon Books.

Goody, Jack. 1961. "Religion and Ritual: The Definitional Problem." *The British Journal of Sociology* 12 (2): 142–64.

Greenhouse, Carol J., Elizabeth Mertz, and Kay B. Warren. 2002. *Ethnography in Unstable Places: Everyday Lives in Contexts of Dramatic Political Change*. Durham, NC: Duke University Press.

Hammami, Rema. 2003. "Gender, Nakba and Nation: Palestinian Women's Presence and Absence in the Narration of 1948 Memories." Essay. In *Homelands: Poetic Power and the Politics of Space*, edited by Ron Theodore Robin and Bo Stråth. Bruxelles: P.I.E. Peter Lang.

Hanafi, Sari. 2008. "Palestinian Refugee Camps in Lebanon as a Space of Exception." *REVUE Asylon(s)*, Palestiniens en / hors camps, 5 (September).

Hannerz, Ulf. 2002. "Several Sites in One." Essay. In *Globalization*, edited by Thomas Hylland Eriksen, 18–38. London: Pluto Press.

Hefner, Robert W. 1983. "Ritual and Cultural Reproduction in Non-Islamic Java." *American Ethnologist* 10 (4): 665–83.

Hefner, Robert W. 1985. *Hindu Javanese: Tengger Tradition and Islam*. Princeton, NJ: Princeton University Press.

Hefner, Robert W. 1998. "On the History and Cross-Cultural Possibility of a Democratic Ideal." Essay. In *Democratic Civility: The History and Cross-Cultural Possibility of a Modern Political Ideal*. New Brunswick, NJ: Transaction Publishers.

Hefner, Robert W. 2000. *Civil Islam: Muslims and Democratization in Indonesia*. Princeton, NJ: Princeton University Press.

Heidegger, Martin. 1971. *Poetry, Language, Thought*. New York, NY: Harper & Row.

Hirschkind, Charles. 2001. "The Ethics of Listening: Cassette-Sermon Audition in Contemporary Egypt." *American Ethnologist* 28 (3): 623–49.

Hirschkind, Charles. 2006. *The Ethical Soundscape: Cassette Sermons and Islamic Counterpublics*. New York, NY: Columbia University Press.

Hirschkind, Charles. (2010, November 15). *Is there a secular body?* SSRC The Immanent Frame. Retrieved June 30, 2016, from https://tif.ssrc.org/2010/11/15/secular-body/

Hirschkind, Charles. 2011. "Rethinking Secularism: Is There a Secular Body?" *Cultural Anthropology* 26 (4): 633–47.

Hobsbawm, Eric J. 1990. *Nations and Nationalism since 1780: Programme, Myth, Reality*. Cambridge, NY: Cambridge University Press.

Horstmann, Alexander. 2011. "Ethical Dilemmas and Identifications of Faith-Based Humanitarian Organizations in the Karen Refugee Crisis." *Journal of Refugee Studies* 24 (3): 513–32.

Hugh-Jones, Stephen, and James Laidlaw. 2001. *The Essential Edmund Leach*. New Haven, CT: Yale University Press.

Huntington, Samuel P. 1993. "The Clash of Civilizations?" *Foreign Affairs* 72 (3): 22–49.

Huntington, Samuel P. 1996. *The Clash of Civilizations and the Remaking of World Order*. New York, NY: Simon & Schuster.

The Internationalist. 2016. "'How Can You Say No?'." New Internationalist. January 2016. https://newint.org/features/2016/01/01/how-can-you-say-no/.

Jayyusi, Lena. 2002. "Letters from the Palestinian Ghetto." *Critical Arts* 16 (1): 47–52.

Jayyusi, Lena. 2007. "Iterability, Cumulativity, and Presence." Essay. In *Nakba Palestine, 1948, and the Claims of Memory*, edited by Ahmad H. Sa'di and Lila Abu-Lughod. New York, NY: Columbia University Press.

Kanaana, Sharif. 1989. *Speak, Bird, Speak Again: Palestinian Arab Folktales*. Los Angeles, CA: University of California Press.

Kanaana, Sharif. 2000. *Still on Vacation! The Eviction of the Palestinian in 1948*. Jerusalem: SHAML, Palestinian Diaspora & Refugee Centre.

Kanaaneh, Muṣliḥ, Stig-Magnus Thorsén, Heather Bursheh, and David A. McDonald, eds. 2013. *Palestinian Music and Song: Expression and Resistance since 1900*. Bloomington, IN: Indiana University Press.

Kanaaneh, Rhoda Ann, and Isis Nusair. 2010. *Displaced at Home: Ethnicity and Gender among Palestinians in Israel*. Albany, NY: State University of New York Press.

Kassir, Samir. 2006. *Being Arab*. London: Verso.

Kaufman, Asher. 2006. "Between Palestine and Lebanon: Seven Shi'i Villages as a Case Study of Boundaries, Identities, and Conflict." *The Middle East Journal* 60 (4): 685–706.

Khaldun, Ibn. 2004. *The Muqaddimah: An Introduction to History*. Princeton, NJ: Princeton University.

Khalidi, Rashid. 1998. *Palestinian Identity*. New York, NY: Columbia University Press.

Khalili, Laleh. 2004. "Grass-Roots Commemorations: Remembering the Land in the Camps of Lebanon." *Journal of Palestine Studies* 34 (1): 6–22.

Khalili, Laleh. 2005. "Places of Memory and Mourning: Palestinian Commemoration in the Refugee Camps of Lebanon." *Comparative Studies of South Asia, Africa, and the Middle East* 25 (1): 30–45.

Khalili, Laleh. 2007. *Heroes and Martyrs of Palestine: The Politics of National Commemoration*. Cambridge, MA: Cambridge University Press.

Knudsen, Are. 2003a. Islamism in the Diaspora: Palestinian Refugees in Lebanon. CMI Working Paper, 2003(10): 23p.

Knudsen, Are. 2003b. *Political Islam in the Middle East*. CMI Report 2003: 32p.

Knudsen, Ari, and Sari Hanafi, eds. 2011. *Palestinian Refugees: Identity, Space and Place in the Levant*. London, UK: Routledge.

Kublitz, Anja. 2016. "From Revolutionaries to Muslims: Liminal Becomings across Palestinian Generations in Denmark." *International Journal of Middle East Studies* 48 (1): 67–86.

Latour, Bruno. 1993. *We Have Never Been Modern*. Cambridge, MA: Harvard University Press.

Lavie, Smadar, and Ted Swedenburg. 1996. *Displacement, Diaspora, and Geographies of Identity*. Durham, NC: Duke University Press.

Leach, Edmund. 1990. "Masquerade: The Presentation of the Self in Holi-Day Life." *Cambridge Anthropology* 13 (3): 47–69.

Leach, Edmund. 2008. *Political Systems of Highland Burma: A Study of Kachin Social Structure*. New York, NY: ACLS Humanities E-Book.

Lewis, Bernard. 2001. *The Multiple Identities of the Middle East*. New York, NY: Schocken Books.

Lindholm, Charles. 1995. "The New Middle Eastern Ethnography." *The Journal of the Royal Anthropological Institute* 1 (4): 805–20.

Lindholm, Charles. 2007. *Culture and Identity: The History, Theory, and Practice of Psychological Anthropology*. Oxford: Oneworld Publications.

Lybarger, Loren D. 2007. *Identity and Religion in Palestine: The Struggle between Islamism and Secularism in the Occupied Territories*. Princeton, NJ: Princeton University Press.

Lévi-Strauss, Claude. 1968. *The Savage Mind*. Chicago, IL: The University of Chicago Press.

Lévi-Strauss, Claude. 1991. "Maison." Essay. In *Dictionaire De L'Ethnologie Et L'Anthropologie*, edited by Pierre Bonte, Michel Izard, and Marco Aime. Paris: Presses Universitaires de France.

Mahmood, Saba. 2005. *Politics of Piety: The Islamic Revival and the Feminist Subject*. Princeton, NJ: Princeton University Press.

Malkki, Liisa H. 1992. "National Geographic: The Rooting of Peoples and the Territorialization of National Identity among Scholars and Refugees." *Cultural Anthropology* 7 (1): 24–44.

Malkki, Liisa H. 1995a. *Purity and Exile: Violence, Memory, and National Cosmology among Hutu Refugees in Tanzania*. Chicago, IL: University of Chicago Press.

Malkki, Liisa H. 1995b. "Refugees and Exile: From 'Refugee Studies' to the National Order of Things." *Annual Review of Anthropology* 24 (1): 495–523.

Mauss, Marcel. 2000. *The Gift: The Form and Reason for Exchange in Archaic Societies*. New York, NY: W.W. Norton.

Mauss, Marcel. 2006. "Techniques of the Body." Essay. In *Techniques, Technology and Civilization*. Berghahn Books.

Micallef, Roberta. 1992. "Israeli and Palestinian Women's Social Movements." Essay. In *The Struggle for Peace: Israelis and Palestinians*, edited by Elizabeth Warnock Fernea and Heather L. Taylor. Austin, TX: University of Texas Press.

Muslih, Muhammad. 2005. "Palestinian Civil Society." Essay. In *Civil Society in the Middle East*, edited by Augustus Richard Norton. Boston, MA: Brill Academic Publishers.

Nordstrom, Carolyn, and A C Robben. 1995. *Fieldwork under Fire: Contemporary Studies of Violence and Survival*. Berkeley, CA: University of California Press.

Peteet, Julie. 1987. "Socio-Political Integration and Conflict Resolution in the Palestinian Camps in Lebanon." *Journal of Palestine Studies* 16 (2): 29–44.

Peteet, Julie. 1994. "Male Gender and Rituals of Resistance in the Palestinian 'Intifada': A Cultural Politics of Violence." *American Ethnologist* 21 (1): 31–49.

Peteet, Julie. 1996a. "The Palestinians in Lebanon: Identity at the Margins." *The Journal of the International Institute* 3 (3).

Peteet, Julie. 1996b. "From Refugees to Minority: Palestinians in Post-War Lebanon." *Middle East Report*, no. 200: 27–30.

Peteet, Julie. 1996c. "Transforming Trust: Dispossession and Empowerment among Palestinian Refugees." Essay. In *Mistrusting Refugees*, edited by E. Valentine Daniel and John Knudsen. Los Angeles, CA: University of California Press.

Peteet, Julie. 2005. *Landscape of Hope and Despair: Palestinian Refugee Camps*. Philadelphia, PA: University of Pennsylvania Press.

Putnam, Robert. 1994. *Making Democracy Work: Civic Traditions in Modern Italy*. Princeton, NJ: Princeton University Press.

Putnam, Robert. 2001. *Bowling Alone: The Collapse and Revival of American Community*. London, UK: Simon & Schuster.

Rappaport, Roy. 2008. *Ritual and Religion in the Making of Humanity*. Cambridge, MA: Cambridge University Press.

Rougier, Bernard. 2007. *Everyday Jihad: The Rise of Militant Islam among Palestinians in Lebanon*. Cambridge, MA: Harvard University Press.

Roy, Olivier. 2004. *Globalized Islam: The Search for a New Ummah*. New York, NY: Columbia University Press.

Sa'adeh, Safia. 1993. *The Social Structure of Lebanon: Democracy or Servitude?* Beirut: Editions Dar An-Nahar.

Sa'ar, Amalia. 1998. "Carefully on the Margins: Christian Palestinians in Haifa between Nation and State." *American Ethnologist* 25 (2): 215–39.

Sa'di, Ahmad. 2007. "Afterword." Essay. In *Nakba: Palestine, 1948, and the Claims of Memory*, edited by Ahmad H. Sa'di and Lila Abu-Lughod. New York, NY: Columbia University Press.

Sahlins, Marshall. 1972. *Stone Age Economics*. Aldine Transactions.

Sahlins, Marshall. 1976. *Culture and Practical Reason*. Chicago, IL: University of Chicago Press.

Sahlins, Marshall. 1985. *Islands of History*. Chicago, IL: The University of Chicago Press.

Said, Edward. 1979. *Orientalism*. New York, NY: Random House.

Salih, Ruba. 2013. "Reconciling Return and Rights: Palestinian Refugees and the Emergence of a 'Political Society.'" Jadaliyya. Jadaliyya. July 10, 2013. http://www.jadaliyya.com/pages/index/10814/reconciling-retur n-and-rights_palestinian-refugees.

Sanford, Victoria, and Asale Angel-Ajani. 2006. *Engaged Observer: Anthropology, Advocacy, and Activism*. New Brunswick, NJ: Rutgers University Press.

Sayigh, Rosemary. 1979. *The Palestinians: from Peasants to Revolutionaries*. London, UK: Zed Books.

Sayigh, Rosemary. 1994. *Too Many Enemies: The Palestinian Experience in Lebanon*. London: Zed Books.

Sayigh, Rosemary. 1998. "Gender, Sexuality, and Class in National Narrations: Palestinian Camp Women Tell Their Lives." *Frontiers: A Journal of Women Studies* 19 (2): 166–85.

Sayigh, Rosemary. 2007. "Women's Nakba Stories." Essay. In *Nakba: Palestine, 1948, and the Claims of Memory*, edited by Ahmad H. Sa'di and Lila Abu-Lughod, 135–60. New York, NY: Columbia University Press.

Sayigh, Rosemary, ed. 2015. *Yusif Sayigh: Arab Economist and Palestinian Patriot*. Cairo: The American University in Cairo Press.

Sayigh, Yezid. 2000. "War as Leveler, War as Midwife: Palestinian Political Institutions, Nationalism, and Society since 1948." Essay. In *War, Institutions, and Social Change in the Middle East*, edited by Steven Heydemann. Los Angeles, CA: University of California Press.

Schielke, Samuli. 2010. "Second Thoughts about the Anthropology of Islam, or How to Make Sense of Grand Schemes in Everyday Life." SSOAR. Zentrum Moderner Orient. 2010. https://www.ssoar.info/ssoar/handle/document/ 32233.

Schiocchet, Leonardo. 2011. "Far Middle East, Brave New World: The Building of the Middle East the Arab Spring." *The Perspective of the World Review* 3 (2).

Schiocchet, Leonardo. 2013. "Palestinian Sumud: Steadfastness, Ritual and Time among Palestinian Refugees." Essay. In *Palestinian Refugees: Different Generations, but One Identity*, edited by Asem Khalil, 67–90. Ramallah: Ibrahim Abu-Lughod Institute of International Studies.

Schiocchet, Leonardo. 2014a. "Suspicion and the Economy of Trust among Palestinian Refugees in Lebanon." *The Cambridge Journal of Anthropology* 32 (2): 112–27.

Schiocchet, Leonardo. 2014b. "Palestinian Refugees in Lebanon: Is the Camp a Space of Exception?" *Mashriq & Mahjar Journal of Middle East and North African Migration Studies* 2 (1): 122–52.

Schiocchet, Leonardo. 2015a. *Entre o Velho e o Novo Mundo: Diáspora Palestina Desde o Oriente Médio à América Latina [Between the New and the Old World: The Palestinian Diaspora from the Middle East to Latin America]*. Lisboa: Chiado Editora.

Schiocchet, Leonardo. 2015b. "Palestinian Steadfastness as a Mission." Essay. In *Building Noah's Ark for Migrants, Refugees, and Religious Communities*, edited by Alexander Horstmann and Jin-Heon Jung, 209–34. New York, NY: Palgrave Macmillan.

Schiocchet, Leonardo. 2016. "Review of 'Refugees of the Revolution: Experiences of Palestinian Exile, by Diana Allan.'" *American Anthropologist* 118 (1): 177–78.

Schiocchet, Leonardo. 2017. "Essay on the Anthropology of the Fiduciary." Essay. In *Mistrust: Ethnographic Approximations*, edited by Florian Mühlfried, 93–104. Bielefeld: transcript.

Schiocchet, Leonardo. 2018. "Critique, Comparison, Suffering, and the Middle East." *Prace Etnograficzne* 46 (2): 1–25.

Schiocchet, Leonardo. 2019. "Outcasts among Undesirables: Palestinian Refugees in Brazil between Humanitarianism and Nationalism." *Latin American Perspectives* 46 (3): 84–101.

Seligman, Adam, Robert Weller, Michael Puet, and Bennet Simon. 2008. *Ritual and Its Consequences: An Essay on the Limits of Sincerity*. New York, NY: Oxford University Press.

Sfeir, Jihane. 2008. *L'Exil Palestinien Au Liban. Le Temps Des Origins (1947-1952)*. Paris: Éditions Khartala et IFPO.

Shipton, Parker MacDonald. 2007. *The Nature of Entrustment: Intimacy, Exchange, and the Sacred in Africa*. New Haven, CT: Yale University Press.

Shryock, Andrew. 1997. *Nationalism and the Genealogical Imagination: Oral History and Textual Authority in Tribal Jordan*. Los Angeles, CA: University of California Press.

Siddiq, Muhammad. 1996. "On Ropes of Memory: Narrating the Palestinian Refugees." Essay. In *Mistrusting Refugees*, edited by E. Valentine Daniel and John Knudsen. Berkeley, CA: University of California Press.

Slyomovics, Susan. 1998. *The Object of Memory: Arab and Jew Narrate the Palestinian Village*. Philadelphia: University of Pennsylvania Press.

Smith, Anthony D. 1986. *The Ethnic Origins of Nations*. Oxford, UK: Blackwell.

Sperber, Dan. 1975. *Rethinking Symbolism*. Cambridge, MA: Cambridge University Press.

Sperber, Dan. 2007. "Rudiments of Cognitive Rhetoric." *Rhetoric Society Quarterly* 37 (4): 361–400.

Stocking, George W. 1982. *Race, Culture and Evolution: Essays in the History of Anthropology*. Chicago, IL: University of Chicago Press.

Strijp, Ruud. 1992. *Cultural Anthropology of the Middle East: A Bibliography*. Vol. 1. New York, NY: Brill.

Strijp, Ruud. 1997. *Cultural Anthropology of the Middle East: A Bibliography*. Vol. 2. New York, NY: Brill.

Suhr, Christian. 2013. "Descending with Angels: The Invisible in Danish Psychiatry and Islamic Exorcism." Dissertation, Aarhus: Department of Culture and Society, Aarhus University. PhD Thesis.

Swedenburg, Ted. 1990. "The Palestinian Peasant as National Signifier." *Anthropological Quarterly* 63 (1): 18–30.

Swedenburg, Ted. 1992. "Occupational Hazards: Palestine Ethnography." Essay. In *Rereading Cultural Anthropology*, edited by George E. Marcus, 69–76. Durham, NC: Duke University Press.

Swedenburg, Ted. 2003. *Memories of Revolt: The 1936-1939 Rebellion and the Palestinian National Past*. Fayetteville, AR: University of Arkansas Press.

Swedenburg, Ted. 2004. "With Genet in the Palestinian Field." Essay. In *Violence in War and Peace: An Anthology*, edited by Nancy Scheper-Hughes and Philippe I. Bourgois. London: Blackwell.

Tambiah, S. J. 1981. *A Performative Approach to Ritual*. Oxford University Press.

Tambiah, Stanley. 1996. *Leveling Crowds: Ethnonationalist Conflicts and Collective Violence in South Asia*. Los Angeles, CA: University of California Press.

Tambiah, Stanley. 2002. *Edmund Leach: An Anthropological Life*. Cambridge: Cambridge University Press.

Taylor, Charles. 1992. *Sources of the Self: Theœ Making of the Modern Identity*. Cambridge, MA: Harvard University press.

Turner, Victor. 1974. *Dramas, Fields, and Metaphors: Symbolic Action in Human Society*. Ithaca, NY: Cornell University Press.

Turner, Victor. 1995. *The Ritual Process: Structure and Anti-Structure*. New York, NY: Aldine Transaction.

Tylor, Edward Burnett. 2010. *Primitive Culture: Researches into the Development of Mythology, Philosophy, Religion, Art, and Custom*. Cambridge: Cambridge University Press.

UN. 2009. Rep. *World Population Prospects: the 2008 Revision*.

UN. 2013. Rep. *World Population Prospects: The 2012 Revision, Highlights and Advance Tables*.

UNRWA. n.d. "Camp Profiles: Wavel." UNRWA. OAD. https://www.unrwa.or g/where-we-work/lebanon/wavel-camp.

UNRWA. Official Website. n.d. UNRWA. Accessed October 10, 2013. https://w ww.unrwa.org/where-we-work/lebanon.

van der Veer, Peter. 1994. *Religious Nationalism: Hindus and Muslims in India*. Los Angeles, CA: University of California Press.

van Gennep, Arnold. 2004. *The Rites of Passage*. Routledge.

Verdeil, Éric, Ghaleb Faour, Mouïn Hamzé, Franck Mermier, and Sébastien Velut. 2007. *Atlas Du Liban: Territoires Et Société*. Paris: CNRS Liban.

Weber, Max. 1949. "Objectivity in Social Science and Social Policy; The Meaning of Ethical Neutrality in Sociology and Economics." Essay. In *The Methodology of the Social Sciences*, edited by Edward Shils and Henry Finch. New York, NY: The Free Press.

Weber, Max. 1998. *Essays in Sociology*. New York, NY: Routledge.

White, Jenny B. 2002. *Islamist Mobilization in Turkey: A Study in Vernacular Politics*. Seattle, WA: University of Washington Press.

World Vision. 2007. Rep. *Basic Assessment of Dbaye Palestinian Refugee Camp in Lebanon*. World Vision Lebanon.

Index

Social Sciences

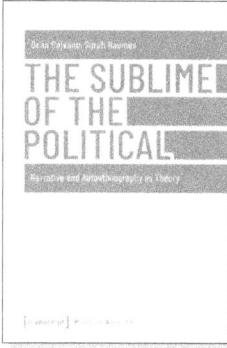

Dean Caivano, Sarah Naumes
The Sublime of the Political
Narrative and Autoethnography as Theory

July 2021, 162 p., hardcover
100,00 € (DE), 978-3-8376-4772-3
E-Book:
PDF: 99,99 € (DE), ISBN 978-3-8394-4772-7

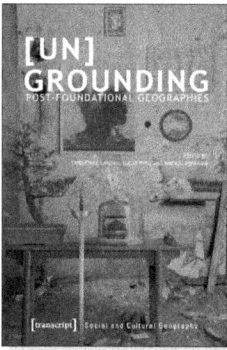

Friederike Landau, Lucas Pohl, Nikolai Roskamm (eds.)
[Un]Grounding
Post-Foundational Geographies

May 2021, 348 p., pb., col. ill.
50,00 € (DE), 978-3-8376-5073-0
E-Book:
PDF: 49,99 € (DE), ISBN 978-3-8394-5073-4

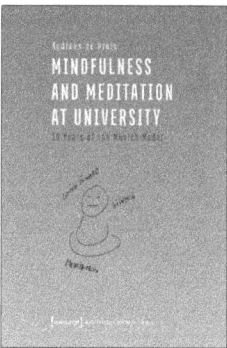

Andreas de Bruin
Mindfulness and Meditation at University
10 Years of the Munich Model

April 2021, 216 p., pb.
25,00 € (DE), 978-3-8376-5696-1
E-Book: available as free open access publication
PDF: ISBN 978-3-8394-5696-5

**All print, e-book and open access versions of the titles in our list
are available in our online shop www.transcript-publishing.com**

Social Sciences

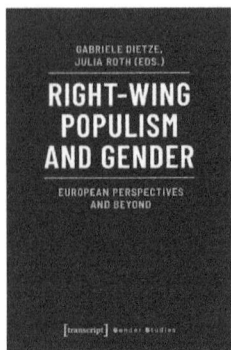

Gabriele Dietze, Julia Roth (eds.)
Right-Wing Populism and Gender
European Perspectives and Beyond

2020, 286 p., pb., ill.
35,00 € (DE), 978-3-8376-4980-2
E-Book:
PDF: 34,99 € (DE), ISBN 978-3-8394-4980-6

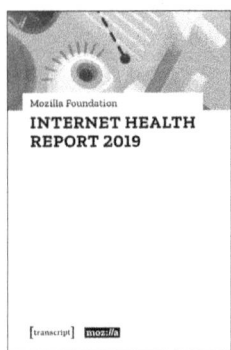

Mozilla Foundation
Internet Health Report 2019

2019, 118 p., pb., ill.
19,99 € (DE), 978-3-8376-4946-8
E-Book: available as free open access publication
PDF: ISBN 978-3-8394-4946-2

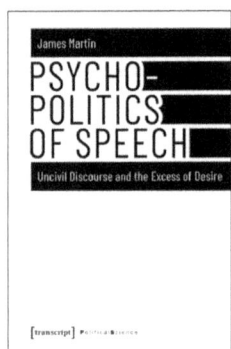

James Martin
Psychopolitics of Speech
Uncivil Discourse and the Excess of Desire

2019, 186 p., hardcover
79,99 € (DE), 978-3-8376-3919-3
E-Book:
PDF: 79,99 € (DE), ISBN 978-3-8394-3919-7

**All print, e-book and open access versions of the titles in our list
are available in our online shop www.transcript-publishing.com**

GPSR Authorized Representative: Easy Access System Europe, Mustamäe tee 50, 10621 Tallinn, Estonia, gpsr.requests@easproject.com

www.ingramcontent.com/pod-product-compliance
Lightning Source LLC
Chambersburg PA
CBHW062131040426
42335CB00039B/1967